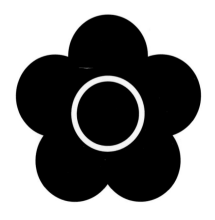

V&A Publishing

Jenny Lister

With contributions by
Johanna Agerman Ross
Beatrice Behlen
Regina Lee Blaszczyk
Susanna Brown
Elisabeth Murray
Janine Sykes
Stephanie Wood

MARY QUANT

Contents

Sponsor's Foreword

The King's Road is one of the world's most famous shopping and lifestyle destinations. Since its origins as King Charles II's private road, it has played a central role in Britain's cultural and social history. It has always been at the forefront of fashion trends – from Mods to Punks, Sloanes and New Romantics – and at the epicentre of London's art, fashion and music scenes. And, of course, a key location and playground for Mary Quant and her brilliant boutique: Bazaar.

Today, it has an abundance of independent shops, galleries and restaurants. Working closely with other local stakeholders, we plan to ensure it remains an inspiring and essential part of London's rich character. Retail is changing, and the King's Road must balance its iconic heritage with an openness to creativity and innovation.

Although we are only one of the King's Road's landowners, it felt vital to us to lead on a central vision to unite the community there. As retail faces a seismic shift with the evolution of online shopping, it is timely to revive the King's Road's fame for pioneering trends and position it at the forefront of the latest retail revolution, ensuring it rightfully remains one of the world's most famous high streets.

It is a particularly pertinent time to focus on the destination as the V&A stages the first international retrospective of Mary Quant in nearly 50 years. Quant was an iconic character central to the King's Road, and revolutionised retail with immense global impact.

The King's Road is proud to sponsor this exhibition and celebrate the Road's rich heritage, as well as looking to its future as a home for the next generation of creative, era-defining pioneers.

Hugh Seaborn
Chief Executive, Cadogan

Director's Foreword

Mary *Quant* explores the extraordinary career of Dame Mary Quant and her contribution to fashion. Quant personified the vibrant, optimistic spirit of the 1960s, popularizing the mini skirt and becoming Britain's best-known designer, as well as a powerful role model for working women. Harnessing the boom in both high street consumerism and the media – in photography, graphics, journalism and advertising – she helped to shape an outward-looking, innovative identity for post-war Britain.

Long overdue, this is the first international exhibition to tell the full story of Mary Quant's journey from stylish London art student, to amateur King's Road boutique owner, to the face of a popular fashion label and the first international lifestyle brand, selling not just dresses but everything from lipstick to duvet covers across the world. The exhibition focuses on the years between 1955 and 1975, spanning post-war gloom, the flourishing of art and design in the 1960s and the economic and political challenges of the later 1960s and early 1970s. It traces Quant's design evolution through 120 key garments, together with accessories, photographs, magazines and film footage, charting the revolution in lifestyles and the democratization of fashion at that time. Many of the exhibits are treasured clothes and photographs donated or lent by women from all over the UK, who responded to the V&A's call-out for Quant clothes and memories in the #WeWantQuant press and social media campaign.

Quant changed the fashion system, overturning the dominance of Paris couturiers and transforming young women just like her into the new leaders of style. The industry has since evolved, thanks to offshore manufacturing and digital technology, but Quant, along with her two business partners – husband Alexander Plunket Greene and friend Archie McNair – anticipated the future dominance of visual branding and marketing, with their instantly recognizable daisy-logoed products. The Quant brand influenced the global identity of UK fashion today, making London an international centre of street style, creativity and fashion education.

The V&A is fortunate to have had the great privilege of working closely with Dame Mary and her son Orlando Plunket Greene, who have generously given the Museum unprecedented access to their private archive of clothes, fashion photographs and marketing materials. We are extremely grateful to them both. This archive has informed the narrative of the exhibition and allowed us to illustrate Quant's work in intricate detail, exploring the reality behind the legends of the mini skirt and 'Swinging London'. In particular, we would also like to thank Heather Tilbury Phillips, a director of Mary Quant Ltd during the 1970s, who has advised during the development of the exhibition and enabled us to tap into a broad international network of ex-employees, manufacturers, models, photographers and journalists. We gratefully acknowledge all their thoughtful contributions. We also appreciate the opportunity to have collaborated with Mary Quant Limited. We are especially thankful to our sponsor the King's Road for their enthusiasm and generous support. I can think of no more fitting partner for this exhibition.

In 1973, Dame Mary, always ahead of her time, said: 'I didn't have time to wait for women's lib' (see p.18). Her satirical dresses with waistcoats and ties, striped trouser suits and brightly coloured, energizing jersey dresses, pre-empted the broader social change of later years. Perhaps Quant's greatest legacy is her vision of fashion as a way of communicating new attitudes and ideas. By bending the rules, imagining different gender roles and identities with affordable clothes to enjoy, empower and liberate, she powerfully articulated the opportunities and freedoms of future generations.

Tristram Hunt
Director, V&A

Prefaces

I remember the day an official-looking man with black shoes and an enormous clipboard came to our home to investigate why I still hadn't been enrolled at a school. 'He is having an amazing education travelling with us!' my mother protested, baffled that the officer didn't share her logic. Until the British government finally caught up with me, I travelled everywhere with the Mary Quant team and the first thing I always heard from people who worked with my parents (and still do to this day) was how much fun they had. Everyone worked like crazy because they were all having so much fun. Even by today's digital standards, the pace was eye-watering. New products were launched on a near weekly basis.

I don't think anyone really knew what they were getting into but my mother had a clear vision of what she wanted and my father, Alexander, had an innate ability to make everything riotously exciting. Thankfully, Archie McNair's legal and business skills managed to wrangle the whole circus into a business.

Amongst the hubbub of the tiny office in Chelsea, I would be sprawled out on the floor with my crayons and toys. Countless times I would hear the phrase 'but Mary, you can't do that'. A momentary flash of defiance in my mother's eyes would quickly turn to a flirtatious and mischievous 'oh come on, YOU can make it happen ... and it will be so much FUN!' Be it a life-long career man from ICI or a fifth-generation artisan perfumer from the south of France, their balance sheets and conventional wisdoms would be tossed over their shoulders like it was the last day of school. Conventional wisdom no longer seemed necessarily wise and most of all, it really wasn't that much fun.

From the grey of post-war Britain, 'necessity' wasn't the mother of invention, fun was. Across Britain a generation decided to risk it; go for it and have fun, unleashing an attitude revolution that changed much more than fashion.

Orlando Plunket Greene

Great fashion designers are those who offer people what they never knew they wanted – until, of course, they see it. The graduate from Goldsmiths College of Art, who married aristocratic Alexander Plunket Greene in 1957, was a poster girl for the 1960s before that post-war era let loose a cacophony of youth. Everything that Quant did with her husband, in partnership with their friend Archie McNair, was about creating a new society. That meant physically turning to London's King's Road in Chelsea, as a haven for fun new coffee shops and fashion boutiques, laced with lively music. Together with like-minded friends, they created the 'Swinging Sixties'.

But mentally, the shift was even more profound, for the young designer realized that her peers no longer wanted to dress – or to live – like their parents. The renaissance of youth brought in simple clothes like slip dresses worn over young bodies, with hemlines that climbed higher up the thighs with each season.

Sex was not new to fashion. But the Mary Quant look not only founded the concept of youthful style with its mix of cheekiness and innocence, it also reflected the iconoclastic change in female behaviour following the invention of the contraceptive pill. One again, the designer was a precursor, not a follower, of what was happening in society at large.

I lived through that era and, as the first woman editor of the Cambridge University newspaper *Varsity*, I asked, with the daring and certainty of youth, to interview Mary Quant in the mid-1960s. I can still remember the journey to London, wearing fishnet tights, square-heeled shoes and a skirt as short as I dared, to meet the famous designer. I recall Quant as a slight woman, deprecating herself by claiming her success was all about 'luck' and 'chance' and leaving her husband to do most of the talking.

A more experienced journalist might have asked her if she felt she had changed society or simply gone with the fashion flow. Approaching that question in the twenty-first century, it is clear that Quant was a crucial part of a cultural revolution that is still churning, half a century on.

Suzy Menkes

Acknowledgements

This book and exhibition have been made possible through the generosity and collaborative spirit of many people. Most of all, I would like to thank Dame Mary Quant and her son Orlando Plunket Greene for their wholehearted support of the V&A, and for allowing us to explore their private archive. It has been the most exciting privilege to work with them and reveal some of the precious clothes, photographs and marketing materials that tell the detailed story of Mary Quant's early career for the first time.

Heather Tilbury Phillips, a director of Mary Quant Ltd during the 1970s, and Advisor to the exhibition, has been instrumental in bringing it to fruition and I am extremely grateful to her for all her assistance, given with kindness, energy and sensitivity. Janey Bain, Dame Mary's personal assistant, has similarly provided constant support. With their help we have developed an extraordinary network of hundreds of people with professional and personal links to Mary Quant and her brand. Many have responded generously with time, as well as thoughtful and informative contributions. Too many to mention by name, this network includes journalists, models, photographers, ex-employees, business people and manufacturers, all of whom worked with Mary Quant.

I would like to thank past donors of Mary Quant garments to the Museum, as well as the hundreds of (mostly) women from all over the UK, as well as from North America, Australia and New Zealand, who responded to the #WeWantQuant campaign – the Museum's call-out to the public for dresses, photographs and memories of wearing favourite Quant purchases. We have been able to add 40 important garments to the permanent collection as a result of the campaign, all of which illustrate the particular social context for, and relevance of, Quant's designs from the 1950s onwards, truly demonstrating her impact on fashion and lifestyles.

Colleagues in museums in the UK and internationally have helped generously with research. I would especially like to thank Beatrice Behlen of the Museum of London, Rosemary Harden and Eleanor Summers of the Fashion Museum, Bath, and Miles Lambert of Manchester City Galleries for their curatorial support, and for accommodating loans of key garments to the exhibition. I am also especially grateful to Phyllis Magidson of the Museum of the City of New York and Alexandra Palmer of the Royal Ontario Museum. Special thanks are due to all lenders, institutional and private, especially Ruth Lowe and Jannette Flood, who have kindly shared objects from their significant Quant archives. The knowledge of all these people has informed the narrative of this book as well as the exhibition. The project has also greatly benefitted from the expertise brought by the book contributors – Beatrice Behlen, Regina Lee Blaszczyk,

Janine Sykes, as well as my V&A colleagues Johanna Agerman Ross, Susanna Brown, Elisabeth Murray and Stephanie Wood.

Other colleagues who assisted with much appreciated contributions towards the early development of the exhibition and book are Christine Boydell, Chris Breward, David Gilbert, Alistair O'Neill and Mark Eastment. Painstaking research has been completed by many valued volunteers including Camilla de Winton and Jennifer Roberts. Lack of space prevents me from listing every volunteer who has helped, but their combined work is the foundation of both this book and the exhibition. Sonia Ashmore, Daniel Milford Cottam, Liz Eggleston and Liz Tregenza have all helped generously with their deep knowledge of fashion from the period.

Co-curator Stephanie Wood, with her tireless attention to detail, unique visual sense, and great collegial spirit has made the shared process of researching, shaping and organizing this multifaceted project an entirely positive experience. Elisabeth Murray provided excellent curatorial assistance and other curatorial colleagues including Victoria Bradley, Clare Browne, Amelia Cimino, Oriole Cullen, Edwina Ehrman, Sarah Medlam, Lesley Miller, Suzanne Smith, Sonnet Stanfill, Dani Trew, Claire Wilcox, Christopher Wilk and Maude Willaerts and have also been extremely generous with their much-appreciated support. The project has benefited from the expertise and enthusiasm of Joanne Hackett, Frances Hartog, Gill MacGregor and Keira Miller of the textile conservation department, and Clair Battison, Victoria Button and Jane Rutherston of the paper conservation department, as well as Richard Davis and Robert Auton of the photography studio, who created the brilliant photographs of the surviving garments in the book. I would like to thank Tom Windross, Coralie Hepburn, Fred Caws and Emma Woodiwiss of V&A Publishing for helping to make this book a reality, and particularly, editor Sophie Sheldrake, copyeditor Rebeka Cohen and designer Raymonde Watkins, who have been a pleasure to work with.

Many other V&A colleagues have given support and professional acumen in order to realize the exhibition, particularly Linda Lloyd Jones, Sarah Scott, Zoe Louizos and Lauren Papworth (Exhibitions), Pip Simpson, Laura Middlehurst, Sam Brown and Heather Whitbread (Design), Nicola Breen (Technical Services), Bryony Shepherd and Asha McCloughlin (Interpretation), and Laura Mitchell, Jordan Lewis and Kate Morais (Press Office). Maria Blyzinsky from the Exhibitions Team provided patient editorial guidance for the exhibition text.

I would also like to record my thanks to Victoria Anthoni, Survjit Cheeta, Rachael Long and the Lister and Hurlston families, especially Jean, Peter, Katie and Susan Lister, Susan Hurlston, Freddie Hurlston and Poppy and Holly Hurlston.

Jenny Lister

Introduction
Making Fashion History

Dame Mary Quant revolutionized the way women dress. From the 1950s, her distinctive look expressed a new attitude to fashion, and a different approach to life, which a whole generation wanted to experience too; and her innovative boutiques helped to make shopping on the high street an exciting activity for men and women. Quant's clothes were often radical for their time. In the late 1950s she used traditional materials in unusual ways, and in the 1960s she utilized modern synthetic materials, bringing manufacturing innovations to the public. Boldly packaged Mary Quant tights, dressmaking patterns and cosmetics made designer style affordable, and her home furnishings subsequently brought fashion to domestic interiors. Before long, her image, name, and daisy logo, represented a global lifestyle brand.[1]

Quant was given an OBE (Order of the British Empire) in 1966 'as a fashion designer and for her contributions to export'[2] and made a Dame in 2015, amongst the many other awards and accolades she collected over her lifetime. She is often credited with many fashion and retailing innovations, particularly for popularizing the mini skirt. Yet as a designer, she underplayed her intuitive vision, stating that her clothes simply reflected the mood of the time. Writing in her first autobiography, *Quant by Quant*, published in 1966, she acknowledged her ability to 'catch the spirit of the day and interpret it in clothes before other designers', but recognized that she started her career at the same time 'that "something in the air" was coming to the boil.'[3] 'The clothes I made just happened to fit in exactly with the teenage trend, with pop records and espresso bars and jazz clubs' [1].[4]

The aim of this book is to uncover the true story behind the fashion legend, tracing the development of Mary Quant's style from the 1950s to the 1980s, using a variety of sources. For the first time, the V&A has been given exclusive access to material from Quant's personal archive. Illustrated with photographs showing selected examples from the V&A's collection, surviving clothes and designs by Quant are complemented by fashion photographs showing how the garments were marketed, sourced from magazines, newspapers and archives, both private and public. The life stories of the original wearers of garments help to demonstrate their particular social context and meaning for fashion consumers.

The ≠WeWantQuant campaign launched by the V&A in June 2018 invited the public to lend or donate specific garments designed by Quant to enable the Museum to represent a more comprehensive range of her designs. This resulted in over 40 new acquisitions for the permanent collection. Each of these garments is enhanced with details about the original wearer and their social background, why Mary Quant designs were specially chosen at the time, and the reasons for treasuring the garments for so long. Over 1,000 people responded offering Quant cosmetics and other memorabilia, some contributing photographs of Quant garments being worn at the time. Jean Scott, who bought her dark red version of the classic 'Footer' jersey dress in 1966, while she was training to be a teacher in Newcastle, described the dress as an 'investment piece, to wear anywhere', and was still wearing it in 1969 when she was photographed with her uncle on the promenade at Penarth in South Wales [2].

Quant's own account in *Quant by Quant* provides a vibrant sense of the experience of making an international success of the brand in the late 1950s and early 1960s. The voices of many of her colleagues and employees, interviewed as part of the research for this book, add new perspectives from the network of skilled workers and specialists which any fashion business relies on, in the linked fields of manufacturing, distribution and fashion marketing. This broader context is vital for assessing the true significance of Quant's career. Throughout this book, additional contributions by fashion, design and advertising historians, focus on particular aspects of Quant's work

1 Mary Quant
Dress with tie, *c.*1966
Wool jersey
V&A: T.28–2018

2 Jean Scott with her uncle, Eddie Armstrong, Penarth, 1969

which were especially forward-thinking at the time, and which remain just as relevant today.

As Quant made plain herself, the success of her fashion brand was underpinned by the contributions of her husband Alexander Plunket Greene, who had a particular flair for marketing and publicity. Likewise, their friend and business partner Archie McNair provided business and legal acumen, and 'rationalised the mood in the air'.[5] Both men understood the potential of Quant's talent for design, and helped this develop into a huge market.

This partnership, the perfect team, had the ideal figurehead to promote the concept and the product [3]. Quant embodied her brand, modelling her own designs as effectively as a professional model. Her photogenic appearance, with very dark reddish hair, cut from 1960 into a 1920s-style bob, and strong, clear features, demonstrated the look, and helped to ensure that the business could take full advantage of expanding media opportunities. Another fortuitous attribute, her unusual but class-less name, short and punchy, also helped to drive the transformation of the amateurish 'Bazaar', a small but dynamic boutique selling accessories and pyjamas to friends in south-west London, into an international fashion brand. The decision to market her clothes under her own name rather than her married name was probably also strategic from a marketing perspective, perhaps underlining her youth and independence. But she was far more than just a front woman. Perhaps most significantly, Quant's ability to talk and write perceptively and provocatively about fashion secured attention from journalists and filmmakers, although she sometimes needed encouragement from her colleagues to overcome her natural shyness. As early as 1960, Quant became an international celebrity, not only as the face of her fashion business, but also as the personification of London and what came to be known as the 'Swinging Sixties'. She defined the ideal 'Chelsea Girl': young, slender, confident, unconventional, and as such she demonstrated the Chelsea lifestyle.

To the south west of central London, bordering the Thames, Chelsea had long been home to artists and provided a London base for the upper classes; by the 1950s, the area attracted both young professionals and students. But it was also a popular area for middle-class families, as the publisher Alexandra Pringle recalled in 1988, remembering the King's Road of her childhood, with its 'tall plane trees, squares of white-fronted houses and red-coated pensioners', and ordinary shops like 'Jones the Grocer, where there were glass-topped biscuit tins, Sidney Smith's the drapers, and the Woolworths with its counters piled high with sweets', and 'sedate expeditions' such as 'missions to Peter Jones for dress patterns or fabric'. Amongst the family homes were also houses divided into bed-sitting rooms or studios, which attracted artists and actors. As Pringle grew into her teens, following the media fame of Mary Quant and Bazaar, and the other boutiques which soon opened up, the King's Road became a cat-walk, with young women wearing 'big floppy hats, skinny ribbed sweaters, key-hole dresses, wide hipster belts.... white lipsticked lips and thick black eyeliner, hair cut at alarming angles, op-art earrings and ankle-length white boots'.[6]

As Quant observed in 1966, 'Chelsea ceased to be a small part of London; it became international, its name interpreted as a way of living and a way of dressing far more than a geographical area.' After the intense development and commercialization of the 1960s, the King's Road remains one of London's prime shopping destinations for well-known fashion brands.

Quant and the Chelsea look began to be noticed in the American fashion industry newspaper *Women's Wear Daily* in 1959.[7] By 1960, her visit to New York was the subject of an article in the American magazine *Life*, which identified Quant and her husband as 'exponents of elegantly way out ways both in clothes and behaviour' and noted their friendship with the Armstrong-Joneses (Princess Margaret and her new husband Antony) observing that: '... their clothes seem wackier than they

are because they come from England, stronghold of the court gown, the sturdy tweed and the furled umbrella' [4]. Quant's clothing and its portrayal in the media certainly capitalized on the subversion of these stereotypes of traditional Britain. The caption to the lead image notes Quant's 'own design tartan suit with easy top, very short skirt'. Barely revealing her knees, and accessorized with a substantial hat, the suit seems formal to contemporary eyes, but was radical in 1960s America. An example of this same tartan suit, in bright yellow and black woven wool MacLeod tartan, is in the collection of the Fashion Museum in Bath.[8] Widespread adoption of shorter skirts took a few years, gaining pace after 1964, and by 1966, designers including Quant promoted the extreme thigh-revealing mini skirt. This garment would eventually dominate fashion for the rest of the decade and is still part of conventional dress, 50 years later.[9]

The 1960 *Life* feature highlighted the sale of a range of Quant's designs to the upmarket New York department store Henri Bendel. Quant's business trip to consolidate this deal was an exciting breakthrough, as she describes in *Quant by Quant*, particularly for experiencing the fast-paced American work ethic, meeting women in business and for seeing American methods for producing clothes in accurate sizes. She and Plunket Greene returned inspired by American sportswear and coordinates, which prompted them to move into mass production. A Mary Quant wholesale range was launched in the UK in autumn 1961, at the same time as a deal to design garments manufactured and retailed by the vast American chainstore JC Penney.[10] This later agreement lasted until 1971 and launched her brand into the international market.

The British ready-to-wear or wholesale industry already had an established export business, with an infrastructure that developed during the post-war period, largely because of the activities of the Model House Group, later known as the Fashion House Group, lead by the designer Frederick Starke. The companies within the group successfully promoted ready-to-wear clothing as an acceptable alternative to couture during the post-war period for high status British customers. They also sold to international buyers who demanded good quality, good value clothing that represented the tradition and prestige of London. Brands such as Susan Small as well as designer Starke, with his Frederica line of 1959, responded to the youthful Chelsea look, as defined by Mary Quant. Trade magazine *The Ambassador*, re-launched in 1946 with government support, helped Britain to promote itself as a global exporter of fashion after the war.[11] Other initiatives, such as London Fashion Week, instigated in 1958, established London as a viable competitor to Paris and New York.[12]

Quant and her fashion business boldly capitalized on the opportunities presented by the international demand for British fashion, and she set up a separate wholesale company, Mary Quant's Ginger Group, in 1963.[13] This range was sold in British department stores and independent boutiques, as well as equivalent retailers in Australia, America, Canada and many European countries. The long-established clothing manufacturer Steinberg & Sons created Quant's designs under license for the Ginger Group line. The vital relationships between business, manufacturing, distribution and designer, so often left out of fashion history, are highlighted here in Regina Lee Blaszczyk's essay 'Doing Business in Transatlantic Fashion: The Experience of Mary Quant' (p.110). Once the success of the licensing business model for the Quant brand was established (whereby manufacturers made her designs at their own cost, paying Mary Quant Ltd a licensing fee), the route to mass production and increasing diversification was clear. Archie McNair perceived the financial potential of this business model early on, realizing that with Mary's design talent and ability to produce large numbers of designs, there was no need to directly employ seamstresses beyond the small team that made samples. The company Mary

4 'A British Couple's Kooky Styles'
Life, 5 December 1960
Photograph by Ken Heyman

Quant Ltd remained based at the same small office at 3 Ives Street, SW3 from 1958 to the late 1990s, with an outpost for Ginger Group at 9 South Molton Street, W1, employing about 30 individuals at any one time.[14] This undoubtedly contributed to the friendly, supportive work ethos consistently described in testimonials by those who were employed by the company.

The precise mix of social backgrounds represented by Quant, Plunket Greene and McNair, was another vital strength of the brand. As detailed in *Quant by Quant*, and explored in more detail in the following chapter of this book, Quant's parents were academically-minded, both grammar school teachers originally from south Wales, working in south-east London. They instilled a strong work ethic in their children, insisting that both Mary and her brother Tony grew up expecting to earn their own living. Meanwhile, Quant's future husband Alexander Plunket Greene was born into one of England's oldest and most influential aristocratic families, through his mother Elizabeth Russell, a cousin of Herbrand, the 11th Duke of Bedford. The family seat of the Dukes of Bedford is Woburn Abbey in Bedfordshire, the Palladian mansion which was at the centre of Britain's social and political life since the seventeenth century, and which opened to the public in 1955. Amongst his many notable relatives on this side of Plunket Greene's family were the philosopher Bertrand Russell, and his father Richard, who was the son of the celebrated singer Harry Plunket Greene.

Archie McNair's family lived in Tiverton, Devon. His father Donald was employed as a mercantile clerk in Exeter in the 1911 census. His maternal grandfather, Thomas Jourdan, was joint owner of a boot polish factory, and made a fortune from the patent for a kit for patching car tyres.[15] He was a strong influence, successfully buying patents and shares in companies, and stimulating his son's interest in business and finance. The McNair family were members of the strict Christian sect the 'Brethren', known as the Plymouth Brethren by the outside world. During the Second World War, while his two future friends and business partners were still children, McNair experienced combat first-hand as a pilot on the Thames in the Auxiliary Fire Service – a highly dangerous occupation.

Meanwhile, Alexander Plunket Greene attended school at Bryanston, where he became close friends with Terence Conran, whereas Quant (according to her autobiography) enjoyed great freedom as an evacuee in Kent and later in Wales, while her parents focused on their multiple responsibilities as teachers of evacuated schoolchildren. As Quant noted, the disruption and upheaval experienced during the war resulted in a liberated childhood for many, while their parents were away or pre-occupied with the challenges of keeping life and limb together. Quant's generation took their wartime experiences forward into adult-hood, turning the necessary attributes of resourcefulness and risk-taking to positive advantage.

Quant's life story follows the transformation of Britain from Second World War austerity to a globalized, post-industrial nation. She designed the clothes that expressed these changes for women, some of whom were able to go to grammar school, and on to university, secretarial college or training as nurses or teachers, later developing careers, often alongside bringing up a family. Many worked in the fashion industry. While there were many other innovative and well known young designers who also harnessed the opportunities of the 1950s consumer boom, such as John Stephen, Kiki Byrne, John Bates and Jean Muir, Quant became the ultimate fashion icon for Swinging London, essentially because she was female, and because she was the first. Her clothes, and eventually the mini skirt, came to symbolize the triumph of youth, freedom and hedonism against the Establishment – the traditional hierarchy of British society, personified by the London businessman in his formal tailored suit and bowler hat. Film footage such as 'Mary (Export) Quant', by British Pathé

of 1966, shows her in action as a strong, assertive influencer, in City meetings with powerful men such as Leon Rapkin of Steinbergs.[16] Quant exercised considerable power as the design source, and maker of decisions, which would generate sales for the business as a whole. Before the 1960s, designers of ready-to-wear clothing were paid little, and received scant recognition but Quant's strong presence in print and in filmed documentaries raised the profile of design and designers in general; at the time, for a woman, this was remarkable.

Although Quant said little that directly connected her views to political feminism ('I didn't have time to wait for women's lib'[17]), she certainly empowered herself and other women. She was a highly visible and successful working woman – designing clothes and shoes which provided an alternative to the 1950s' tight-waisted hourglass, high-heeled silhouette, and which were unrestricting, natural and 'suited to the actions of normal life.'[18] Her 1966 autobiography provided a kind of career manual for young women, particularly those who wanted to work in fashion [5]. Design consultant Barbara Fowkes described how the book inspired her:

> When I finished design school it gave me the confidence I needed to get my first industry job with Puritan Fashions, the company that produced the Mary Quant collection in the US. No question, she revolutionized women's fashion....If it weren't for Mary Quant, I imagine women might still be fiddling around with dangling garters and other binding hardware, however for me, it was her impact on the female workforce that I found most commendable... every once in a while when I'm feeling stuck I leaf through my very used copy of *Quant by Quant* to remind me that all things are possible.[19]

Quant's powerful brand and this wider social significance was promoted by the media, which was itself going through a revolution, as more

5 Portrait of Mary Quant, used on the cover of the first edition of *Quant by Quant*, 1966
Photograph by David Bailey

As his assistant Annabel Mackay (née Taylor) recalled, he was 'a wizard at public relations, much sought after by the ladies of the fashion press' (see Mackay's account in Part 3). From the late 1950s Mary Quant enjoyed the support of senior fashion journalists including Caterine Milinaire (of *Queen* magazine, daughter of the Duke of Bedford and so related to Plunket Greene), Clare Rendlesham of *Vogue*, and Ernestine Carter of the *Sunday Times*. Other newspaper journalists such as Meriel McCooey (also the *Sunday Times*), Prudence Glynn (the *Times*), Marit Allen (*Queen* and *Vogue*) and Felicity Green (*Daily Mirror*) regularly reported on Quant's fashion shows, bringing news of her inventive designs to a broader audience. Suzy Menkes reported on Mary Quant as a young journalist at Cambridge University, and designs by Quant were in her fashion collection, auctioned in 2013.[20] Journalists and fashion editors working for new magazines aimed at younger women such as Deirdre McSharry for *Cosmopolitan* and Brigid Keenan for *Nova* (Keenan worked at the *Times* and *Sunday Times* first), featured Quant designs, leaving a legacy of many fascinating fashion images and articles which document the popularity and target audience for Mary Quant designs.

The Quant team were at the centre of the overlapping worlds of journalism, photography and modelling from the start – McNair having established his own portrait studio at 128 King's Road, later moving it upstairs once his coffee bar opened. The fashion photographers Quant worked with are discussed by Susanna Brown in her contribution (p.80), while Stephanie Wood reveals some of the stories of the models who appear in a number of the many iconic photographs produced for the brand for their own publicity use, and as created by fashion editors for publication (p.61).

The Mary Quant cosmetics range, manufactured by Gala Cosmetics from 1966 at their large factory in Surbiton, captured the brand's irreverent attitude with products such as 'Come Clean' cleanser and 'Starkers' foundation.

and more people gained access to television sets and magazines. Developments in the quality of photography and colour printing meant that tabloid newspapers incorporated more visual imagery than ever before, using photography more than illustration, and so bringing information about designer fashion to a mainstream audience. Traditional magazines such as *Vogue* and *Queen* were revamped, featuring new pages about fashion specifically for younger consumers, while new magazines were launched targeting working class girls, such as *Honey* (1960) and *Petticoat* (1966). The novelty of designers like Mary Quant provided vital celebrity stories as well as adding expensive and appealing colour pages with the advertising provided by their licensees. From 1965 this included her Alligator rainwear and Youthlines underwear ranges, which was followed in 1966 by Mary Quant cosmetics.

Quant's ability to secure publicity for herself and her shops on magazine pages was partly founded on Plunket Greene's innate charm.

6 *Mary Quant's London*, London Museum exhibition catalogue, 1973

6 *Mary Quant's London*, London Museum exhibition catalogue, 1973

In her essay on this aspect of the business (p.154), Beatrice Behlen explains how specially trained advisors sold these cosmetics in department stores. The make-up in particular was promoted around the world by distinctive advertising that relied on the common currency of the Mary Quant brand; a shared knowledge of Quant's appearance and what she was like, and the humour and attitude she represented. Janine Sykes looks at the distinctive advertising strategies for the brand in her essay on p.164.

In 1969 the Bazaar shops closed,[21] signifying the company's commitment to the global brand and licensing model, rather than selling direct to customers, and extending beyond fashionable dress into many other areas. Mary Quant designs and ideas, all personally approved by Quant, were instead sold for others to manufacture, resulting in more collaborations such as the Daisy dolls, 9 inches (23 cm) high and produced by Model Toys in Hong Kong, making 1970s glamour affordable for girls with just 10 pence a week for pocket money. Mary Quant style was brought to interiors, with duvet covers and coordinated soft furnishing ranges produced by Dorma, part of the Carrington Viyella group, and the manufacturer ICI (Imperial Chemical Industries) which also produced Dulux paint. Johanna Agerman Ross provides a view of these and other 'lifestyle' ranges from the perspective of an interior and product design historian, as well as looking at the innovative interiors of the Mary Quant boutiques (p.194).

On 29 November 1973 the London Museum (now the Museum of London) opened a retrospective exhibition, *Mary Quant's London* [6]. Choosing to focus on fashion was an innovative step for the Museum's director, John Hayes, although the public demand for fashion in museums had been clearly indicated by the response to the exhibition *Fashion: An Anthology*, curated by Cecil Beaton at the V&A in 1971.[22] Both exhibitions were designed by Michael Haynes. *Mary Quant's London* was

seen to be an appropriate and popular subject for marking the London Museum's final year in the borough of Kensington and Chelsea (before its move to the Barbican Centre), and also for reflecting on the social and cultural shifts from 1955 to 1965. Amidst high inflation and economic depression in the UK, the exhibition may also have fulfilled a nostalgic desire to look back at a time that was perceived to be full of optimism and change. As Professor Brian Morris reflected in 1973, commercialism and consumer culture was taking over, and in the eight years since its conception, the 'revolution' had 'lost its impetus. Some Pop idols have been declared bankrupt, espresso bars have disappeared, the Beatles have disbanded. But much of what they stood for has passed deep into the fabric of British culture, and for ten years at least, "Swinging London" was the envy of the world'.[23] The success of the exhibition was demonstrated by the fact that its run was extended for two months beyond the planned closing date of 30 June 1974.[24]

In the decade between 1963 and 1973, Mary Quant and her team had expanded the licensing business to incorporate stockings and tights, underwear, sunglasses, hats and shoes, home furnishings and other functional and fashionable products which could be produced on a truly industrial scale. The London Museum's exhibition celebrated Mary Quant's special place in fashion history, not for the mini skirt, for tights or even hot pants, but for her unconventional attitude, for 'blast[ing] an opening in the wall of tradition through which other young talents have poured … in every area of fashion she opened windows which had been sealed tight for too long.'[25] This sense of her brand representing an attitude, or a set of ideas, has become the most pervasive of her influences in contemporary life. The daisy motif, wherever it was seen, represented fun and life-enhancing rebellion, as the London Museum's poster and catalogue cover, showing London's Big Ben with a daisy replacing the clock face, both demonstrate [6]. The daisy cypher anticipated the globalizing force of purely visual signs representing brands such as the Macintosh apple and the Nike 'swoosh'. As Kevin Roberts (who began his career at Mary Quant cosmetics, later becoming the Chairman and CEO of Saatchi & Saatchi, and author of Lovemarks, The Future Beyond Brands) has said: 'Mary Quant created something much bigger than a Brand. She created a Movement. A Movement of Freedom, Confidence, Fun and Optimism. A Movement of Hope and Liberation.'[26]

As the 1970s progressed, Mary Quant went on to develop more ranges, reaching further into lifestyle areas, including wine and carpets, as well as designing clothes for the London Pride label and Viyella House. She worked increasingly in Japan where her minimal style and British heritage found instant connection with consumers. Simultaneously, European fashion reflected the influence of Japanese designers with Rei Kawakubo and Yohji Yamamoto showing in Paris for the first time and deconstructing traditional ideas about the fashionable body, with monochrome,

asymmetrical shapes. Back on the King's Road, at number 435, Vivienne Westwood and Malcolm McLaren's shop SEX became the centre of London's emerging punk movement. Androgynous and spontaneous, it embodied the next generation's challenge to the British Establishment. Designers like John Galliano and others graduating from British art schools in the 1980s, who went on to secure high profile careers for couture labels such as Givenchy and Dior, demonstrated the creative legacy nurtured by the British art school system and the prestigious fashion courses in London which have developed since Quant's own art school training.

Mary Quant was key to promoting British fashion on the international stage, and her work contributed to the popularization of Western style. She built her own distinctive brand, which helped to define a quirky, youthful and rebellious Britishness, which is still part of the national identity today. Her visionary understanding of the mass appeal of affordable style helped to change the fashion system, making it into a medium that many more people can choose to enjoy. As Quant wrote in 1966: 'fashion is not frivolous; it is a part of being alive today.'[27]

Over 50 years later, this statement is still relevant. Designers work across international borders. Time and space have been transformed by digital technology, enabling instant fashion communication. Social media has turned typical consumers into streetstyle bloggers and fashion authorities to rival the long-established magazines, and everyone can present themselves online as a brand – an ideal version of themselves. This is a kind of empowerment, a democratic movement: anti-mainstream and anti-corporate brands. Paradoxically, the essence of Mary Quant and the appeal of her brand, was that it was in itself anti-brand, representing individual style and self-expression rather than a faceless corporate identity; Quant understood and harnessed the commercial potential of style, and of democratizing fashion.

MATITA

Erik Hat

PART ONE

1919–1955

Before Bazaar

The history of Mary Quant Ltd begins with the birth of Archie McNair, on 16 December 1919. The First World War had ended just over a year before; his father Donald had fought in Palestine, and his mother Janie-Grace Jourdan had already given birth to an older son.[1] McNair was to be the second of six siblings – four brothers, and two sisters. McNair's childhood, as previously noted, was unusual, as the family was part of the Plymouth Brethren, a world-renouncing Christian sect which did not socialize beyond the group, and did not allow modern inventions such as wireless sets or gramophones in the home. Despite this, the McNairs led a comfortable middle-class lifestyle, in a large Queen Anne-style villa in Tiverton, Devon, with nine bedrooms and six servants, and McNair was a day pupil at nearby Blundell's School. His later interest in, and aptitude for, business seems to have stemmed from his maternal grandfather, Thomas Jourdan, who made a fortune from his business acquisitions, which included the patent for a car tyre repair kit from Alfred Dunhill. Thomas Jourdan owned a bright yellow Rolls Royce open tourer, and was driven around in it by his chauffeur. McNair described this as one of the enduring memories of his 1920s childhood in a series of interviews recorded with the fashion historian Alistair O'Neill for the British Library in 2008.

After leaving school, McNair trained as a solicitor in Exeter, to comply with his parent's wishes rather than his own (a spinal injury meant that sedentary work was excruciatingly painful). The outbreak of the Second World War interrupted this training, and as a conscientious objector, he moved to London and volunteered as a pilot on the Thames for the Auxiliary Fire Service – one of the most risky occupations of the Civil Defence Service. He returned to Exeter after the war, in order to continue studying for his legal qualifications, but eventually decided to leave the Brethren in 1947 and launch a new career in photography. He moved back to London in 1950, buying a requisitioned shop with a flat above – 128 King's Road – from Kensington and Chelsea council. This was converted into his photography studio and named Alister Jourdan. This prime location on the sunny side of the King's Road, bought for a bargain price of £1,750, became the focus of the Chelsea set when McNair opened a coffee bar on 4 July 1954 [8]. The Fantasie had an Italian Pavoni espresso machine – one of the first in London – and functioned as 'a sort of common room' for the actors, artists and aristocrats who lived in the houses and bedsits on the surrounding streets and squares [9]. McNair's particular friends and neighbours included Antony Armstrong-Jones (later Lord Snowdon), the Hon. Robert Erskine, the Marquis of Bristol and the influential publisher, Mark Boxer, who later worked on the revitalized *Queen* magazine. McNair's description of the lively social and musical events centred around the Fantasie contrasts greatly with that of his conservative upbringing, which seems to have left all the McNair siblings with an 'irreverent' attitude to life, in reaction to the 'obviously dotty' rules of the Brethren. His determination to enjoy life was shared by many who had lived and worked through the war.[2]

Three weeks after the Fantasie opened, on 7 August 1954, McNair married Catherine Fleming at Lavenham church in Suffolk.[3] The couple had met in Chelsea in 1953;

PREVIOUS PAGE
7 Advertisement for Matita suit with hat by Erik
Tatler and Bystander, 7 June 1950

8 Fantasie coffee bar, 128 King's Road, 1955. Film still from *Food for a Blush*, released in 1959

9 Archie McNair at Fantasie coffee bar,
with writer Nick Tomalin (far left),
128 King's Road, 1954

Fleming had been a nurse in the Royal Navy, and was working as a ceramics teacher. By this point, McNair was at the centre of the Chelsea set and perfectly equipped with the energy, creativity and entrepreneurial spirit to invest in property development.

McNair's business and legal brain was fundamental to generating the future success of Mary Quant's designs. But it was the wit, humour and social prowess of Alexander Plunket Greene that enabled the team to generate headlines and fashion stories, and market these to the fashion press of London and their readers. The chance meeting of Plunket Greene and Quant while at Goldsmiths College generated a kind of chemical reaction between two style leaders, and the true beginning of the Quant brand. In *Quant by Quant* the designer devotes the first pages to describing her future husband's unique approach to dressing, and his impact on those around him: he wore silk pyjama tops as shirts, with narrow, short fitted trousers, apparently borrowed from his mother, which revealed white calves above his Chelsea boots.[4]

Quant attended Goldsmiths College, probably from around 1949, or possibly a little earlier. Records have not been found which confirm this, but she may have taken a two year National Diploma in Design, followed by a one year Art Teachers' Diploma, which was a suitable compromise, as her parents refused to allow her to work in fashion. Plunket Greene joined later to study Illustration. He had just left Bryanston – the public school in Dorset encouraging liberal and creative values that Quant described as 'a sort of mock Eton except that the boys there seem to have an extraordinary amount of freedom.'[5] Born on 17 June 1932, he was an only child, and his parents, Richard Plunket Greene and Elizabeth Russell, were at the centre of the Bright Young Things – the fashionable young elite fictionalized by Evelyn Waugh in novels such as *Vile Bodies* (1930) and *Brideshead Revisited* (1945). Waugh became friends with the Plunket Greene family after meeting at Oxford, and was best man at the wedding of Richard and Elizabeth on 21 December 1926 at Holy Trinity, Sloane Square.[6] According to Quant, Richard Plunket Greene, his brother David and sister Olivia sometimes travelled to New York, to go to jazz clubs in Harlem and to have trousers tailored there, anticipating the American connection later established with the Mary Quant business venture. Waugh described Richard as:

> Piratical in appearance, sometimes wearing ear-rings, a good man in a boat, a heavy smoker of dark, strong tobacco, tinged, as were his siblings, with melancholy, but also infused with a succession of wild, obsessive enthusiasms. He brought to the purchase of a pipe or a necktie the concentration of a collector.[7]

Richard and Elizabeth's marriage brought together two families, both of which had nurtured illustrious and unconventional society figures including musicians and authors: Richard was the son of Harry Plunket Greene, a well-known concert baritone singer, and Gwendoline

Parry, daughter of the composer Sir Hubert Parry. Alexander's mother Elizabeth Russell was descended from the Dukes of Bedford, and her relations included Bertrand Russell, the philosopher, and her aunts were Flora and Diana Russell (who in their youth were at the centre of artistic circles in late Victorian London). As Quant pointed out in *Quant by Quant*, for Alexander to go into 'trade' and run a shop, was very shocking for his family. His great aunts were 'prepared to put up with the Army or the Church or being a farmer … or simply pottering about being a duke. But selling dresses was too much.'[8] Nevertheless Aunt Flora left her home in Surrey to her great nephew Alexander in her will, and the house became a vital retreat for the family as the business of Mary Quant grew.

Richard and Elizabeth Plunket Greene enjoyed motor racing, and published two detective novels together: *Where Ignorance is Bliss* (1932) and *Eleven-Thirty Till Twelve* (1934), although the couple divorced when Alexander was eight years old.[9] His memories of his father, as told to Quant, were of 'an exciting stranger, a tall, handsome, buccaneering man in naval uniform who turned up out of the blue at rare intervals with exciting stories.' Alexander spent the war years living with his maternal grandmother, Lady Victoria Russell, at The Ridgeway, Shere, near Guildford, along with 16 girl evacuees. His cousins Rachel and Caroline Blakiston were living nearby at Clandon House, where their father Noel Blakiston was in charge of the temporarily rehoused Public Record Office.

Alexander's many relations and their rich cultural life exerted a strong influence on him. This blend of elegant bohemianism, with intellectual and political activity, found natural expression in the coffee bars of Chelsea and was part of the background to the Mary Quant brand. The Plunket Greenes treated everyone equally, as family or friends, as customers and staff of Bazaar testified from its earliest days.[10] The same sense of inclusion, wit and fun characterized fashion photographs and later on, advertising for Mary Quant products. Mary Quant's designs of the early 1960s literally looked back to the exuberance of the Bright Young Things of the previous generation. Quant often reinterpreted the boyish flapper styles in her designs, and even had her hair cut into a 1920s-style bob in 1960.

Quant adeptly describes the profound contrast between her own family background and that of her in-laws in *Quant by Quant*. Her parents, John Quant, always known as Jack and Mildred Jones[11] were born in Tonypandy, Glamorgan and Kidwelly, Carmathenshire – both deprived coal-mining areas of South Wales. The 1911 census records Mary Quant's paternal grandfather Henry Quant as an Insurance Agent at Prudential, living in Pontypridd with his wife Caroline, two daughters and a son: Jack (officially John), Mary's father. Mary's mother Mildred Jones was the daughter of Thomas and Amy-Mary, both Elementary (Primary) school teachers, who employed a live-in servant. It is not known where Jack Quant and Mildred Jones met, but both went to grammar school and then Cardiff University, achieving first class degrees, and dedicating their lives to teaching in the grammar school system.[12] By 1925 they had moved to London, marrying in Woolwich[13] and settling at 43 Eaglesfield Road in Plumstead near Blackheath, where their children were born: Barbara (Mary) on 11 February 1930, and John Anthony (known as Tony), in 1933. According to her brother, Quant refused to answer to the name Barbara as a child.[14] The children were brought up to value the rewards of hard work and academic success; at home 'it was a sort of sin to sit around doing nothing….' So, with none of the inherited social advantages of the Plunket Greene family, Jack and Mildred Quant were nonplussed by the lifestyle represented by their daughter's new art school friends – people who prioritized 'the pursuit of pleasure and indulgence' over work. They found Plunket Greene's 'uninhibited language and behaviour' incomprehensible.[15]

Mary Quant's early education was interrupted by the outbreak of the Second World

there. Despite the rebelliousness and confidence Mary Quant seems to have shown in some situations, her memoir also reveals something about the shyness and reserve in her character, and also an early interest and awareness of fashion and love of sewing. One of her sketchbooks from 1944 survives in the family, showing her aptitude for drawing figures, albeit stylized children in the vein of Mabel Lucie Atwell [10].

Writing in her 1966 memoir, Quant describes constant embarrassment about her clothes as a child especially when forced to wear a cousin's 'ornate' dresses. Quant could already imagine her own designs. Inspired by the dance uniforms worn by a friend for tap lessons: very skinny black sweaters, short black pleated skirts and long black tights, white ankle socks and black patent ankle strap shoes. The girl had 'the sort of fringe now favoured by Vidal Sassoon. How I envied her!'[16]

Another early influence, after the family had moved back to London, was her father's sister, Aunt Frances, who would visit for shopping trips and stay at the Quant family home. According to *Quant by Quant*, Aunt Frances was a professional medium, who described both future husband and career in uncannily accurate detail to the teenaged Quant. Perhaps Quant inherited a kind of intuition, or feeling for what people want next, from her aunt.

After leaving school, Quant studied at Goldsmiths College where she was taught figure drawing by Sam Rabin who was tutor to Bridget Riley at the same time.[17] Quant's ability to produce fashion drawings was clearly nurtured here. Although the school did not teach fashion specifically, her course, probably the National Diploma in Design, entailed a wide range of study. In 2014 a sketchbook from her time at Goldsmiths was sold at auction. This included a series of fashion drawings, including a range of sinuous black evening dresses with contrasting bodices with the broad shoulderline of the 1940s [11].[18] Goldsmiths had developed a reputation for advanced instruction in fine art under Headmaster Clive Gardiner, and teacher

War and in about 1940, the whole family was evacuated to West Malling in Kent, with Jack and Mildred Quant in charge of a large group of Blackheath schoolchildren. Mary and her younger brother Tony enjoyed the freedom of the countryside, and often found themselves in charge of games and causing 'havoc' with the rest of the children. The constant presence of the war was exciting, especially as they were situated under the flight path of enemy planes heading towards London. These formative experiences may have nurtured resilience and an entrepreneurial spirit – after moving schools no less than four times while in Kent, the family relocated with Jack Quant and his evacuated schoolboys to Tenby in Wales, where Mary and Tony set up a profitable service cleaning boats and teaching sailing to children on holiday

training (both in art and other subjects) was another strength. The college was part of the University of London, but had a distinctive identity and considerable autonomy, and was also convenient, being only five miles away from Eaglesfield Road.[19] During her last year at college, Quant and Plunket Greene spent all their spare time together in central London or Chelsea, which meant that she would stay out until the last possible train from Charing Cross, to be home by 11pm, as agreed with her father. Lively details of elaborate practical jokes and nights out with Plunket Greene and their friends can be found in *Quant by Quant*, where she also describes the bohemian squalor of Plunket Greene's residence at his absent mother's house in Beaufort Gardens, Chelsea, and extravagant meals with champagne at Quaglino's in St James's on the days his allowance was paid.

Quant decided to leave Goldsmiths before qualifying for her Art Teachers' Diploma, determined she would never teach, despite her parents' wishes. Still living at home, she found a job as a junior apprentice in the workroom at

Erik's. 'Erik', the son of a Danish count, was the designer and proprietor of a high-class millinery shop situated next to Claridge's Hotel in Brook Street, at the heart of London's couture fashion quarter. Patricia Stacey (née Chilton), who worked for Erik as a copyist (an experienced milliner, who copied Erik's original designs, adapting them to suit individual clients) remembered Quant as a 'slight, slip of a girl', with 'long brown hair, usually tied back in a pony tail … quietly spoken and very shy…. But she was a good listener who never had to be told instructions twice. And as a result, she was quick to learn.'[20] In the early 1950s hats were an essential everyday accessory, not just reserved for the events of the London season, and Stacey's full account describes a busy working environment, thriving before the full impact of the post-war shift towards mass produced, informal clothing, which resulted in women dispensing with formal accessories [12]. Recalling the return to fashion of feminine, small hats after the end of clothes rationing in 1949, she then describes the room where Quant worked:

All the cutting, steaming, shaping and stitching took place in our workroom. This was a large basement room, which ran underneath the shop floor and housed the hotel boiler. It was warm and smelled of the cow gum used to stick on decorations. Bolts of fabric jostled for space with jars of buttons, spools of ribbon and boxes of thread. Every surface was littered with swatches and name tags, with a sprinkle of pins.[21]

While at Erik's, Quant would have visited the London haberdashers with a matcher, whose job was to collect samples, 'pieces of lace, netting, feathers … a simple reel of cotton or a special pelt of fur … the matchers had to have a marvellous eye … [Quant] had a good, natural eye of her own and became a neat stitcher, introducing the use of a curved needle which she borrowed from her brother who was studying dentistry at Guys Hospital.'[22] As Stacey concludes, Quant's days at Erik's were:

… the days of a diminishing world, and not the world which Mary wanted to cling on to. She was young, and wanted to enable people like herself to enjoy fun, affordable fashion. I would like to think that during the time Mary worked for Erik – which were undoubtedly formative years – she learned more than hat-making skills. Things like the importance of a good window display, a simple but memorable logo, or a well-executed fashion show. Perhaps, also, the ability to mix and match different accessories and try out new, synthetic materials, or – more important than all of these – the benefit of a happy, close-knit team.[23]

Stacey often observed Quant meeting Plunket Greene for lunch or for a drink in the bar at Claridge's, and had been told that they lived together – 'a pretty forward thing to do at such a young age in that era'. This may have been true, although the electoral register for 1955 records both Mary and Tony at their parents' address in Plumstead.[24] By this time, Quant and Plunket Greene spent most of their free time socializing in Chelsea, particularly at Finch's, a pub on the Fulham Road (a high street or radial road into central London, north of the King's Road). Here, they met many creative people: '… very clever young architects, painters, musicians, sculptors, film directors and layabouts congregated there', people who were 'positive and go-ahead', and passionately involved in their work, unconsciously creating what later became known as the Chelsea set.[25]

It was at Finch's, in 1954, where they were introduced to Archie McNair. Quant very precisely defined his role in making possible the local coffee bars, restaurants, and even Bazaar, although his appearance – with suit and umbrella – set him apart.[26] The three decided to work together and open a shop, with McNair and Plunket Greene both investing £5,000 (Plunket Greene had received an inheritance from his grandmother Lady Victoria Russell, who died on 11 February 1953, Quant's 23rd birthday). When Markham House, a corner shop with a basement at 138a King's Road, became vacant, after much negotiation, they bought the freehold for £8,000, and in early 1955 Quant left her job at Erik's.[27]

PART TWO

1955–
1962

Boutique
to
Wholesale

The story of Bazaar, and its transformation from a boutique run by amateurs in late 1955, to a flourishing designer label with a growing wholesale line and export market in America by 1962, is described in animated detail in *Quant by Quant*.[1] From the beginning, Quant and her two partners had clear ideas about how they wanted the shop to look, replacing the existing front windows with a plain glazed shop front, and taking away railings to leave a large forecourt. These alterations, which provoked strong objections from the London County Council planning department and the Chelsea Society, took six months, during which time Quant moved from her parents' home to a bed-sitting room in Oakley Street, nearby. Quant was paid £5 a week by McNair and Plunket Greene (twice what she had earned at Erik's) while she bought

stock for the opening, got to know wholesalers and visited art schools to buy jewellery made by students. The name 'Bazaar' was a clever choice, implying that their shop sold odd and interesting (bizarre) things, and also recalling the eclectic mix of artefacts to be found at a market or church bazaar. Bazaars are important in the history of retailing, going back to the eighteenth century; the first bazaars were covered walkways where exhibitions as well as shopping stalls encouraged shopping as a leisure activity.[2] This approach of creating edited selections for well-informed consumers to browse is successful today, in individual stores such as Colette in Paris (1997–2017), or Rei Kawakubo's Dover Street Market in London (opened in 2004).

Initially, rather than designing clothes for the shop, Quant gave herself the task of buying rather than designing – stocking the shop with

Nightshirts
for the
New Year

Photographed by
BERT HARDY

Grandpapa's nightshirt is
back with a difference—
and what a difference!
But one feels that grand-
papa, who was used
to having even the legs
of his chair draped for
propriety's sake, would
secretly have approved
of this borrowed fashion.

*Here are the details (from left
to right):*

*Striped and spotted shirt in
non-iron cotton, made like a
cami-knicker.(Fenwick 29s.6d.)*

*Short nightshirt in non-iron
cotton.* (Fenwick 29s. 8d.)

*Long nightshirt in fine flannel,
also in royal blue* (Bazaar,
King's Road, Chelsea.£5 9s.6d.)

*Short nylon nightshirt and
bloomers.* (Fenwick £5 5s. 0d.)

*Ankle-length cotton night-
shirt, which can also be worn
as a housecoat.* (Woolland's,
Knightsbridge. 75s. 9d.)

15 'Nightshirts for the
New Year'
Picture Post, 24 December
1955

Photograph by Bert Hardy

a 'bouillabaisse of clothes and accessories ...
sweaters, scarves, shifts, hats, jewellery and
peculiar odds and ends'. Black stretch tights and
small white plastic collars selling at 'two-and-six'
were sold in 'literally thousands'.[3] In 1959 she
recalled that: 'We opened with imports from
Italy and Austria which were really newsy ... and
kept selling out in the first few weeks. The next
step was getting London wholesale houses to
make up my own designs and eventually I was
able to open my own workroom.'[4] It appears to
have taken a year or so to get to this stage. From
the beginning, nightwear was included in an
eclectic mix of garments, including a bright red
nightgown featured in the Christmas edition of
Picture Post, 1955 [15]. Bert Hardy's photograph
now appears fraught with contemporary attitudes
to gender and race, showing infantilized models
with children's toys including a black doll.

Giving a slightly different account to Archie
McNair, Quant describes the shop opening after
the restaurant, with a party which spilled over
into a marquee outside [14]. Either way, a
notice in September's *Harper's Bazaar* suggests
that the opening was later than planned.[5] Old

friends from Finch's pub mixed with junior
assistants from fashion magazines; and from
that point the party atmosphere was revived
every night, with Alexander's club-like restaurant fuelling sales in the shop upstairs.

The blurring of work with social life meant
that Bazaar initially opened late, even on
Saturdays, in an era when many shops closed at
midday on Saturday. After a visit from a Shop
Act inspector,[6] Bazaar had to close on Saturday
evenings, and this became the time when Quant
and Plunket Greene would change the shop
window displays. Initially just a place where
they could pin blouses or hats flat to boards,
these windows became an art form, a brilliant
form of marketing, intended to shock people:
'We wanted to entertain people as well as to
sell to them', as Quant wrote. Occasionally
they would make some 'colossal, extravagant
gesture meant as a pure joke', wanting 'the old
ladies who had no intention of buying anything
to stop and stare ... we had to be arrogant then.
We had to make a sharp shocking statement
at the beginning to be noticed at all'.[7] The
windows, and the whole ethos of Bazaar

16 Bazaar, King's Road, shop window, December 1960
Photograph by Mark Peppe

17 Bazaar, Knightsbridge, shop window, c.1961
Mary Quant Archive

shared a spirit of irreverence and satire with the new theatre, television and publishing: *Beyond the Fringe* had opened in London in 1961, the same year that *Private Eye* was first published, and in 1962 *That Was the Week That Was* was broadcast on BBC television.

Sometimes the subject of a display would purposefully appeal to husbands and boyfriends, such as the Christmas window of 1960, which was photographed by an art student who worked in the opposite building. A mannequin, dressed in monochrome separates with white bodice and black skirt, was posed opposite a Harley Davidson motorbike, emerging out of a huge, gold foil wrapped parcel. A handwritten speech bubble caption reads: 'THINKS: just what I've always wanted' [16].[8] Such Christmas windows, which required a special effort for all retailers, could involve logistical challenges for the Plunket Greenes' friends, as Shirley Conran recalled:

Once, Alexander woke me at about midnight just before Christmas, to frantically ask, 'Have you got a stuffed partridge?', 'No, only a stuffed squirrel or stuffed fish, in glass cases.' 'No good.... How about a pear tree...?'[9]

Other windows employed surrealist tactics, such as one with a figure leading a large (dead but clean) lobster on a lead. Another showed a photographer figure hung upside down, his camera pointed at a mannequin hung at an obscure angle. Bazaar brought a distinctive, dry British sense of humour to the art of shop window display. American department stores were firmly established as the leaders in the field of visual merchandising, which had reflected art movements such as Surrealism at least since the 1930s. By the 1950s, artists including Roy Lichtenstein, Claes Oldenburg

and Andy Warhol were working on the window displays of stores such as the New York department store Bonwit Teller. In Britain, the Reimann School of Art and Design, initially established in Berlin but which moved to London in 1937, was the first to focus on commercial display. A teacher there, Natasha Kroll, became display manager for the innovative clothing store Simpson's of Piccadilly, creating ground-breaking new displays, sometimes topical, or often minimalist, from 1942 to 1956; Quant and Plunket Greene would undoubtedly have been aware of her work.[10]

At Bazaar, the mannequins themselves were unconventional. Quant worked with display artist John Bates, and a company called Barway Display, to create figures with 'contemporary high cheek-boned, angular faces and the most up to date haircuts. I wanted them with long, lean legs, rather like Shrimpton's,' she explained: 'made to stand like real-life photographic models in gawky poses with legs wide apart, one knee bent almost at right angles and one toe pointing upwards from a heel stuck arrogantly into the ground.'[11] Surviving photographs of these early windows on the King's Road and in the Knightsbridge shop, which opened in 1958, illustrate the flow of ingenious ideas for generating interest in Quant's designs [16, 17].

In 1966 Quant looked back on the early days of Bazaar as 'an awful hand to mouth existence' – the accounting was haphazard, and the trio were not taken seriously by the fashion trade.[12] But the demand for fashion for young people, chosen by people of a similar age, proved the potential of her unique approach, and slowly, the brand became established as a growing force, although its clothes were not necessarily cheap. High-end fashion magazine *Harper's Bazaar* was an early supporter of the shop. A small photograph in the 'Shopping Bazaar' feature of September 1955 shows a pair of 'smart tan pyjamas' with 'big penny spots' for 4 guineas. Published before Bazaar had opened, the caption mentions the 'wonderful range of hats by a young milliner, Mary Quant'.[13] Quant

mentions a pair of 'mad house pyjamas', with a retail price of almost £5, her entire weekly wage, in *Quant by Quant*, as one of her first designs for the shop. Quant recalls that she was then inspired to focus on designing clothes herself, especially as they were apparently bought by an American who openly stated that he would be copying them for mass production in the US. Equipped with only basic dressmaking skills, Quant began adapting Butterick patterns and making clothes in her bedsit, using fabric she bought at Harrods, and later finding three dressmakers and a cutter to help. The dresses were sold as soon as they were made, and Quant moved her belongings and her cottage industry to the flat over the Fantasie, a few doors up the road, towards Sloane Square.[14] Bazaar continued to stock clothes and accessories from other wholesale ranges such as O'Keefe and Michelle Deliss, which reflected Quant's particular style and vision of what her customers wanted to buy.

Quant's customers were initially a small group of friends and local residents of Chelsea, but increasingly, as the area became more developed, she attracted a more diverse clientele. As Quant famously said, 'snobbery has gone out of fashion and in our shops you will find duchesses jostling with typists to buy the same dress.'[15] She detected a gap in the market, for women like herself, who rejected existing stereotypes such as the debutante, needing formal dresses for dances or silk afternoon dresses for Ascot and Henley. As Fiona MacCarthy has described in *Last Curtsey: The End of the Debutantes*, the daughters of the British aristocracy, for centuries the focus of media attention each summer party season, were presented at court in a centuries old rite of passage, now represented a bygone era; a new social order was on its way. 1958 was the last year of court presentation, which fittingly, was the same year as the Knightsbridge branch of Bazaar was opened.[16] But formal parties continued for some, and the required debutante wardrobe came from Mayfair couturiers such as Norman Hartnell or Victor Stiebel, or reputable department stores such as

19 Tea towel printed with a map of Chelsea.
Original map designed by Mardie Madden for *Tatler
and Bystander*, May 1959, then produced as a
tea towel by the department store John Lewis, 1960
Museum of London: 89.70

Harrods, Woollands or Harvey Nichols. Cheaper dresses might be found in the Knightsbridge 'Madam shop' Norah Bradley, or Wakefords on the King's Road, or by having a style made up by a local dressmaker for a few pounds. A typical party dress of grey denim, as modelled by Mary Quant in July 1960, cost 15 $\frac{1}{2}$ guineas, or about £341 today,[17] while a cocktail dress by the well-known brand Susan Small in the same feature cost 12 guineas. A couture party dress might cost £250 or 238 guineas.[18]

An article in *Tatler and Bystander* magazine, 'The Young Face of Old Chelsea' – which provided a useful conceptual map of the area – highlighted the social hot spots as well as recent social changes and the young newcomers [19]. It focused on the wealthy pseudo-bohemians converting and updating old houses and

driving fashionable cars, as well as the 'ladies' wearing 'exaggerated fashion ... short skirts and eccentric coiffeurs, fur-lined leather coats and mink cloches; the gentlemen, languidly confident in natty suits, livid suede shoes, curly-brimmed trilbies pulled down over the eyebrows, bow-ties and long, low roadsters.'[19] This group contrasted with an opposing Chelsea tribe: impoverished students, rotating between coffee bars, nightclubs and 'each other's box rooms'; Beatnik-style women with long hair and 'black rimmed eyes, parchment faces and pale mouths, and long hairy sweaters pulled down over tight knee length skirts ... gentlemen in uniforms of well-worn jeans, floppy hair merging into a floppy jersey, and often a beard'.[20]

Exploiting the gap between these two extremes, Quant drew most inspiration from

20 'The Young Outlook in Fashion Design'
Harper's Bazaar, July 1957

Photograph by Tom Kublin

what may be the first time her portrait appeared in a fashion magazine, in *Harper's Bazaar* in July 1957. The accompanying article, 'The Young Outlook in Fashion Design', was written by Janey Ironside, professor of the three-year Fashion Design Diploma at the Royal College of Art (RCA). The article highlighted the new demand for 'clever young designers' and the professional training delivered by the course, with teaching from experts from the couture and wholesale industries; precisely what Quant had needed, but learned the hard way. Impressively, Quant was given a whole page colour photograph, wearing what is described as an 'Irish wool sweater', with 'tapering trousers' she designed to wear with it [20]. Her designs for the shop are described as 'work stamped by her feeling for subtle colouring and ease of movement.' While 'for her own copper colouring, she chooses off-beat shades of violet and blue'. On the following page, the article also featured RCA graduates working at Marks and Spencer, Berketex and Cresta, alongside influential textile designer Bernard Nevill.[24]

Around this time, Quant, Plunket Greene and McNair decided to open a second shop, in close collaboration with their friends Terence and Shirley Conran, on the prestigious shopping street Knightsbridge. This was a nerve-wracking financial commitment, but a lease was signed for a suitable premises at number 46, boldly positioned directly opposite Harrods, and the team plunged into the planning and designing of the new shop. This clearly placed the Bazaar brand as a major force in London retail. In the midst of all this activity, Plunket Greene and Quant finally decided to get married, in a very low-key civil ceremony at Chelsea Registry Office, witnessed by Jack and Mildred Quant and Elizabeth Plunket Greene. While on honeymoon in Ibiza, Quant bought a bright green 1930s swimming costume with 'singlet style shoulder straps and four-inch legs', which provided the source for designs of a 'series of pinafore or jumper dresses', which subsequently became one of her most successful styles. The

'the unprejudiced, international, forward-thinking generation' she described in 1966 as 'the Mods', and she delivered the simple, stylish clothes these young women required. The original modernist look, 'cool, sharp, almost anonymous' was classless and inclusive, as opposed to the arty, beatnik look associated with university graduates.[21] Today, mod is a sub-cultural style that has endured for both men and women, and perhaps can be seen as an attitude that transcends fashion: it is a look which 'fuses convention and rebellion', and involves a careful attentiveness to creating a whole image with subtle details of appearance.[22] In author Paul Gorman's words, 'Mary Quant's clean lines and new approach embodies the mod aesthetic'.[23]

Quant's attitude to self-presentation and her taste for casual clothes was encapsulated in

21 Mary Quant and Alexander Plunket Greene, 1960
Photograph by John Cowan
Mary Quant Archive

22 Model holding a Bazaar carrier bag, c.1959
Mary Quant Archive

Knightsbridge shop was open by the autumn of 1958, with a press party and fashion show making the most of the mezzanine gallery and stairs, organized with the help of fashion editor Clare Rendlesham. The shop is first mentioned in *Vogue* in December 1958.[25]

The new shop brought the Bazaar format of surprising window displays and lively fashion shows to a more mainstream audience. Publicity photographs show both Quant and Plunket Greene as the faces of the brand, now incorporat-

ing the shop name in bold capital letters on the Bazaar van, carrier bags, receipts and letterheads, with very effective use of graphic design [21, 22]. This field of design was flourishing in the early 1960s, with agencies like the Design Research Unit and Fletcher, Forbes and Gill creating influential corporate identities. The lettering (Bureau Grotesque) for the Bazaar identity was probably specified by Plunket Greene,[26] perhaps in consultation with the art director Tom Wolsey, who is likely to have been responsible for the occasional adver-

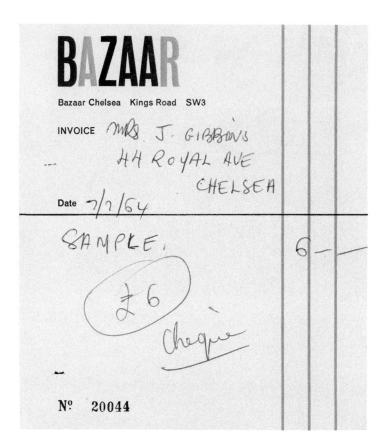

tisements for Bazaar (1960) and Mary Quant (1962) as seen in fashion magazines from the early 1960s.[27] Wolsey assisted with developing the daisy logo, from Quant's initial sketches, for branding and advertising for the Mary Quant cosmetics range from 1966.[28] Labelled garments from the 1950s and 1960 are branded with a simple white label, woven with 'BAZAAR'. From 1961 a new label reading 'BAZAAR/DESIGNED BY MARY QUANT' was introduced, clearly indicating the growing name recognition and prominence of Quant as a designer, although this was only a transition; from 1962 the labels simply had her name woven in bold capitals (see Appendix for further details).

Indeed, very few garments survive from these first years of Bazaar, before 1960. The 'Pinafore Pleats' style, a pinafore with a narrow line of swinging pleats at the hem was characteristic by 1959, and illustrated in the *Daily Mirror* on 24 October 1960, where Quant's interest in 'out-of-date school uniforms' and the 'moving effect of very short pleats' is described, along with her own collection of eight gym tunics, in denim, suiting cotton, flannel and linen.[29]

One of the earliest dresses designed by Mary Quant in the V&A collection is a straight pinafore, made from fine striped wool for men's formal dress trousers (known as the 'Alexander stripe') with belt and pockets. This dress was donated by Carola Zogolovitch, one of architect Sir Hugh Casson's three daughters. Norman Parkinson photographed a similar dress for a double page *Vogue* spread showing how it could be worn differently for day and night in a 'Young Idea' feature called 'Double Take' [25, 26].[30] Styled for day, the model (Suzie Leggatt) wore it over a black polo neck sweater, and accessorized it with LP records by Count Basie, Tom Lehrer and Ken Nordine, flat shoes and a large shopping bag. For evening, the same dress is worn with heels, a clutch bag and a man: Alexander Plunket Greene.

Quant was singled out as 'undiluted 1960' that year and Bazaar was receiving growing

attention from the fashion press.[31] In February 1960, *Queen* magazine, which was transforming its traditional image under the management of Jocelyn Stevens and art direction of Mark Boxer, with fashion editor Beatrix Miller, published a feature 'Beat the Beatniks – eligible clothes for debs'.[32] Parkinson photographed carefully posed models wearing prim shirtwaisters, immaculate tailored suits, carefully accessorized with hats, gloves and bags, against a backdrop of madly partying figures in black. A straight, drop-waisted 'cocktail dress for the young individualist in kingfisher blue Thai silk' from Bazaar indicates fashion's new direction, away from rules and regulations and towards increasing informality [27]. A similar silk dress in purple is in the V&A collection – a gift of Nicky Hessenberg, who described buying a first dress from Bazaar as a 'coming of age' landmark. The sister of Carola Zogolovitch, Hessenberg left her boarding school at 18, and on the fringes of the fading world of the debutante, she was bought the dress by her mother as a kind of bribe to help her navigate the ordeal of being launched in society as an adult. She went on to secretarial college, and later worked on the magazine *House and Garden*.[33]

Mary Quant's name as a designer was becoming so well known in 1960 that she was invited by Edward Rayne, celebrity shoemaker to the Royal Family, and chair of the INCSOC (Incorporated Society of London Fashion Designers) to design for his 'Miss Rayne' range. A private collector owns the only known surviving example of this collaboration, a pair of white court shoes with punched decoration, with distinctive Bazaar lettering stamped inside.[34] Quant also worked with the knitwear manufacturer John Laing of Hawick in the Scottish Borders in the early 1960s, producing the casual sweaters she preferred, often with masculine details such as the V-necked sweater owned by the V&A (T.1707–2017). The fur coat makers S. London appear to have made her designs too.[35] With ever more demands on her time, in the months before October 1960, and her trip to New York, Quant changed her hairstyle,

having it cut into a swinging bob, an early form of the famous Vidal Sassoon five point style, as her friend Shirley Conran recalled: 'Mary had wonderful hair – shoulder length, bell shape, the colour of a conker. She told me she cut it off because it took up too much of her time. I was awed by this brutal example of time and motion efficiency.'[36]

At a time when most women only wore trousers at very informal occasions or in private, Quant was a great advocate of trousers for fashionable dress. A rare pair of 'Mary Quant London' labelled trousers survive in her own archive. Made from striped worsted wool, the 'Alexander stripe', they clearly borrow from traditional tailoring for men, but are cut with a low waistline, described as 'cowboy style' by Quant. A fashion photograph from about 1962 shows how they were styled with a blouse and tousled hair to create an unconventional new

OPPOSITE
25 Mary Quant for Bazaar
Pinafore dress, 1960
Worsted wool
Given by Carola Zogolovitch
V&A: T.71 2018

26 Suzie Leggatt modelling 'Alexander
stripe' pinafore dress with Alexander
Plunket Greene
'Young Idea: Double Take'
Vogue, January 1960
Photographs by Norman Parkinson

look [29]. Appropriating trousers remained a strong theme in Quant's designs, although surviving examples are very rarely found now, perhaps because they were popular and consequently worn out before being discarded. Other designs, such as her distinctive grey flannel knickerbocker suits and tweed Norfolk jackets, parodied Victorian upper class male dress, borrowing garments and traditional British fabrics to create clothes which challenged the class system and promoted female independence [30].

In late 1960 or early 1961, with ever-growing demand for Quant's designs, McNair hired a secretary and PA named Shirley Shurville. Shurville was born in 'Cockney-land' in the Elephant and Castle, south of the Thames, and was awarded a place at a grammar school. There, in her own words, she 'changed her accent, pulled herself up by the bootstraps', and attended night school at St Martin's School of Art while working as a buying assistant at Simpson's in Piccadilly. Having also worked as PA to Barry Reed of Austin Reed, Shurville arrived at Bazaar Workshops Ltd (the registered company name before Mary Quant Ltd, when the wholesale line was introduced in 1962) well-equipped with versatile skills and relevant experience. Apart from a break of six months for the birth of her son, she stayed at the company for nearly a decade, at the helm of Ginger Group, based in South Molton Street, until 1968, when she went to work for Biba.

Initially Shurville helped Quant with buying from other wholesale ranges, but when the Mary Quant wholesale range was launched, she worked more closely with Plunket Greene on selling and marketing. Shurville recalled the task of expanding the number of stockists in 2017:

> Initially Mary was wary of me but began to relax after we had all had lunch together on my first day at La Popote – later on she began to trust my instincts after Archie had asked me to select some knitwear designs from a collection which

she had an appointment to view at Ives Street but wasn't able to attend. She liked them and ordered some for the two Bazaar shops.

The first Mary Quant wholesale range was launched in autumn 1961 and I worked with Alexander on the PR and Sales to a very limited group of stockists – 11 in that first season, such as Liberty's, who would know how to show the clothes as a group and not split them up on the general racks with garments from other suppliers. Alexander was brilliant with both the ladies from the press and the buyers – they all loved him, as did I. John Bates

30 Jean Shrimpton and Celia Hammond modelling
Mary Quant designs
Daily Mail, 16 August 1962
Photograph by John French

garments from the first collection and our utter belief that we were offering them pure gold!

I loved Mary's version of a Chanel-type suit in burgundy tweed, the low-necked jacket was edged with ochre wool braid overlaid with a narrow black silk ribbed-ribbon which I wore with one of our lined black crepe polo neck tops and had a Gladstone-type handbag made in the burgundy tweed by a great American guy who was making some handbags for the two shops. I felt so good and confident in that outfit and John and I both had very successful trips.

I covered the North and East country from Newcastle, Liverpool, Chester, Leeds and Hull and even included a boutique in an out of the way village of Southwold which became one of our best stockists, while John covered the West Country and Wales. Our stockist list was built up very gradually as we only wanted those who could show our clothes as a group and to their best advantage.[38]

(NOT the fashion designer) joined us to help Mary with the Bazaar shop windows and other displays as she now spent far more time on designing. He and I shared an office and by now I was busy assisting Alexander and Mary so Archie engaged Bernadette to take over his work.[37] The first MQ Wholesale range was very successful and it was decided to expand the number of stockists for the second range – so John and I set off around the country by train, bus and taxi to check out prospective stockists who had applied to us and to keep our eyes open for others who we thought might be suitable. We each simply had a small case containing just some handout photographs of the major

In 1962, as the wholesale brand took off, Quant achieved a publicity coup when Ernestine Carter featured her designs not only in a double page spread, titled 'Into the Big Time' but also on the cover of the first edition of the *Sunday Times* colour magazine [31]. The timing was perfect, with a collection of her wholesale clothes bringing the Chelsea look into 'the more conservative provinces'. Photographed by David Bailey, the clothes were worn by three models including Jean Shrimpton with Quant and Plunket Greene as shadowy figures in the foreground. Together they created intriguing and beautiful fashion images that would entice interest in the brand (and its designer) from readers of the new supplement. Stockists included Woollands in London, at its in-house boutique '21 shop', opened by managing director Martin Moss in 1961, with Vanessa Denza as buyer. The wholesale range could also

31 'Into the Big Time'
Sunday Times magazine, 4 February 1962
Models: Jean Shrimpton, Jill Stinchcombe
and Maryrose McNair

Photograph by David Bailey

be bought at Marshall & Snelgrove in Leeds and Darling's in Edinburgh. Some of the designs featured survive in the V&A collection, including a bold striped wrap dress named 'Georgie' [32, 33, 34], donated by Sarah Robinson, who described it as a 'happy, fun dress to wear, and beautifully made', and bought her dress from a shop called 'Elizabeth' in Truro, Cornwall, which specialized in the 'latest from London'.[39] The grey flannel skirt suit 'Tutti Frutti' is also in the V&A collection (specially made for the London Museum exhibition *Mary Quant's London* in 1973), while the the printed cotton dress 'Greenery Yallery' is only known to survive as a design.[40]

Ensuring that there was little motivation for London's copyists to target Quant's designs, the wholesale range made her work available to more people at lower prices. Initially the clothes were made in a small manufacturing facility on Fulham Road which had previously been an underwear factory. The range enabled the company to expand, without developing a chain of shops.[41] This development paved the way for the collaboration with JC Penney, launched in 1962, which was manufactured in Steinbergs' vast modern factory in South Wales (see p.110), and also led to the establishment of Mary Quant's Ginger Group, initially based in Conduit Street, and at 9 South Molton Street from 1964.

The V&A owns a rare group of Mary Quant garments all bought in the early 1960s by textile collector Elizabeth Gibbons. Married to architect Peter Gibbons, she travelled widely, living in India, Singapore and Kuala Lumpur with their young children. She purchased a range of outfits including the 'Coal Heaver' ensemble modelled by Celia Hammond in 1963 [45], a summer party dress of printed silk [35], and 'Stampede', a linen dress with asymmetrical front with large buttons, which is accompanied by a design, and has been matched to a fashion photograph in Mary Quant's archive [37, 38, 39]. Some of her choices were especially radical, such as the grey tweed pinafore dress with waistcoat effect,

What do you need to be of the Sixties? First, you should be under 30. Second, you should be in tune with your times. And it helps if you are on the same wavelength as New York and a step ahead of Paris. These specifications fit dress designer Mary Quant (above left), of Bazaar, like one of her own dresses. She and her husband, Alexander Plunket Greene (right), are both 28. Like a good dancer, she accommodates her steps to the changing rhythms of fashion. Together they have conquered New York; and they have had the heady excitement of anticipating the massed oracles of Paris. Now the success of their second wholesale collection will spread the Bazaar Look past Chelsea and Knightsbridge into the hitherto more conservative provinces.

In 1955 Mary Quant and Alexander Plunket Greene ope[...] they opened their second Bazaar shop in Knightsbridge [...] mass-production. From the first, they have had an easi[...] windows of their two shops are consistently witty and w[...] a ball, with model girls out-Grocking Grock. Even t[...] megaphoned barker on the pavement exhorting a d[...] pioneered the taste of her generation and opened the wa[...] language. Now, with this second wholesale collection, sh[...] of the dress trade. Her impudent, kooky clothes are left [...] the trend to the pretty. But the handwriting is all her ov[...]

3

4

All Mary Quant wholesale clothes can also be bought at Bazaar, Knightsbridge and Chelsea.

...azaar in Chelsea. In 1958, ...t summer, they went into ...tifiable thumbprint. The ...Their dress collections are ...les are different—with a ...d crowd. Mary Quant ...others who speak the same ...s her place with the giants ..., and she has moved with **Ernestine Carter**

PEOPLE! OF THE **60**s

MARY QUANT

Telephone: Kensington 5037

"Georgie"

Striped cotton dress with frill
trimmed crossover bodice. Stripes
are vertical on the bodice and
horizontal on the gathered skirt
and wide sash.
Colours — black with orange stripes
and navy with red stripes.
Lined with cotton batiste.
Retail Price 12½ gns.

"Rosie"

Same style in chiffon lined with
taffeta. Available in black, pink
and jade.
Retail Price 22 gns.

176/-

Bazaar Workshops Limited
Directors: Mary Quant Alexander Plunket Greene Archibald McNair Catherine McNair Francis Morley

32 Mary Quant
Fashion drawing for 'Georgie'
and 'Rosie', 1962
V&A: E.255–2013

33 Maryrose McNair
modelling 'Rosie', 1962
Photograph by Michael Wallis
Mary Quant Archive

OPPOSITE
34 Mary Quant
'Georgie', 1962
Cotton with woven stripe
V&A: T.74–2018

35 Mary Quant for Bazaar
Summer dress, *c.*1962
Printed silk
Worn by Elizabeth Gibbons
V&A: T.41–2014

36 'The Arrogant Arrogant
from Chelsea'
Women's Wear Daily,
19 September 1962
Illustration by Gladys Perint Palmer

complete with shirt and exaggerated tie, also modelled by Celia Hammond for an advertisement [40, 41]. A pinafore dress with ginger coloured bodice and straps over a black and white striped skirt would also have required some nerve to wear, even in London. Gibbons recalled in 2013:

> Having seen articles about Mary Quant in magazines from England and US, especially one in *Life* magazine ... I was struck by her vibrant and young style, very new and exciting and different. So when we returned to UK in 1960 as part of our world tour, I immediately rushed off to stay in a hotel in London for three days where I bought several outfits from Mary Quant's shop Bazaar on King's Road, Chelsea (one of which I wore to return to my husband who was 'stunned and delighted' by my new clothes). In 1962 we came to live in Swinging Chelsea, in Royal Avenue, just off King's Road and almost opposite Mary Quant's shop Bazaar. It was interesting to see her racks of clothes hanging out on the pavement, with loud speakers advertising her goods until quite late into the evening. Her husband's restaurant, underground, was just next door. King's Road itself was a

fashion parade, especially on Saturdays, with processions of veteran and exotic cars adding to the scene.

Before passing them to the V&A 50 years later, with considerable foresight, Gibbons carefully stored a flimsy paper bag, and receipts and letters from McNair and Shurville responding to her requests by mail-order between Kuala Lumpur and Ives Street in 1961 and 1962. The correspondence, from Archie McNair and Shirley Shurville (one reads 'what a very nice person you sound!') reveals the very personal level of service Bazaar offered [23, 24].

By the end of 1962 the marketable name of Mary Quant become more well-known than that of Bazaar, and her name could be found in bold letters on all the labels of the garments she designed. Quant designs appeared regularly in *Vogue* and *Harper's Bazaar*, and in America, in *Women's Wear Daily* and *Seventeen* [36]. Bridging the gap between haute couture and high street fashion, her clothes were dashing and sporty, and Quant energetically promoted them at fashion shows in Paris and New York. With the technical know-how and factories of clothing manufacturer Steinbergs ready to put Quant's designs into mass production, in multiples of thousands, she was ready to expand further into the wholesale market.

MARY QUANT

Telephone: Kensington 5037

"Stampede"

75% Linen/25% Terylene interlined
with lightweight Vilene. Buttons
are brass/gold. Available in
white, navy, black and brass (a
small cutting of brass attached).
A 'top-super' dress!
Retail price 18½ gns.

148/-

Bazaar Workshops Limited
Directors: Mary Quant   Alexander Plunket Greene   Archibald McNair   Catherine McNair   Francis Morley

37 Mary Quant
Fashion drawing for 'Stampede'
with fabric sample, 1962
V&A: E.250–2013

38 Maryrose McNair modelling
'Stampede', 1962
Photograph by Michael Wallis
Mary Quant Archive

39 Mary Quant
'Stampede', 1962
Linen and Terylene
Worn by Elizabeth Gibbons
V&A: T.42–2013

40 Celia Hammond modelling for a
Mary Quant advertisement
Harper's Bazaar, October 1962

Photograph by Terence Donovan

41 Mary Quant
Waistcoat effect pinafore dress
with shirt and tie, 1962
Wool tweed, cotton and silk

Worn by Elizabeth Gibbons
V&A: T.38:1 to 3–2013

Modelling Quant

Stephanie Wood

Mary Quant's models, along with Quant herself, came to define and popularize the 'look' and ethos of the Mary Quant brand on an international scale. The photographic models, who appeared in the iconic images of Quant's designs produced for the press, and those she employed to model the collections at presentations and fashion shows each season, were at the forefront of a revolution in modelling styles during this period.

The modelling profession emerged from humble beginnings in the 1870s when couturiers such as Charles Frederick Worth began to use living models, or 'mannequins', to present garments to clients within their fashion houses. The term 'model' had different connotations in France, where it was used to refer to women who posed nude for artists.[1] Within polite society, modelling was generally seen as unsavoury, and the term 'modelling' was used euphemistically to conceal less favourable professions for women. It was not until the 1940s that the profession gained some legitimacy, and by the 1950s was established as a respectable occupation for women of good reputation.

The modelling world of the 1950s was dominated by upper class, society women who often went on to make 'good' marriages to members of the aristocracy – Lords and Barons, or as in the case of couture model Jean Dawnay, a Prince.[2] The fashion world had long celebrated the mature sophisticate as the ultimate woman all young girls should aspire to be, and so the poised, often-aloof modelling style favoured by the couture fashion houses reflected the refined, mature elegance of the houses' clientele. This resulted in models appearing far older than their years as they sought to emulate older women.

For the leading fashion photographers of the day such as Clifford Coffin, Norman Parkinson and particularly John French, the arched eyebrows, wasp waist and unsmiling hauteur of British model Barbara Goalen perfectly embodied the spirit of post-war couture [43]. Seen here wearing customary pearl necklace and opera gloves, the stiff and imperious style adopted by models such as Goalen, also perfectly suited the outdated, rather elitist image fostered by the 'glossies' such as *Harper's Bazaar*, *Tatler* and *Vogue*. Through her work with John French, Goalen became a household name as his high fashion images reached a broad audience, widely distributed through mass-circulation newspapers such as the *Daily Express*. As Brigid Keenan, one-time fashion editor of the *Daily Express* and the *Sunday Times* said: 'these girls were the darlings of the newspapers. They were the last society girls in a world that was about to be blown apart by the pop explosion that was the Swinging Sixties.'[3]

Many of the most successful models of the period began their career training at one of a handful of elite modelling schools, where they were taught the arts of grooming, make-up, posture and etiquette; learning a staid range of conventional fashion poses and how to expertly remove a coat and gloves while walking.[4] In America, the most prestigious school was the Ford Modeling Agency, established in 1946; by the 1950s, Britain's most celebrated institution was the Lucie Clayton Charm Academy. Founded in 1928 as a finishing school, Lucie Clayton counted many of the most celebrated British models including Fiona Campbell-Walter and Barbara Goalen among their alumni, but it was from the class of 1960 that their greatest star was born: Jean Shrimpton.

Jean Shrimpton

Seen here alongside her fellow classmates Fiona Laidlaw Thompson (left) and Celia Hammond (centre) on their graduation day, Jean Shrimpton, affectionately known as 'the Shrimp' in the fashion press, went on to become one of the most recognizable and highly-paid models of the 1960s [42]. She was the first of a new breed of models who rejected the

42 Fiona Laidlaw Thompson, Celia Hammond and Jean Shrimpton, on the day of their graduation from Lucie Clayton Charm Academy, 1960

formality and convention of the previous generation; whose young, natural, tomboyish style embodied the spirit of 1960s London and the ethos of the Quant brand. As Quant explained: 'I want model girls who look like real people ... I want girls who exaggerate the realness of themselves, not their haughty unrealness like the couture models do.'[5]

Both Hammond and Shrimpton featured in some of the most iconic images promoting Quant designs in the early 1960s. Celia Hammond was chosen to promote the brand in one of the first Mary Quant advertisements in 1962, and both Hammond and Shrimpton were regularly photographed together wearing Mary Quant, including in two of John French's photographs for the *Daily Mail* that year [30, 45].

Born in 1942 and raised on a farm in Buckinghamshire, Shrimpton was far more interested in horses and dogs than fashion, describing herself in her early years as 'gawky and tomboyish, more like one of the ponies I loved than a girl, with a lot of leg, a lot of hair and a lot to learn.'[6] She came to London in 1959, aged 17, to complete a secretarial course. However, having been approached by multiple people suggesting she become a model, the seed was sown, and Shrimpton enrolled at Lucie Clayton not long afterwards. For Quant, Shrimpton was the perfect model to promote the Quant look and she went as far as modelling the mannequins in her Bazaar boutiques on Shrimpton's 'long, lean legs.'[7] As she explained: 'the most beautiful of all the models I have known was Jean Shrimpton. To walk down the King's Road, Chelsea with her was like walking through the rye. Strong men just keeled over right and left as she strode up the street [44].'[8] In her own autobiography Shrimpton could almost be referencing Quant's designs when she said 'the unladylike, tomboy, off beat fashions came in just as I started and were responsible

Fitch coat with optional belt by Mary Quant at Debenham & Freebody, 360 gns.; the hat to match, 30 gns. Gold Antron knit dress from the Ginger Group Collection, 10 gns. at Fenwicks; Brown Muff, Bradford. Topaz and gold ring, brooch, Hooper Bolton.

Fitch reefer

Gold over gold

46 Jean Shrimpton modelling 'On Target' dress
'Young Idea Goes West'
Vogue, April 1962
Photograph by David Bailey

in some way for my success. I know how lucky I was to arrive on the scene just at that time.'[9]

Shrimpton's arrival on the modelling scene coincided with developments in photographic style and magazine publishing that reflected the shifting cultural landscape of post-war Britain and the emerging youth culture. This newfound celebration of youth at the heart of both developments had a profound effect on modelling styles during this period. Quant had already begun revolutionizing fashion in 1955, anticipating the needs of the new generation of young consumers. British fashion publishing was also undergoing a transformation with *Vogue* introducing the 'Young Idea' pages in 1955 that helped to promote young models wearing designs by fresh, emerging designers such as Quant. 1957 saw *Queen* magazine overhauled from an old Establishment journal into a witty and youthful magazine, geared to the burgeoning youth market. The arrival of the next generation of fashion photographers including John Cowan (see p.80) and 'The Terrible Trio' of David Bailey, Terence Donovan and Brian Duffy saw a shift towards dynamic, reportage-style photography that resulted in modelling increasingly happening outside the photographic studio.[10]

Shrimpton's work and her relationship with Bailey, with whom she collaborated almost exclusively between 1960 and 1964, is the stuff of fashion legend and undoubtedly raised their profiles to stratospheric heights. Her renowned photoshoot with Bailey for 'Young Idea Goes West' in *Vogue*, April 1962, features her modelling several Mary Quant designs on the streets of New York [46]. It was completely groundbreaking at the time because of its spontaneous, documentary style that captured Shrimpton in natural lighting with natural poses, surrounded by real people. Shrimpton's relaxed, girl-next-door look came to define the Quant look of the early 1960s: a democratic kind of beauty, refreshingly at odds with what had gone before. Now every girl wanted to look like Jean Shrimpton.

Grace Coddington

Although better known as the creative director at large of American *Vogue*, Grace Coddington began her career as a model in 1959. She left her home on the island of Anglesey, north Wales, aged 18 and began working as a waitress in Knightsbridge to afford her modelling school fees.[11] After winning a modelling contest for *Vogue*, she swiftly established herself on the London scene, befriending photographer Terence Donovan and, like many models, became part of the same social circle as Quant and Plunket Greene. Coddington remarked: 'the artistic Chelsea people I usually ran around with congregated each evening at the Markham Arms, a rowdy pub next door to Bazaar, Mary Quant's King's Road Boutique, where I became a serious shopper....'[12]

Seen here in 1967 wearing Quant's favourite design 'Banana Split', 'The Cod' as she became known, recalled the dangers of traversing stairs on buses while wearing the Quant look with its progressively shorter hemline [47].[13] She was Quant's favourite model because of her 'mixture of fashion know-how, beauty (and) stylish simplicity.'[14] Her tomboyish appearance and cropped hair perfectly reflected the increasingly androgynous direction of Quant's designs of the 1960s. She personified the Quant look, not least because she was an early house model and muse for Vidal Sassoon and sported the iconic Vidal Sassoon five point hair cut that became Quant's signature look in 1964 [93].[15] In a 2012 interview she highlighted the contribution that Sassoon and Quant made to women's lives saying: 'Vidal came along and liberated hair after Mary Quant liberated clothes.... He cut my hair in a bowl cut and totally changed hair – everything before then was lacquered and stiff. Suddenly you could shake your head – it was a defining moment of the Sixties.'[16] Quant herself deplored the lacquered, overblown and unnatural hairstyles that dominated fashion in the 1950s and early 1960s, stating: 'I find it arrogant to ... wear

47 Grace Coddington modelling 'Banana Split' dress, 1967
Mary Quant Archive

48 Jill Kennington modelling white PVC rain tunic and hat by Mary Quant
Photograph by John Cowan, commissioned by Ernestine Carter for the *Sunday Times*, 1963
Ernestine Carter Archive, Fashion Museum Bath

49 Jill Kennington modelling 'Candytwist' dress 'Designed by Mary Quant in Courtelle', knitting pattern, c.1966
Mary Quant Archive

wanted to promote a strong, cohesive image for the brand.

Like Coddington, Kennington also became a serious shopper at Bazaar and described herself as 'always a Quant girl', going so far as having her Mini car painted to match her beloved Mary Quant purple suit in the early 1960s. She first discovered Mary Quant aged 18 on her lunch break as a buyer for Harrods, when she regularly window-shopped at the Knightsbridge branch of Bazaar. But it was once she was established as a model that she became friends with Quant personally, introduced by her close collaborator, photographer John Cowan. In her years as a model from

very elaborate, ornate, hairstyles that look like wedding cakes or hats ... which are obviously so stiff that if you touch them they're not hair.'[17]

Jill Kennington

The Vidal Sassoon bobbed cut was such a signature part of the look that by 1966 many of Mary Quant's models sported it and were encouraged to shake their heads during fashion shows to fully showcase the freedom of movement. British model Jill Kennington, whose hair was significantly longer and fairer, was encouraged to wear a bobbed wig made by Sassoon when modelling for Quant fashion shows and products such as the Mary Quant Courtelle knitting patterns [49]: Quant

DESIGNED BY
Mary Quant
IN
COURTELLE®

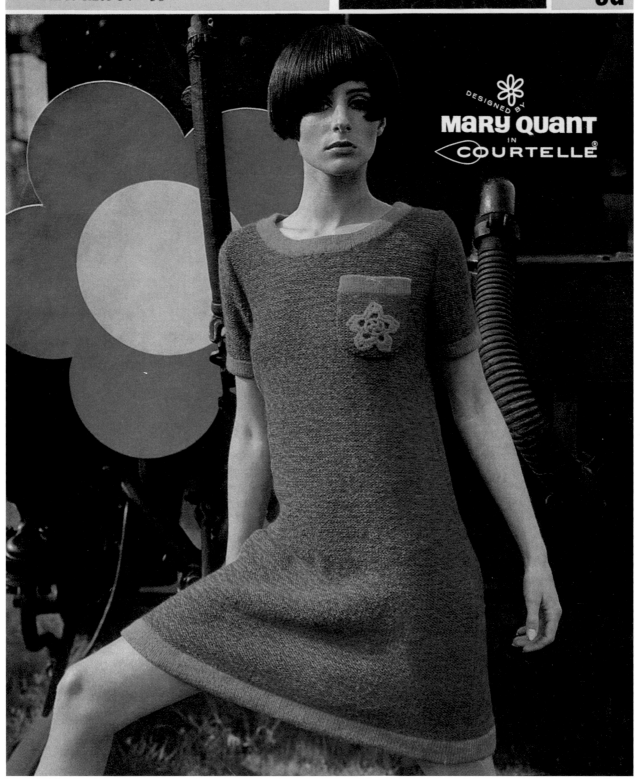

1962 to 1967 she would regularly appear in
the fashion press, bringing her trademark
energy and youth to promote the Quant look,
and in her later career as a photographer,
she would go on to capture portraits of both
Quant and Plunket Greene in 1987 [190].

Twiggy

Twiggy or 'the Twig' was born Lesley Hornby
in 1949 in Neasden, north London to working
class parents,[18] and at just 16 years old she burst
onto the fashion scene, going from Saturday girl
at a hairdresser's to being named 'the face of
1966'.[19] Her child-like, boyish appearance was
often highlighted in the fashion press with
Paris Match proclaiming *'Garçon ou fille? Non!
C'est Twiggy.'*[20] This 'new kid on the block'
as Kennington described her,[21] with waif-like,
adolescent frame, skinny legs and doll-like
face, accentuated by painted on mock-eyelashes,
was perfectly suited to Quant's playfully
androgynous designs. Having long borrowed
from traditional menswear and childrenswear,
Twiggy's arrival in 1966, with her knock-knees
and spindly legs, emphasized Quant's hemlines
– which were well above the knee [136].
Quant's continued celebration of youth culture
was mirrored in Twiggy's exaggerated child-like
image; in her brief career as a model from 1966
to 1970, she came to define the Quant look,
taking on the mantle from her idol, Jean
Shrimpton. Her androgynous look is particulary
evident in this 1966 photograph of her in signature gawkish pose wearing a Ginger Group
waistcoat and shorts ensemble with white shirt
and black tie [51]. Her working class roots and
cockney accent contrasted refreshingly with
the image projected by the society girls who
had dominated the modelling profession in the
1950s. As photographer Cecil Beaton remarked:
'today's look comes from below. The working-
class girl with money in her pocket can be as
chic as the deb. That's what Twiggy is all about.'[22]

Catwalk modelling

From the very first fashion shows that Quant staged, she recognized the need to present her collections differently. The paired back, simple lines of her designs, which were so radical when first introduced, demanded an equally radical presentation. This was particularly important when having to compete at international trade shows alongside 'the grandees of the British Fashion world.'[23] Quant remarked of one show in the late-1950s in St Moritz: 'the only possible way was to break the tempo of the whole evening with one great burst of jazz and let the girls come in at terrific speed in the zany, crazy way in which my clothes should be seen.'[24] She

concluded: 'Nobody in the audience had ever seen this sort of thing before.'[25]

Quant's fashion shows were a far cry from the established salon-style presentations as followed by the leading designers of the time. She preferred to use photographic rather than salon models to present the collections because they swung rather than paraded down the catwalk, taking up dramatic poses en route. It is interesting to note that both Grace Coddington and Jill Kennington, who were predominantly photographic models, still chose to do Mary Quant fashion shows in the mid-1960s, citing how fun they were compared with other designer's shows.[26]

These shows were characterized by fun,

52–5 Mary Quant's Ginger Group fashion show, 1966
Mary Quant Archive

52–5 Mary Quant's Ginger Group fashion show, 1966
Mary Quant Archive

energy, high-speed and movement with models dancing wildly to the 'hot jazz' that Quant and Plunket Greene loved so much.[27] Quant said of her presentation style: 'When I showed the collection, I knew I wanted the girls to move ... to jump, to be alive.'[28] A series of photographs of a 1966 fashion show captures the sense of energy and movement conveyed in her presentations [52–5]. The playful celebration of youth embodied in Quant's designs is mirrored in the models' poses with one licking a lollipop as she walks [54], and another sporting pigtails as she does the splits in her towelling child-like romper suit [52]. Quant freely acknowledged this celebration of youth in her designs and preferred an informal, playful presentation style

that often emphasized the theme of adolescence: 'I didn't want to grow up, perhaps that's something to do with it,' she noted, adding that:

the way rather young adolescent girls ... 12, 13 year olds, walked and moved, with that ease and grace ... more like dancers, was much more attractive than the ... rather paralysed, stilted high-heeled walk, and hobbled-skirt walk.... And this means ... short skirts, in fact with wide hems ... so you can walk![29]

With its mezzanine level and feature staircase, the Knightsbridge Bazaar shop was well designed to stage press shows [181] (see p.196)

and following the excited reaction to Quant's
progressive way of presenting her collection at
the store's launch in 1958, subsequent collections were often presented there each season
with a small number of favourite models.

But with the closing of Bazaar Knightsbridge
in 1969, the seasonal press shows relocated to a
restaurant setting or, quite frequently the Savoy
Hotel. Heather Tilbury Phillips, public relations
manager at Mary Quant during the 1970s,
recalled that:

> We worked with very few models –
> perhaps only four ... maximum six which
> meant really quick changes. Pamela
> oversaw the running order, but I tended
> to do the choreography.[30] The dressers
> were from the workroom or the office
> staff.... There wasn't always a catwalk and
> often the girls walked amongst the tables,
> where the press were sitting, chatting to
> them as they all knew each other well.
> They often included regular favourites

like Carina Fitzalan-Howard, Lorraine
Naylor, Hazel Collins [56], Ulrika, Marie
Helvin, Vicki Hodge and Ika Hindley
[57]. The shows were mainly at breakfast
time so that the pictures would be in the
Evening Standard and *Evening News* by
just after lunch and also got picked up by
the regional press as well as the nationals
and internationals the following morning.
The "standard" Quant girl was about 5'8"
and measured 34" bust, 24" waist and
34" hips – with a boyish, rather than
hourglass, figure. Mary often favoured
an androgynous look although she flirted
with girlie dresses and trimmings.[31]

Exporting Britishness

Jan de Souza, seen here second from left alongside Quant (centre) and three other models all
wearing Quant designs in 1966, was employed
full-time by Mary Quant from 1962 to 1964 as

a Ginger Group house model (pp.2–3). She was based predominantly at the Ginger Group Showroom, 9 South Molton Street, where she modelled the collections to buyers in addition to modelling in press and international tradeshows.

The Mary Quant 'look' was so important to the brand that house models such as de Souza and favourite regular models like Sarah Dawson [117] and Kari-Ann Muller, who had perfected the 'rangy',[32] relaxed way of modelling she preferred, played a fundamental role in selling the Quant brand to the rest of the world. When presenting internationally, Quant always preferred to fly out her own models rather than using local 'big bosomed types' who were not her 'idea of the model girl shape.'[33] For the Puritan fashion 'Youthquake' collaboration in 1964 (see p.118), Quant and Plunket Greene embarked on a whirlwind multi-stop promotional

tour across America that involved fashion shows at each venue. To save money the organizers proposed using locally sourced models for each show, but Quant was so concerned about the negative impact of doing so that Plunket Greene demanded to use their regular models Sarah Dawson (right) and Sandy Moss (centre) [102]. He noted that 'the only way this tour is workable ... is if we have our own girls with us who have 'the Look', know us, know the clothes, know the way to show them.'[34] Internationally, and particularly in America, Quant's set of models, with hemlines above the knee, free-moving hair and modern attitudes, were the epitome of Quant's quirky brand of Britishness. Quant recognized the cultural cachet of this distinct brand of Britishness. As a result, models were increasingly photographed alongside recognizable symbols of the British Establishment

58 Sarah Dawson, Jenny Boyd, Sandy Moss and
Pattie Boyd with Puritan Fashions vice president,
Paul Young on the Youthquake campaign trail, 1965
Mary Quant Archive

59–62 Chelsea Pensioners and models wearing
ensembles by Mary Quant's Ginger Group, c.1966
Photographs by Gunnar Larsen
Mary Quant Archive

such as Chelsea Pensioners [59–62], horse-guards, routemaster buses, telephone boxes and Union Jack flags [51]. By 1968, the Lucie Clayton Charm Academy itself had produced a book capitalizing on the global appeal of the London model-girl look.[35]

Diversity of models 1965–75

The evolution of Quant's style from the late 1960s into the 1970s reflected the eclecticism and nostalgia popularized in fashion more generally during that period, and in turn was reflected in the diversity of the models chosen to promote the brand. Donyale Luna, born Peggy Ann Freeman in Detroit in 1945, moved to London in 1965 and made history as the first black model to appear on the cover of British *Vogue* in March 1966, photographed by David Bailey.[36] Despite the racial segregation and violence being experienced at that time in her native America, in Europe Luna became a highly sought-after model, regularly working with Mary Quant among other leading designers. In the same year that Twiggy was named 'The face of 1966', *Time* magazine in America published an article proclaiming it 'The Luna Year', describing her as 'unquestionably the hottest model in Europe' and referencing her 'striking singularity'.[37] She is seen here contorting her willowy body in a zip-front Mary Quant jumpsuit for this 1966 advertisement taken out by Quant to help raise funds for the Campaign Against Racial Discrimination [63]. Luna would go on to appear in a number of art-house and fashion films, including *Who Are You, Polly Maggoo?* (1966), alongside fellow Quant model Peggy Moffit, until Luna's untimely death at the age of 33.

Kellie Wilson was another photographic model who made the leap across the pond at the height of the Civil Rights Movement in the mid-1960s in search of better work opportunities. Part Polynesian, part African–American, Wilson graduated with a bachelor's degree in psychology from Chicago but struggled to find reliable modelling work in New York.[38] Upon relocating to Paris she swiftly became highly sought after, live modelling at a number of Parisian couture houses and regularly featuring as a photographic model promoting Quant in the fashion press in 1966 [61]. This photograph of Wilson wearing a Mary Quant purple satin shirt and matching shorts with strawberry motif was taken by Brian Duffy for the *Sunday Times* magazine in 1966. Her relaxed stance, emphasized by sucking an ice-lolly, reflects the playful nature of this leisurewear ensemble and the ease of movement it would have afforded the wearer [64].

Possibly the most versatile of all Quant's models was Amanda Lear who regularly worked as both a photographic and catwalk model for Quant from the late 1960s to the early 1970s [156]. Little is known about her early life but it is widely agreed that Lear began modelling professionally in 1965 and established herself at the heart of the swinging London scene. Her varied career spanned stints as a model, painter, Europop singer, actress and television presenter. She featured on the now-iconic cover of Roxy Music's 1973 second album *For your Pleasure*, and for nearly 15 years was the muse and close friend of surrealist artist Salvador Dalí.[39]

It has long been suggested that before her modelling career began, Lear worked under the stage name Peki d'Oslo, performing drag acts at Le Carrousel Club in Paris. According to the famous transgender model and entertainer April Ashley, Lear's birth name is Alain Tap and in the 1950s and early 1960s they worked together at Le Carrousel.[40] Lear's supposed transgender background is alluded to in Quant's recollection of the JC Penney promotional tour in which Lear featured:

Double rooms had been booked so that the models shared with each other. But a great whispering campaign started up amongst the girls: 'I am not sharing with her – she is a man.'

Mary Quant, David Bailey, Donyale Luna, David Anthony
and Tom Wolsey got together to make this picture
because they're all terrific C.A.R.D.s

... There had always been rumours
about this.... Amanda was certainly
tall and had the right bone structure....
Of course, as the trip progressed there
were outraged squabbles amongst
the girls, who were saying, 'It's my
turn with Amanda', 'No, it's mine!'[41]

What is certainly true is that Lear remained
one of Quant's favourite models and in addition
to representing the brand internationally as part
of the tour, she was also chosen to represent
the brand alongside Quant and Plunket Greene
in the *Sunday Telegraph* magazine, wearing
Quant's favourite design from her autumn–
winter 1973 collection [65].[42]

Quant's choice of models reflected the
shifting ideals of beauty at the time. Each model
that would come to define the Quant look
would successively symbolize the feminine ideal
of the era. This was a new world order for the
modelling profession, where youth, movement
and freedom of expression were prized above all
things: models became increasingly younger

and started to look their own age, if not
younger; hair became more natural and moved
freely; mask-like make-up became playful and
fun; and the controlled, static poses mastered
by the previous generation of models in photography studios were replaced by relaxed and
natural, and later gawky and child-like poses
increasingly captured on the streets.

There is a strand of energy and movement
that runs through the catwalk modelling
and is captured in the photography of the
time. The simple shapes and freedom of
movement allowed by Quant's garments
enabled the models to dance and run freely,
and as the hemlines became increasingly
shorter, the movement of the models' legs
became more visible and more important.

Quant's ethos in promoting fashion for
all, rather than for the elite few, was echoed in
her choice of models, who increasingly came
from more diverse backgrounds. Modelling
was no longer the preserve of the upper-class
society girls as it had been in the 1950s.

Photographic Interpretations

Susanna Brown

'It seems very fashionable just now to treat photographers like film stars.'[1]

The unnamed teenage protagonist of *Absolute Beginners*, a 1959 novel by Colin MacInnes, is an ambitious freelance photographer. The centre of the action is London in the summer of 1958 – the cool coffee shops, rock 'n' roll clubs and smoky jazz bars frequented by the emerging youth culture. His is a world where mods in Italian sportswear rub up against teddy boys in drape jackets, Caribbean residents of Notting Hill, Chelsea rent boys, prostitutes, musicians and drug addicts. He dreams of success and wealth and his heroes are the new generation of British photographers, vibrant and virile men who sleep with beautiful women. He aspires to make money publishing his pictures in magazines and newspapers, perhaps even having 'a fabulous exhibition somewhere'.[2]

This essay explores the work of the real photographers that MacInnes's fictional character sought to emulate. The author's inspiration included the likes of Antony Armstrong-Jones, whose witty, light-hearted images shook up the established order and enlivened British *Vogue* in the 1950s, when it still retained a somewhat elitist approach and an old-fashioned look. The marriage of Armstrong-Jones to Princess Margaret in 1960 brought prestige to the photographic profession and reinforced the image of British photographers as celebrities in their own right. Armstrong-Jones worked for a time at the Alister Jourdan Studio at 128 King's Road, launched in 1952 by Archie McNair. It was in the newly hip area of Kensington and Chelsea, focused on the King's Road, that McNair first met Mary Quant and Alexander Plunket Greene.[3] The trio immediately understood the crucial role photography could play in shaping the identity of their fledgling company and promoting the brand to the widest possible audience. Photographs of Quant clothing, and later cosmetics too, were presented not only to a high-fashion audience

in the 'glossies' – such as *Harper's Bazaar* and *Vogue* – but also to a much broader demographic through images in mainstream newspapers. This essay will discuss how leading photographers responded to Quant's clothing, capturing 'the look' and philosophy of the brand.

In the 1950s and 1960s, numerous fashion and portrait photographers chose to position their studios in Kensington and Chelsea, and Quant counted several of them among her friends. They formed part of the fashionable crowd which congregated in Alexander's restaurant below Bazaar, as Quant recalled in 2009: 'Everybody came there, from Brigitte Bardot to all the photographers ... and all the film directors.'[4] One of them was John Cowan, who opened a studio at 98a Oakley Street, Chelsea, in 1958, and moved to 426 Fulham Road the following year. He captured Quant and Plunket Greene working and socializing, including a shot of them preparing a new window display and as the archetypal young Chelsea couple, jiving in 1960 [66].

Cowan was a tall, blonde, charismatic daredevil who attempted various careers – pilot, shop assistant, chauffeur, travel agent – before taking up a camera. Quant admired his 'immediate charm, energy, passion for life', and they enjoyed long conversations 'about photography, style, fashion, jazz'. She recalled that 'he was always game for anything. We had that kind of exuberance in common. I do associate him with planes and cars.'[5] Energy crackles through Cowan's pictures as his models dance, dive and leap with a dynamism barely contained by the limits of the magazine page. The effect is heightened by graphic composition and high contrast printing – bright highlights and dark, punchy shadows. As photographic historian Philippe Garner explains in his superlative monograph on Cowan, Armstrong-Jones' book *London*, published in 1958, could have served as an inspiration.[6] In the introduction,

66 Mary Quant and Alexander Plunket Greene in a New York dance hall, 1960

Photograph by John Cowan
Mary Quant Archive

Armstrong-Jones describes his attitude: 'I believe that photographs should be simple technically, and easy to look at ... their point is to make ordinary people react – I use a very small camera, little apparatus, and no artificial lighting at all ... [photographs] have to be taken fast. It's no good saying "hold it" ... like trying to hold a breath, you find you've lost it.'[7]

This technique chimes with that of Martin Munkácsi, who had first encouraged a reportage approach to fashion photography in the 1930s, writing in *Harper's Bazaar* in November 1935: 'Never pose your subjects. Let them move about naturally. All great photographs today are snapshots. Take back views. Take running views. Our cameras today allow us one-thousandth of a second. Pick unexpected angles, but never without reason.'[8] While their predecessors had been confined to the studio by cumbersome large-plate cameras mounted on heavy tripods, the new generation took up portable cameras such as the Leica, using 35mm roll film, embracing the opportunity to work outdoors with greater speed and realism.

Cowan took his photojournalistic aesthetic onto the streets of the metropolis, using London's landmarks as a backdrop for animated shoots. The resulting pictures are a thrilling collision of new and old, bringing together youthful fashions and traditional symbols of the British Establishment. In a photograph entitled 'Stealing a march on the Guards', model Marie-France marches past Buckingham Palace in Quant's check coat, frogged in black, accessorized with a bearskin-style hat [67]. The geometric pattern of the coat is echoed in the verticals and horizontals of the iron railings, shadows and paving stones and her wide-legged stance conveys a sense of purpose and freedom, reminiscent of Munkácsi's famous shot 'Jumping a Puddle', published in 1934.

Cowan's reportage approach and daredevil attitude brought him success in both fashion magazines and national press and he found his greatest inspiration collaborating with Jill Kennington, who began modelling in early 1962. Most photographic models in the 1940s and 1950s learnt a fixed repertoire of decorous and sophisticated poses which would be held, statue-like, under the glare of hot studio lights while the photographer loaded a single sheet of film into the large-plate camera. In the hands of a master, the resulting picture could be sublimely elegant, but it could also appear haughty or rigid, an effect accentuated by mask-like make-up and heavily lacquered hairstyles. In contrast, Kennington moved about naturally in front of the camera, her athleticism and tousled hair perfectly suited to the freedom of movement that Quant's designs allowed. Brave and spirited, she was part of the new wave of models in Britain who embodied the ethos of the Quant brand.[9]

Kennington's chemistry with Cowan resulted in a close collaboration lasting more than four years, with their most active period spanning 1962 to 1964; as Kennington later explained: 'Our teamwork elevated the usual status of model from clothes horse to action art form.'[10] On 1 April 1964, Cowan's exhibition *The Interpretation of Impact through Energy* opened at the premises of Gordon's Cameras in Kensington High Street. Quant and Plunket Greene attended the opening party and the show received positive reviews with a feature in the *Daily Express* highlighting the major role of his 'outdoor, dare-anything model'.[11] As well as photographing models in Quant's designs, Cowan documented some of her extraordinary window displays. In her 1966 autobiography, Quant described one such display, that might well have been inspired by Cowan's passion for unexpected vantage points and his ability to push his models to new limits: 'Dressing the window on Saturday night was something we really looked forward to. We had enormous fun. Once we used the model of a photographer strung up by his feet to the ceiling with the most enormous old-fashioned camera focused on a bird also suspended at the most incredible angle. We wanted to give the impression that here was a dress so

outstanding that it was worth while getting into any position to have a good look at it.'[12]

It was Cowan who was chosen to film Quant's first show in Paris – the PVC 'Wet Collection' – which was presented at the Hôtel de Crillon in April 1963 by the models Jill Kennington, Penny Patrick, Maryrose McNair, Vicki Vaughan and Jill Stinchcombe, plus Gully Wells, the 11-year-old daughter of American journalist Dee Wells. Cowan's film was brimming with his characteristic liveliness:

> He wanted to get the whole atmosphere of the thing and not just the clothes so he was shooting all over the place and going up to the grandees to take close-ups.... The show went on at colossal speed with jazz playing in the background. We showed about sixty dresses and suits in fifteen minutes flat.... There was none of the mincing up and down, stop and start, stylized movements of the usual fashion models. These girls were all primarily photographic models so that when they stopped in their tracks, they automatically took up the sort of arrogant positions you see in the fashion pages of the glossies. This type of showing was still something of a shock treatment.[13]

As Quant's shows in Paris became more regular, she took to arranging lunch parties on the Monday before the shows in January and July at Le Relais Bisson hotel. As well as Cowan and Kennington, guests included Ernestine Carter, Eugenia Sheppard, Iris Ashley, Barbara Griggs, Sally Kirkland, Percy Savage and Norman Parkinson.[14] Parkinson belonged to an earlier generation of gentleman photographers that included Cecil Beaton and John French in Britain, and Horst P. Horst and Irving Penn in America. After training with the court photographers Speaight Ltd, Parkinson opened a studio on London's Dover Street in 1934,

68 London fashion designers
Life, 18 October 1963

Photograph by Norman Parkinson

'Young designers clamber on Chelsea Embankment. First row from left to right: Mary Quant, 29, and her husband Alexander Plunket Greene, moustachioed Kenneth Sweet, 34. Behind are Jean Muir, 29, of Jane and Jane, Gerald McCann, 29, Kiki Byrne, 26, and David Sassoon, 29. Hanging from lamp-post Sally Tuffin, 25, Marion Foale, 24 and milliner James Wedge.'

joining *Harper's Bazaar* the following year, then *Vogue* in the early 1940s. Like Beaton, he had sartorial flair and aristocratic aspirations, eschewing his somewhat pedestrian given name of Ronald Smith. Both men went on to enjoy long careers, but while Beaton revelled in a theatrical artifice that often referenced eighteenth- and nineteenth-century painting, Parkinson adopted the new reportage style.

Parkinson's contract with *Vogue* ended in 1959, a pivotal year for the photographer and for British fashion magazines, as Robin Muir explains:

> *Vogue*'s last issue of the 1950s contained a photo-essay by Roger Mayne on the rise of the teenager. That same year he had photographed the dust jacket for Colin MacInnes's prototypical London novel *Absolute Beginners*. Cultural change was so palpable that *Vogue* had no alternative but to put its weight behind it. And so too for Britain's 'leading fashion magazine' the 1960s started fractionally early. Martin Harrison has rightly perceived that two of Parkinson's last contributions to *Vogue* – a jocular representation of a Mary Quant dress for 'Young Idea' and a portrait of the playwright Shelagh Delaney, a proponent of the 'kitchen-sink' dramas of British working-class life – 'belong equally in the cultural climate of the new decade'.[15]

The cultural change was similarly embraced by *Queen* magazine. As contributing editor from 1959 to 1964, Parkinson worked with publisher Jocelyn Stevens and editor Beatrix Miller to steer *Queen*'s metamorphosis from sober society magazine to cutting-edge fashion publication. Debutantes and high society beauties in stiff ball gowns were gradually replaced by more relatable models in boutique

69 Melanie Hampshire and Jill Kennington modelling 'Bank of England' and 'Eton'
Life, 18 October 1963
Photograph by Norman Parkinson

wear by Quant and her contemporaries [68]. Quant herself declared 'Snobbery has gone out of fashion';[16] MacInnes's teenage photographer put it more bluntly: 'I'm just not interested in the whole class crap.'[17]

Some of Parkinson's most memorable pictures of this era depict women as independent jet-set travellers, shot in tropical locations and foregrounded against planes, helicopters, sports cars and boats. For the May 1961 issue of *Queen*, he photographed Swiss actress and model Dolores Wettach at the stern of a speedboat, wearing a Quant sailor suit, comprising linen trousers buttoned to a white linen top [85]. In the 1960s, colour camera film and printing were expensive, and many fashion pictures were still shot in black and white. The accompanying description was therefore essential to build a full picture of the garments, which Quant often created in vibrant shades such as scarlet,

ginger and grape. The sailor suit trousers seen here are pale orange, and Wettach poses with her left leg positioned to show off the slight flare of the trouser leg. She appears supremely confident and relaxed, apparently disinterested in the water-skier's show of skill behind her.

In contrast to this international aesthetic, Parkinson created other pictures firmly rooted in British life, playfully juxtaposing glamorous models with humble settings – rural pubs and quintessentially English farms. And, like Cowan, he frequently took his models onto London's bustling streets. One such example was published in *Life* magazine on 18 October 1963, in a feature entitled 'Brash British Designers: New Styles from London will Give American Girls the Chelsea Look' [69]. The composition is striking in its symmetry: Melanie Hampshire and Jill Kennington are face on, framed by tall policemen in profile.

stands alongside, holding a hammer poised to close the crate.[18] Parkinson and Beaton worked hard to adapt to the ethos of the pop generation – to remain 'with it', as Beaton said – but John French was most comfortable working in the style he had perfected in the late 1940s and 1950s.[19] During the Second World War, French had served as an officer in the Grenadier Guards, cultivating a respect for formality and meticulous precision that would serve him well in his photographic career. French's characteristic sense of discipline is evident throughout his archive of negatives, photographs and related documents from nearly 10,000 sittings, now cared for by the V&A [70]. His preferred camera was a medium format Rolleiflex and during a typical day he would shoot up to a dozen outfits, using two to three rolls of films of 12 exposures per outfit. In the studio he favoured natural light over tungsten and was one of the first fashion photographers to use bounced light, positioning multiple reflectors around a carefully posed, static model to produce flatteringly soft illumination and very little shadow. Each print would be carefully retouched by hand before publication, to straighten hems and creases and smooth the skin.

French rarely worked with make-up artists or hairdressers but was fortunate in having the assistance of studio stylist Janet Campbell, whose artful use of hidden bulldog clips, hat pins and lead weights created clean lines and neat shapes. Favourite props included a chic cigarette holder, bouquet of flowers, winter muff and demure clutch purse. In French's studio the radical nature of Quant's designs was occasionally undermined by the addition of 'ladylike' accessories – pearl earrings, gloves, a handbag and heels – but he helped to bring Quant's clothes to the masses through papers such as the *Daily Express*, *Daily Mail* and the *Sunday Times*. His crisp pictures and Quant's strong, graphic shapes reproduced well, even on cheaply printed paper. Felicity Green, one-time assistant editor at the *Daily Mirror* noted 'his ability to

Their figures fill the length of the frame, Quant's striped wool dresses emphasize the vertical thrust of the picture. The women's dark-brimmed hats and white collars frame their faces and reference the men's uniforms. Hampshire bites her lower lip, Kennington opens her mouth wide; these fleeting expressions give the picture an un-staged look, heightened by the blur of moving traffic.

Exporting the 'Chelsea Look' to America, and across the globe, became big business for Quant in the 1960s and the international reach of the brand was humorously pictured by John Adriaan in his photograph 'A Crate Full of Quant' [71]. A wooden shipping crate is filled with models and nine of the 25 countries to which Quant was by then exporting are prominently listed on the side. The designer herself sits atop the crate proudly clutching examples of her new cosmetics while Plunket Greene

THE Tatler

& Bystander   2s.6d.   weekly   27 Dec. 1961

PARTY
TIME

72 *Tatler and Bystander*, 27 December 1961
Photograph by Barry Warner

73 Pattie Boyd modelling 'Miss Muffet'
with the Rolling Stones, 1964
Photograph by John French

was 'The Autumn Girl' of 1960: 19-year-old model Paulene Stone kneeling among dry leaves in a short skirt, puckering her lips towards a stuffed squirrel. Casual and surprising, the image had a major impact on Quant's approach to fashion shows, as she later explained:

> It was just like no fashion picture
> had ever been taken like that before.
> It was just a great slap of excitement.
> It was tremendous. And certainly,
> from that time on, when I showed
> the collections, I knew that I wanted
> the girls to move – move like Bailey
> photographs, to jump, to be alive.[22]

Music was essential to the live presentation of Quant's clothes and was the pulsing heart of photographs by Bailey and his contemporaries, played loud in their studios and almost audible in their pictures. Unexpected camera angles like syncopated jazz rhythms. Girls reacting joyously to the carefree sounds of pop. After a day shooting, photographers, models and friends danced the night away at clubs such as the Saddle Room in Mayfair, Britain's first discotheque.[23] Musicians themselves often featured in fashion images of the 1960s: in 1964 John French photographed Pattie Boyd posed in a Mary Quant dress surrounded by the Rolling Stones, two years before her marriage to George Harrison of the Beatles [73]. Duffy brought Ronnie Scott's 'All Star' jazz group into the studio to play alongside models posed in evening gowns and encouraged Joanna Lumley to sing while he photographed her. Duffy's British *Vogue* cover of 1 October 1963 features Tania Mallet playing an imaginary trumpet in Quant's red PVC raincoat, and an earlier cover of *Tatler* depicts a model in simple black Quant dress, her cherry red necklace perfectly matched to the glossy drum kit she sits behind [72].

Like Bailey, Terence Donovan honed his photographic skills while undertaking national service – Donovan in the Royal Army Ordnance Corps at Catterick, and Bailey in

make a three guinea dress look a million dollars', and when one of his photographs appeared in the early edition of a national newspaper, the garment usually sold out within a few hours.[20]

Fashion editor Brigid Keenan at the *Daily Express*, and later the *Sunday Times*, recalled how French's demeanour seemed at odds with the assistants he employed: 'He was a very aristocratic figure, always immaculately dressed, very grand … but he took on all these young men as his assistants from the East End.'[21] The young cockneys included Terence Donovan and David Bailey, who, along with Brian Duffy, were christened the 'Black Trinity' by Parkinson and became among the most celebrated and highly paid of the new generation of rebel photographers in London.

Bailey set up his own studio in April 1960 and was soon shooting young fashions for the *Daily Express*. Bailey's first picture for the paper

74–7 'Yes, la mode anglaise is good for you…' *Elle*, 20 October 1966

Photograph by Terence Donovan

the RAF. After assisting Adrian Flowers and John Adriaan at French's studio, Donovan opened his own studio in 1959 at Yeoman's Row, a short walk from Quant's Bazaar. Just a month later he was photographing for the hairstylist Vidal Sassoon, a fellow working-class boy and one of Quant's close friends. For London's young photographers, women – not clothes – were their primary interest and the close relationships between photographers and models in the 1960s brought a sensual intensity to fashion images which was lacking in the polite distance assumed by John French.

Bailey's first muse was Jean Shrimpton; Duffy adored red-haired Paulene Stone; Donovan favoured Celia Hammond, whom he compared to the actress Julie Christie. She described him as 'very earthy and very strict…. He frightened me because he looked quite fierce … he was barking orders at me…. I realised his bark was worse than his bite.'[24] Grace Coddington also modelled for Donovan and recalled how he drew inspiration from the high contrast images of London's suburbs and slums by Bill Brandt, taking his 35mm camera to gritty and industrial locations, 'out of Belgravia to the streets of his youth in the East End…. Shoots were always a pleasure. With Terry, one would spend one's day laughing until one's sides ached. But he always had such a great command of the situation, no fussing about, always so direct.'[25]

Coddington appeared alongside Twiggy in one of Donovan's most striking editorials for French *Elle* on 20 October 1966 [74–7]. Across eight pages, he combined colour fashion shots with black and white photographs of quintessentially British tropes – The Beatles, Grenadier Guards, policemen, judges in traditional wigs and robes, a lion and a crown – and flat planes of vivid pink. These collages pay homage to artists such as Eduardo Paolozzi, Richard Hamilton, Peter Blake and Tom Wesselmann, who used press and advertising photographs torn from magazines in combination with painted elements. Under the tenure of artistic director Peter Knapp, French *Elle*'s pages frequently riffed on the themes of Pop Art, and Donovan admired Knapp for his creative talent and frank attitude. The first page of the editorial incorporates a shot of Twiggy in moiré taffeta waistcoat and skirt, white satin shirt and black tie from Quant's Ginger Group, originally photographed for *Woman's Mirror*.[26] In the original shot, Twiggy stands before a vast Union Jack flag, symbolic of Britain's role at the forefront of fashion and the teenage embodiment of the 'London Look' [51].

Twiggy was best known for her huge eyes, cropped hair and long thin legs, which photographers accentuated by shooting from a low vantage point or with a wide-angle lens. In the same year that Twiggy rose to fame, swiftly eclipsing every model that had come before her,

À gauche, le fameux lion britannique. La reine
jupe l'a d'abord fait rager. Mais la reine vient
de décorer Mary Quant au nom de l'Empire,
alors ! Justement une petite « Mary Quant »
en jersey pleine d'astuces : emplacement
boutonné, col plat, cravate géante (195 F.
au Bon Marché). À droite : hello, Bob-
bies ! Ils viendront de là-bas
aider leurs collègues lyon-
nais à régler la circula-
tion pendant la « Se-
maine ». Et redon-
pour Mary Quant
robe en jersey à
col roulé zippé
et petites poches
passepoilées
(149 F. chez
Nit - Paradol,
Bas Echo.

Quatre garçons très dans le vent : Ils
n'ont pas 100 ans à eux quatre, ils sont co-
tés en Bourse, ils sont bannis en Australie ,
on a tout dit sur les Beatles. Conferment, pour le
plaisir, que, malgré des bruits alarmistes, Paul Mc
Cartney (à gauche bien sûr) est plus célibataire que jamais.
Et regardez de plus près ces deux robes très « Carnaby
Street » : On ne les plus démente de Londres, derrière Regent's
Street) : ci-dessus, en crêpe, sweater à col roulé sur jupe à gros
plis, casque en crêpe, ceinture d'argent (John balms sur Jean Varon,
87,30 F., chez Veg). Bas lamés Mary Quant, Escarpins Charles Jourdan. À
droite, robe chemisier en jersey de laine, taille basse, surpiqûres, très pe-
tits plis et près d'en vent (Mary Quant, 195 F. aux Galeries Lafayette), Bas Echo.

En 45,
Rose et He-
bea sont reçus
en grande pompe à la
Chambre des Lords. Ce sont
les premières Anglaises à porter le
parisien. Depuis Vidal Sassoon il y
en eut beaucoup d'autres. Aujourd'hui,
chez elles, les Anglaises portent vo-
lontiers des pyjamas en jersey comme
ça. Nous aussi. Celui-ci sweater ca-
plat, sur un certain mossif Finès
and Tuffin, 249 F. chez Dorothée)

Une belle journée de belle couvée : voici
quatre elégants haut ce volante Mary
Quant, 265 F., chez Nit-Paradol, JC, sur
le tartare la « Cérémonie Der Colonels » au
se grand défilé des Horse Guards plus
impressionnant de la place. C'est ce jour-
là que la reine prend chaque année
les 31 jours en tenue d'émotion que po-
tour, mouse seins en tagoa entremelre,
parisimatnetée et ses newspapers.

Quant was appointed OBE for her outstanding contribution to the fashion industry, and Italian director Michelangelo Antonioni released his stylish thriller *Blow-Up*. The film was set in Youthquake's epicentre and David Hemmings played the role of the photographer Thomas, partly based on Bailey, alongside a cast that included actresses Vanessa Redgrave and Jane Birkin. The Yardbirds and Verushka appeared as themselves, as well as numerous uncredited models, Melanie Hampshire, Jill Kennington and Peggy Moffitt among them. Antonioni carried out exhaustive research in the capital, and selected John Cowan's new studio at 39 Princes Place, west of Notting Hill, as the principle set: 'a vast and lofty barn, once a carriage works, more recently a furniture store.... It must be the most amazing studio in London.'[27]

The critical reception to *Blow-Up* was positive: the *New York Times* called it a 'stunning picture – beautifully built up with glowing images and color compositions that get us into the feelings of our man and into the characteristics of the mod world in which he dwells.'[28] However, Quant was underwhelmed by the film, commenting: 'I was quite disappointed with *Blow-Up*. I talked to Antonioni about it at the time – he spoke to everyone, including Bailey. It had less style and chic than I had hoped for.'[29] Quant was not involved in the costume design for *Blow-Up*, but worked on numerous other films including *The Haunting* (1963), *Georgy Girl* (1966) starring Charlotte Rampling, and *Two for the Road* (1967) starring Audrey Hepburn, one of Quant's favourite actresses.

The sexy photographer's life that *Blow-Up* presented inspired many to take up the profession. The German–Australian photographer Helmut Newton recalled that after the film's release in Paris: 'the young people, everybody, wanted to be a fashion photographer. It became a big cult.'[30] Newton photographed Twiggy for the 'Young Idea' pages of *Vogue* in 1966 and 1967 and a comparison of the two reveals the versatility of both model and photographer.[31] In the earlier image Twiggy lies on a bed, photographed from above, appearing as a space-age babydoll in thigh-skimming metallic dress and Quant's sparkling tights. In the latter shoot she takes on an androgynous dandy look, her body concealed by dark suiting topped off by a finger-wave hairstyle by Vidal Sassoon that harks back to the 1920s [136].

In the late 1960s fashion trends began to shift towards diaphanous floral fabrics, romanticism and exoticism. In 1967's 'Summer of Love' the hippie movement came into full bloom and Penelope Tree became Bailey's new muse. Black models gained greater prominence and African–American Donyale Luna was the first black model to appear on the cover of British *Vogue*.[32] Both Luna and Hazel Collins modelled Quant and in the 1970s a greater number of black models helped to give the brand a more diverse appeal. In spring 1972, Terry O'Neill photographed Collins alongside Quant and Plunket Greene at their Surrey home [56]. O'Neill's contact sheet reveals how he experimented with different groupings of the figures within the leafy landscape and picturesque outbuildings.

Models' careers are often short-lived and the faces of the Mary Quant label were many. It was the designer herself who became the ultimate brand ambassador, shot by the leading photographers of each decade in which she worked, always wearing her latest designs. She was photographed in her home, her office, shops and at fashion shows. She posed grouped with her models and fellow fashion designers, or with Plunket Greene as the ultimate modern couple. Portraits of Quant alone show her in confident wide-legged stance or seated with her cheek against her hand, pensively peering out from under an immaculate Sassoon fringe [78]. The naturally camera-shy Quant became one of the most recognizable women of her generation and understood from the start photography's immense power as a universal language.

PART THREE

1963–1964

Into the Big Time

I n 1963 Mary Quant became a house-hold name with her innovative designs hitting headlines, achieving her first cover of British *Vogue*,[1] and winning awards and accolades reflecting her impact on the international fashion market. In the same year she launched a new wholesale range, Ginger Group, which would become a sought-after label for every young woman's wardrobe. The first major challenge of the year was staging a fashion show in Paris at the Hôtel de Crillon, an eighteenth-century palace on the Place de la Concorde, where many historic political meetings and fashion events have taken place.

Quant describes the chaotic preparations and travel arrangements for the five models and the collection of clothes, the PVC 'Wet Collection', in cardboard boxes and grocer's crates, arriving at the hotel with its 'masses of chandeliers and marble walls … a staggering contrast to the extreme and outrageous clothes I had made…. Stimulated and probably over-excited by the success we were having in America and by the challenge of the Ginger Group, I had let myself go on this collection.'[2] The pressure was great, as the fashion show was attended by fashion editors and other key figures such as Lady Dixon, the wife of the British ambassador to France, encouraged by the efforts of the *Sunday Times* journalist Ernestine Carter. The show lasted just 15 minutes, with jazz playing in the background and the five models apparently showing 60 dresses and suits, a manically fast rate of changing outfits, compared to conventional fashion shows which were sedate and staged, allowing viewers to see clothes at all angles. After an oddly silent reception to the show and sleepless night, Quant was relieved to find the next day that several journalists called to borrow the clothes for features in their magazines; the critical response was positive.

This publicity generated great demand for the Wet Collection clothes, which unfortunately Quant could not supply in large numbers,

as the team had not perfected the technical process for sealing PVC seams in mass production. It was another two years before a collaboration with Alligator Rainwear of Stockport resulted in the very successful range of Mary Quant raincoats: 'by that time other designers on both sides of the Channel were as bewitched as I still am with this super shiny man-made stuff and its shrieking colours, its vivid cobalt, scarlet and yellow, its gleaming liquorice black, white and ginger.'[3]

The other key development that year was the launch of Mary Quant's Ginger Group, a second wholesale label (alongside the Mary Quant label) which was a separate company with joint interest held by the manufacturers Steinbergs. An advertisement for the label appeared in *Vogue* on 15 September 1963,

PREVIOUS PAGE
79 Mary Quant and Alexander Plunket Greene, Bazaar, Knightsbridge, 1964

80 Mary Quant's Ginger Group, swing tags, c.1963 Figures designed by Maureen Roffey

Museum of London: 74.330/41f–h

featuring the distinctive doll-like figures drawn by Maureen Roffey which were reproduced on Ginger Group merchandise materials and dress labels [80]. The dotted lines separating the figure at the neck and hips indicate the principle of interchangeable separates that was initially fundamental to the Ginger Group concept.[4]

The strapline 'Quant clothes at budget prices to buy a piece at a time everything goes with everything else in Mary Quant's Ginger Group' elaborates on this idea, designed to be modular and so as affordable as possible, piece by piece. The advert lists 59 different stockists in the UK, from Beckenham to Yeovil, with 16 additional shops in London, a mix of department stores and independent boutiques. In the same edition of *Vogue*, Young Idea ran a four-page spread showing the Ginger Group collection on location in Cambridge, clearly pitching the range at the wealthier student market. The popular magazine *Honey* also promoted the new label, in October 1963. Prices ranged from 29sh 11d for a pair of tights, to 3 guineas for a shirt, and a long crepe dress at 8 $\frac{1}{2}$ guineas. With colours and textiles carefully planned to allow for different looks, fabrics used included plain weave cotton, flannel, crepe and

a heavy jersey. This early form of what became Quant's signature fabric had a wool face, with a synthetic knit backing, and was a significant find, Quant having brought a small piece back from America for sourcing in the UK. An equivalent was found by Shirley Shurville (see p.142) by chance when a fabric manufacturer's rep, a Mr Eatough, who worked for Ames Mill,[5] turned up with a single sample. As Quant's designs simplified and moved ever closer to the very short shift dresses of 1966, this and other types of bonded jersey fabrics were used in very high volumes for Ginger Group, JC Penney, and the Puritan Fashions range of 1965.

Quant's designs for her mainline 'Mary Quant' label continued to thrive alongside the wholesale ranges, and appropriately, when Doris Langley Moore, owner of the Museum of Costume in Bath, inaugurated her Dress of the Year award in 1962, the Mary Quant design 'Rex Harrison', was the first to be chosen [82]. This was a longline buttoned pinafore dress inspired by the actor's cardigans as Professor Higgins in the stage production of *My Fair Lady* which showed for five years from 1958 at London's Theatre Royal. Further evidence of the mainstream media's increasing focus

82 Jean Shrimpton modelling 'Rex Harrison' pinafore
dress, 1963
Photograph by John French

83 Mary Quant's Ginger Group
Pinafore dress, 1963
Jersey
Mary Quant Archive

on fashion was shown by the establishment of
another prize, the *Sunday Times* International
Fashion Award. Quant was given this in a
ceremony at the Hilton Hotel on 15 October in
1963, the occasion of another nerve-wracking
fashion show, comprising Quant's ready-to-wear
clothes together with the couture collections of
Pierre Cardin and Norman Norell. Preceding
this, Quant had attended a lunch at the
French embassy where she was seated next to
Elsa Schiaparelli. 'Thrilled' to meet this great
couturier, Quant's shyness led to a difficult start
to the lunchtime conversation, but they found
common ground when she described a visit to
Debenham's fur storage vault, where she had
been excited to see Schiaparelli coats made in
the 1920s and 1930s, and the two designers
apparently had a wonderful time telling stories
to each other. Soon after this award ceremony,
Quant was awarded 'Woman of the Year'.[6]

The public fascination with Quant's story
was fuelled in a feature by Jill Butterfield in
the *Daily Express* in November 1963, which
highlighted the success of Mary Quant Ltd's
wholesale and export trade that year. It quoted
the fact that her business sold over 200,000
garments a year to shops in Britain, America,
Kenya, South Africa, France and Switzerland
(this territory also included New Zealand and
Australia).[7] Butterfield's article also reveals
much about the entrenched attitudes of the
time towards women, identifying Quant as
'young, tiny ... looking like a Pollyanna among
a staff composed of the toughest professionals
in the fashion world'.[8] Despite the patronising
tone, articles like this helped to promote the
visibility of women with careers, providing young
women and girls with valuable role models.

Although Quant's contemporaries, female
designers like Jean Muir, Kiki Byrne and
Marion Foale and Sally Tuffin also enjoyed press
and media attention, Quant and her success
story was earlier, and generated more features
and more arresting headlines. Presumably,
therefore, she helped to sell more newspapers,
although newspaper journalists like Butterfield,

and Felicity Green of the *Daily Mirror*, had to
compete with their male colleagues to gain
page space for her fashion stories.[9]

The *Daily Express* article, and the
accompanying photograph by David Bailey
[84], captures the unique spirit of equality,
camaraderie and energy of working for Mary
Quant, which in turn contributed to the brand's
persuasive appeal. From Archie McNair, on the
left, describing himself as 'Mary's business

nanny', with Plunket Greene and Quant, to Tom Tottham on the right, driver of the Bazaar 'gown van', the photograph shows ten colleagues who worked together to translate Quant's work from pencil sketch to shop floor. In the foreground, the pattern cutter, Mikki Katz, is wielding a large pair of scissors. Katz emphasizes the designer's perfectionism, saying 'She will never compromise on design, and to convince her an idea is impractical you have to have every point in your favour.' The photograph also features fitter Pura Garces, model Jill Stinchcombe, shop managers Joan Zimbler and Anne Cossins, together with Robert Peet (accounts), George Kersen (business manager), and Anthony Stanbury, from Steinbergs, manufacturer of the Ginger Group label, and at the back of the photograph Annabel Mackay (née Taylor) can just be seen. Taylor's role was to assist with buying from other wholesale ranges to complement the Quant designs sold in the Bazaar shops, and also shared responsibility for selling the clothes to independent store buyers. Jill Butterfield quotes

Taylor directly: 'I get livid with people who don't like her designs, I've never had this sense of identification with a firm before.'

Taylor's strong feeling of personal identification with Mary Quant as an employee in 1963 has often been echoed by customers too – pinpointing the underlying appeal of buying the clothes, and later the tights, make-up and other products, as a way of being more like their designer, or perhaps, more like themselves.

She retained vivid memories of working for Quant. Her family owned the Cambridge department store, Joshua Taylor, and at the age of 19, it was decided that before joining the family business that she should gain experience by working at Harrods. In 1957 she attended an interview there, travelling with her mother. They both wore a tweed coat and skirt, hat and gloves. Taylor's account follows:

I was employed as a Selling Reserve, had to clock in and out, and worked a five and a half day week. At the end of two and

84 'Pollyanna and the Professionals'
Daily Express, 1963
Photograph by David Bailey
Mary Quant Archive

a half years I was Buyer's Clerk to Miss Phillips in Budget Coats, who always wore a mink hat when she was going out buying. It seemed to me that Harrods had not changed since before the war, the décor was all pale green and beige. I then went on to be a supervisor in Evening Dresses at Dickins & Jones in Regent Street, part of the Harrods Group. There was a pink carpet on which I stood all day, waiting for irate customers to bring back botched alterations! I stuck it out for two and a half years and then left to travel. From Kenya I wrote to Mary Quant Ltd applying for a job.

My knowledge of Mary Quant at that time was based on admiration for the quirky windows at Bazaar, Knightsbridge and the purchase of a pair of white linen trousers from Bazaar for £5 in the sale. To my delight Archie McNair replied to my letter and invited me to go for an interview with him, which I did, wearing a MQ grey flannel dress, a grey tweed coat and a rather furry ginger trilby hat. I was asked to return for a further interview with MQ and APG, wearing a different outfit including a hat. I was offered a job as secretary to APG, accepted it with glee and started work in the autumn of 1962.

To reach the offices of Mary Quant Ltd you had to go through a garage where the Bazaar van was kept and find a small Alice-in-Wonderland door. You then found yourself in a corridor stacked high with copies of the first *Sunday Times* colour supplement which featured an article by Ernestine Carter about MQ, on many copies of which, the colour had gone wrong. Three small offices belonging to Mary, her assistant Margaret, and Archie plus a large room where there were Eileen the bookkeeper, her assistants Bridget and Norma and Bernadette (Snell), later to be the invaluable and discreet assistant

to Archie for the whole of her career. After a time ... I found myself running the MQ wholesale showroom and acting as PA to APG, who was a wizard at public relations, much sought after by the ladies of the fashion press. I also took over the buying of other young designers such as Jean Muir, Gerald McCann and Roger Nelson to fill the gaps between MQ ranges for the two Bazaar shops in Chelsea and Knightsbridge.

By this time I had realized how fortunate I was to be part of the MQ workforce. Irreverence was the norm and enthusiasm for the business and independent thought were universal. It was an eye-opener, both sartorial and social, so different from 'Big Department Store' behaviour. My furry ginger trilby was ditched and I was dressed entirely in MQ samples and enjoying every minute.

The most important sample range which appeared in my office in 1962 was that designed for the JC Penney group of stores. Made of heavy cotton in white, azure blue and black, dresses, tops, Bermudas, dungarees and skirts co-ordinated with Baker-boy caps; it was very new and sporty and found a ready market in America.

Fairly early on we were invited to dress the debutantes (along with Belinda Belville) for the annual debs dress show at the Berkeley Hotel. The Duke of Bedford, a kinsman of APG, was compèring. Things did not go smoothly as the mothers of the debs, who were mostly pink and plump, liked their daughters to wear the pretty Belville party frocks and only a few could, or would, wear our more sporty and dashing oufits.

Being part of the Quant 'family' was enormous fun thanks to Mary, Alexander and Archie who commanded great affection and loyalty. When I reluctantly left MQ in 1969 to join my family business, Mary was on the crest of a wave and had my eternal gratitude for a dreamlike work experience.[10]

The wide appeal of Quant's designs was becoming very clear. From 1964 paper patterns were produced by the New York-based company Butterick which enabled Quant to extend her reach to into the wardrobes of thousands more young women. As she stated in *Quant by Quant*, several of her patterns sold over 70,000 copies.[11] Dressmaking was a skill practiced by many and the simple shapes of Quant's designs were straightforward for home dressmakers to copy. 'Miss Muffet' for instance was a simple pattern that worked well when reproduced with plain or patterned fabric. When the first Habitat shop opened on the Fulham Road in May 1964, female staff wore dresses from Bazaar, and photographs show Pagan Taylor wearing 'Miss Muffet' in black crepe trimmed with white [86, 87]. Butterick, established in 1867, had been producing patterns for home dressmaking based on couture collections since 1937, and in 1961 purchased the rights to use the name and trademark *Vogue* Patterns from Condé Nast.[12] Under the 'Young Designer' banner, Butterick marketed designs by Quant, Jean Muir, Gerald McCann and Prue Acton, a designer from Melbourne, Australia.

A natural partnership with Liberty of London was established from 1964, when Quant chose their distinctive small-scale printed cottons for shirts and shirt dresses which featured in many magazines [89].[13] The overall feeling of Quant's designs that year was feminine, using light fabrics such as crepe and cotton lawn, often incorporating details from traditional children's dresses, such as smocking and rounded Peter Pan collars.[14] Flannel produced in Welsh mills was another key fabric that provided the basis for distinctive

designs for autumn and winter [88]. Perhaps surprisingly, many of Quant's designs that year were ankle-length and included perhaps ironic references to Victorian and Edwardian dress, continuing a strand of inspiration which Quant had used since the first Victorian pyjamas featured in *Harper's Bazaar* in 1956.

In contrast, other designs for autumn and winter 1964 exploited the modernizing force of masculine tailoring and the graphic qualities of woven tweeds and checked wool, resulting in Op Art-style coats and dresses. Research by curator Hanne Dahl into the archives at Trowbridge Museum and Wiltshire and Swindon History Centre has revealed the stimulation for the British textile industries provided by Mary Quant and her contemporary designers in the 1960s. As textile designer Alistair Gauld said in 1992: 'the 60s I would say looking back on it were probably the real boom time for designing, in the times of Mary

86 Mary Quant for
Butterick
Paper pattern 3287, 1964
V&A: NCOL.438–2018

87 Terence Conran and
Habitat staff, dressed in
Mary Quant, 1964
Photograph by Terence
Donovan

Quant and people such as her, and I don't
think it's ever been quite so good since.'[15]

In the 1960s Trowbridge sold cloth to
70 countries around the world. They sold the
'bread and butter' grey flannel (wool with
a soft nap or brushed finish), which Quant
used for many tailored outfits at least from
1960 [30]. This could be produced within
a short lead time. Trowbridge mills could
also respond quickly to special requests to
match fabrics and dye particular colours to
suit a client's requirements. The reputation
of West of England cloth for very high quality
flannels and other wool cloth was built on
centuries of experience. The 'West of England'
labels with a woven white horse emblem,
added inside garments shows the value to a
purchase given by the source of the fabric.[16]
A Tattersall's checked wool woven at Salter's
Mill in Trowbridge, Wiltshire, was the vehicle
for a favourite design, worn by Quant herself

in 1964. This was a clever hybrid of a dress,
with cable knitted collar and sleeves, joined
to a Tattersall's check pinafore. Letters in the
archives record Archie McNair negotiating
over colours and price with the mill, as the
Ginger Group collections were finalized. The
following year, once orders were placed, similar
checked wools were ordered directly from
the mill by the manufacturers, Steinbergs.[17]

Quant was pictured wearing the Tattersall's
check dress on one of several occasions when
journalists and photographers were invited to
see Vidal Sassoon cut her hair in his famous
five point bob, which was perhaps a weekly
occurrence for such a precise style [93]. She
recalled in her 2012 memoir that she had
discovered Sassoon's salon while still working
at Erik's, braving a rackety lift up to his salon
in Mayfair to watch him perform, 'like a
four-star chef'. He was also the hairdresser
she chose to cut her hair initially into a 1920s

flapper-style bob in 1960, before the trip to New York documented in both British and American newspapers. As Quant described 50 years later, Sassoon 'completely changed hair', seeing that:

> Hair could be cut into shapes and textures that not only flattered the character and texture of the hair, but projected the best qualities of the head and face – pointing out the cheekbones and focusing on the eyes and making the maximum impact on the individuality of the face and personality.

Sassoon is widely credited with liberating women from tedious hours spent under a hairdryer hood with rollers forcing hair into waves and curls fashionable in the 1950s, and promoting the beauty of natural hair. Sassoon's customers, like Quant, 'found the freedom to swim in the sea, drive in an open-top car, walk in the rain…. Your hair did not forget the shape and chunky curves he created, and it simply returned to base.' Sassoon's five point bob was particularly closely linked with the fashion designer, although he had created it earlier for other customers and models including Elizabeth Gibbons (see p.50) and Grace Coddington.[18] Quant and Sassoon's stories are forever intertwined, with equal roles in creating iconic fashion imagery: for Quant, he 'produced the perfect cap on my leggy mini-skirted designs and the frame for my Colour Cosmetics'.[19] The photographs of Sassoon in action, and Quant admiring her finished look, created valuable publicity for both brands, ensuring that they are both credited with defining the decade.

91 Mary Quant
Fashion design for dress with cable-knitted
neck and sleeves, 1964
Given by Mary Quant
V&A: T.107E–1976

92 Mary Quant
Dress with cable-knitted neck and sleeves,
1964
Woven and handknitted wool
Given by Mary Quant
V&A: T.107–1976

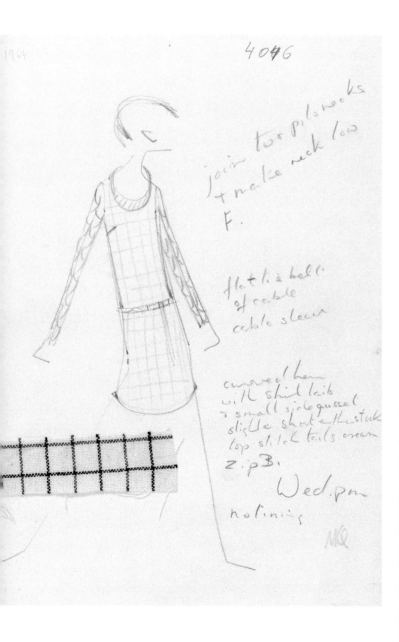

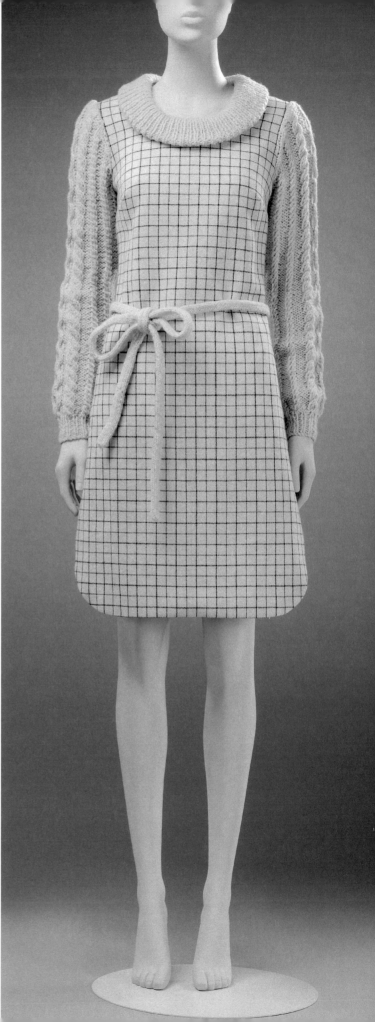

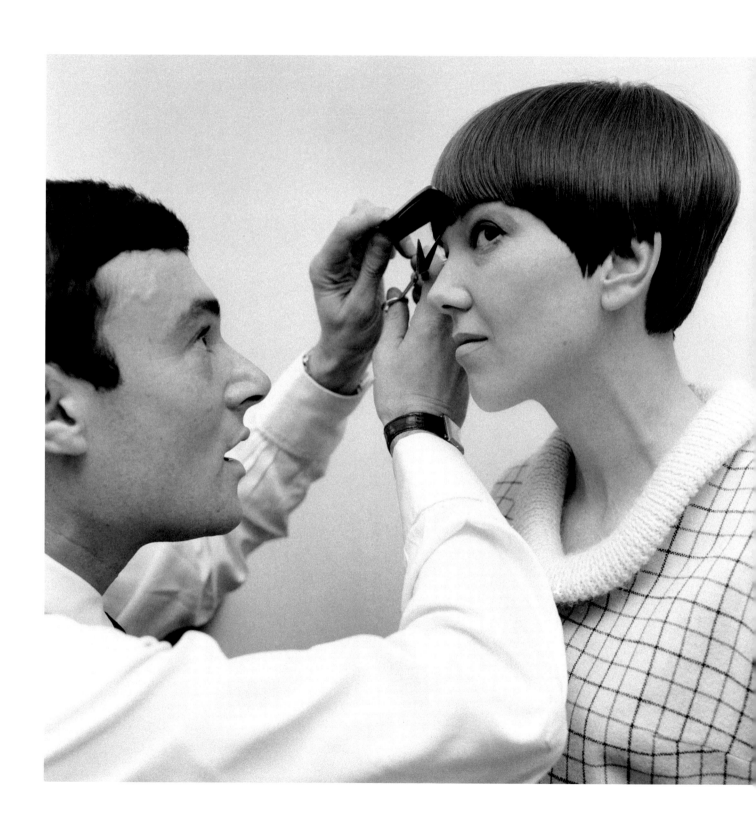

94 Mary Quant
Shirt dress, 1965
Printed cotton
Given by Mrs C.L. Archer
V&A: T.383–1988

95 Grace Coddington and Sue Aylwin
modelling Mary Quant's Ginger Group
ensembles, 1965
Photograph by Terence Donovan

Doing Business in Transatlantic Fashion: The Experience of Mary Quant
Regina Lee Blaszczyk

I n September 1962, the smartly dressed Mary Quant posed beside a British Overseas Airways Corporation (BOAC) cardboard wardrobe filled with ladies' clothing [96]. The apparel had been designed by Quant in London, manufactured by Steinberg & Sons in a South Wales factory, and commissioned by the JC Penney Company, a major American retailer with stores from coast to coast. The shipment was headed for the British Embassy in Washington, D.C., where Quant would attend a press launch on 27 September sponsored by JC Penney. The sheer novelty of the affair – the transatlantic flight, the attractive young female designer and the offbeat London styling – all made for a good photo opportunity on behalf of JC Penney, who used the image to promote its new fashion partnership with the rising celebrity designer.[1]

This essay places some of Quant's apparel business ventures of the 1960s within the broader context of the post-war ready-to-wear industry. Quant developed business relationships with JC Penney, with Steinbergs, and with the Puritan Fashions Corporation (a large American apparel manufacturer) to advance the modern idea that every woman could wear playful and stylish apparel, every day. Quant's venture into affordable fashion hinged on several wider developments: the rise in disposable incomes and the upsurge in consumer spending; the influence of American sportswear and the concept of separates; the introduction of synthetic materials and easy-care fabrics; and the population spike between 1946 and 1964 caused by the high birth rate among a generation later known as the 'Baby Boomers' in the US and the UK. Quant capitalized on these changes and turned ready-made clothing into a new type of fashion: edgy, egalitarian fashion that owed its cachet to London, to street style and to persona of the designer.

The Ready-to-Wear Revolution

The 30 years between 1950 and 1980 saw the triumph of ready-made apparel over home-sewn and tailor-made clothing and the reorientation of fashion around global brands associated with figurehead designers. At the start of the period, the French haute couture houses still lorded over the world of fashion, producing made-to-measure dresses, small runs of boutique wear and export models that foreign retailers and garment manufacturers were authorized to copy or adapt for their local markets. Haute couture enjoyed a renaissance after 1947 when Christian Dior introduced the New Look, but by the time Dior passed away in 1957, elite French dressmaking for the wealthy few was in a life-and-death struggle. A nascent French ready-to-wear industry had grand ambitions but was too wedded to handicraft to compete in the mass market.

America had the world's largest, most advanced ready-to-wear industry, serving an internal market of 180 million people by 1960. It is impossible to generalize about the typical American fashion consumer because there was no such thing. This vast market was segmented by factors such as locale, climate, income, occupation, age, race, ethnicity, marital status and subculture. The Seventh Avenue garment district in New York was the major design and production centre, accounting for 66 per cent of the industry's output. In descending order, secondary clusters were located in Los Angeles, Philadelphia, Chicago, Boston, St. Louis, Dallas, Cleveland, Kansas City, Cincinnati, Baltimore, Milwaukee, San Francisco and Miami.[2]

The Americans had perfected techniques for the quantity production of garments, and had evolved a distinctive style of informal clothing known as 'sportswear'. Los Angeles was the pioneer of casual styling, but hubs like Cleveland were also major producers. Cleveland's top house for sporty, young ready-to-wear was Bobbie Brooks, Inc., which had cornered the market for teenage school

96 Mary Quant with
her JC Penney collection
for the press opening
at the British Embassy,
Washington, D.C.,
27 September 1962

Mary Quant Archive

clothes with a system of inexpensive colour coordinated separates called 'go-togethers'. Sales grew from $9.8 million in 1952 to $44 million in 1961. The 16-year-old teenager who spent her weekly allowance on a Bobbie Brooks high-school wardrobe was buying versatility [97]. She could mix and match five or six separates, changing the combination of top, bottom, jacket and accessories for a different look each day.[3] Bobbie Brooks had adapted Henry Ford's idea of interchangeable parts to casual clothing to become one of the most successful apparel companies in the United States. Along the way, the firm helped to make separates into a hallmark of American style.

The British fashion business sat squarely between that of France and America. Its salient characteristics were a strong commitment to workmanship inherited from the tailoring tradition, quantity production methods copied from America and a symbiotic relationship with major high-street retailers. During the war, the British government consolidated apparel production into the most efficient firms for the duration. Makers-up like Steinbergs, which had factories in the East End of London and in South Wales, sewed long runs of soldiers' uniforms and civilian Utility garments in a small number of styles to strict specifications. The Utility scheme, in effect from 1941 to 1952, mandated precision in manufacturing – and precision had a lasting impact. Quality became the emblem of British ready-to-wear.[4]

The synthetics revolution introduced modern fabrics to the clothing industry. Britain was home to some of the world's great rayon producers – Courtaulds and British Celanese (which merged in 1957) – and their man-made fibres had been used for decades. Nylon, the world's first synthetic fibre, was simultaneously

how many looks can you make with Bobbie Brooks

LOOK [checkered] Shell top, zipper back. About $4. Back-wrap Skirt, lined, big patch pockets. About $8.

LOOK [catchy] Cowl-topped yoke on overblouse. About $5. Knee-Highs, fly front, fully lined. About $7.

LOOK [catchable] Sleeveless cardigan, 2 waist-high pockets. About $5. Jamaicas, fly front, fully lined. About $5.

ALL COTTON KNITS, TOPS S-M-L, BOTTOMS 5-15. COMBINATIONS OF WHITE/RED, WHITE/SURF BLUE.

LOOK [chipper] Rear view of the same cardigan under "unlimited." About $5. Swingy back-wrap, lined. Big pockets in front. About $8.

LOOK [captivating] Hooded cardigan, ties snugly, hood lined. About $7. Capri pants, fully lined. 2 hip pockets. About $7.

LOOKS UNLIMITED Roll-up sleeve Cardigan, check Bermuda collar. About $5. Jamaicas, fly front, fully lined. White only. About $5.

invented in the United States and Germany in the late 1930s, while polyester was developed in Britain during the Second World War. In In the post-war era, the DuPont Company, the American inventor of nylon, launched a major marketing effort to promote nylon, polyester, acrylic and spandex in markets around the world. Fabrics made from the new miracle materials were easy to launder, wrinkle-free and stain resistant.[5] By the 1960s in Britain, a wide range of synthetics went into children's apparel, school uniforms and high-street apparel for men and women.

The British clothing industry grappled with a major demographic shift that was transforming consumer society. In the mid-1950s, the London-based social scientist Mark Abrams undertook research on the newfound prosperity among blue-collar consumers and young people aged 15 to 34. By 1956, the backbone of the clothing market consisted of blue-collar consumers, who spent £600,000 annually out of a national total of just over £1 million. On top of this, young consumers accounted for only 35 per cent of the population but they bought nearly half of all clothing.[6] Some makers-up created teen models in the 1940s, but the major push occurred after 1955 with the formation of the Teenage Fashion Group, a trade association for makers-up in the Baby Boomer market. Steinbergs belonged through one of its subsidiaries, Alexon & Co., Ltd.[7]

Young British consumers took style inspiration from American music, movies and magazines. A few London wholesalers had imported American apparel in the 1930s, but the inflow stopped during the war and was later kept low by government mandates. After restrictions were lifted in 1959, American fashions entered the UK and began to capture the imaginations of teenagers (aged 16 to 24) and young women (aged 25 to 34) who appreciated the reliable sizes and the casual sportswear look.[8]

97 'How many looks can you make with Bobbie Brooks', *Wardrobe Magic* booklet, Bobbie Brooks Inc., 1960

The Western Reserve Historical Society, Cleveland, Ohio

With a widening home market, the British ready-to-wear industry looked to apply its penchant for precision to clothing sizes. No one worried about standard sizes in the days when ladies went to tailors or did their own sewing, but sizing became a major problem with ready-to-wear. In America, efforts by trade associations, home economics groups, and government agencies to quantify female measurements had been underway since the interwar years. In 1939–40, the United States Department of Agriculture (USDA), in collaboration with other federal agencies, state governments and educational institutions, sponsored a scientific study that collected data on the body dimensions of women and children. The federal government used this data to develop commercial standards on body measurements that were widely adopted by the clothing industry in sizing apparel. As a result of this effort, the Americans had better standardized sizes than anyone else, albeit far from perfect.[9] In the 1950s, the American and British clothing industries each undertook new sizing research, and although strides were made, improved diets and changing populations meant that the average woman was a moving target for the statistician with a tape measure.[10]

Some major national retailers, including the Marks and Spencer Company in Britain and JC Penney in America, had a higher degree of success in their efforts to standardize sizes. In America, JC Penney kept abreast of consumer needs through a professional home economics department that worked closely with university and high-school domestic science teachers and their students. Through market research, JC Penney came to understand that American women came in all sizes and shapes, and developed five basic size ranges: junior, junior petite, misses, misses petite and half sizes.[11] Similarly, Marks and Spencer scientifically studied the British woman's figure, applied what it learned to clothing design, and developed a reputation for having the most reliable sizes on the high street.[12]

Finally, the British makers-up looked beyond the home market with the idea to expand sales in North America, Europe and the Commonwealth. British goods had prestige abroad – and clothes were no exception. Steinbergs was a longtime exporter, which strengthened its American position by opening a sales office in New York.[13] Collectively, the makers-up harnessed their British-ness in order to entice foreign retail buyers to London. In January 1956, they hosted a 'London Week' for buyers en route to the major shows in France and Italy.[14] This became a semi-annual event, and London developed an international reputation for ready-to-wear. Following the autumn 1961 shows, the Fashion House Group of London Ltd, a trade association for makers-up, reported export sales of more than $1.82 million, with $1 million of the goods going to Europe and the rest to the Commonwealth and North America.[15]

The Green Light Means Go

America was the most coveted market for British fashion businesses looking to sell their products overseas. Frederick Starke, a designer, exporter, and chair of the Fashion House Group from 1959 to 1966, had been to America and knew the market.[16] Writing in the *Board of Trade Journal*, Starke described the high living standards in America and the 'increasing demand for the snob value of an imported label and the urge to buy something which is not to be found in every shop.' For fashion exporters, these factors added up to 'a situation where all the lights are green'.[17]

The United States had the world's most advanced retailing system, a fact that is little noted in the fashion history literature. The range of stores was mind-boggling: there were stand-alone urban department stores; fashion specialty retailers; regional department store chains; specialty store chains; mail-order houses with retail branches;

national chains with mail-order divisions; suburban discount retailers; and one-of-a-kind shops. Starke believed that Americans were the toughest retail buyers around: 'Buyers in America are more scientific then European buyers,' he told *Women's Wear Daily*, 'and they understand merchandising much better'.[18]

American buyers were always on the lookout for unique merchandise that would attract customers. Seventh Avenue had 'the greatest organized mass-production fashion industry in the world', wrote Starke, with 'more good designers than anywhere else'. But quantity production had bred design complacency. 'There's a stereotyped look from many houses,' he said, 'because they cut in such numbers'.[19] The realities of the American scene – the high standard-of-living, superior retailing practices and conservative designers – gave the London ready-to-wear industry the confidence to launch a British fashion invasion.

Selling British Style

It was in this context that Mary Quant and Alexander Plunket Greene first visited America on a reconnaissance mission in October 1960. Quant's designs caught the eyes of journalists at *Seventeen*, a fashion and beauty magazine for teenagers, and *Women's Wear Daily*, the major American newspaper for the fashion business. The Lord & Taylor fashion specialty store on Fifth Avenue placed an order. But the real coup came two years later when forward-looking managers at JC Penney approached Quant directly.[20]

JC Penney was a large national chain with headquarters on Seventh Avenue, 1,695 stores in 48 states, $1.4 billion in sales, and a visionary CEO who was leading the firm through a major metamorphosis.[21] Back in 1957, William M. Batten, then a JC Penney vice president, had stunned the board of directors with a memo that became legendary in American business circles. JC Penney was established in 1902 as a dry-goods store selling reliable staples to Main

Street shoppers, but by the post-war years, this *modus operandi* had become obsolete due to changing markets. Concerned about the store's declining profits, Batten challenged JC Penney to remake itself around the major demographic trends that were transforming America: rising prosperity, the population shift to the suburbs and the expanding teen market with plenty of spending money. During Batten's term as CEO from 1958 to 1974, JC Penney revamped its image from stodgy to stylish. The store never stopped selling practical apparel for the entire family, but it augmented these basic lines with new, trendy designs for young suburbanites. JC Penney expressly targeted young married couples and teenagers with innovative fashions that could be purchased from some of its upmarket suburban stores or from a 1,252-page mail-order catalogue that was launched in the summer of 1963.[22]

Most JC Penney fashions were produced by American garment manufacturers and sold under the store's house label, but the ambition to capture teenagers' dollars led JC Penney to capitalize on the youthful preoccupation with

99 *The Look to Be Looked At: Youth Power Sets the Rules with . . . Penneys Young International Designer Collection*, fashion forecast leaflet for sales associates, June 1968

JC Penney Company Archive, DeGolyer Library, Southern Methodist University, Dallas, Texas

popular culture and celebrity. American retailers had a tradition of promoting French and British couturiers, Italian ready-to-wear creators and American sportswear designers, but the JC Penney venture was distinctive for its focus on the youth market.[23] As part of its reinvention, JC Penney offered upscale women's apparel adapted from Paris couture models or specially designed for the American lifestyle by Seventh Avenue.[24] But while Jackie Kennedy elegance appealed to young adults, it didn't resonate with teenage pop culture aficionados who religiously read *Seventeen* and *Mademoiselle*, flocked to the movies to see Gidget films, and swooned over pop music stars on *American Bandstand*. JC Penney sportswear buyer Paul Young, a young Brit who had worked on both sides of the Atlantic, was tasked with finding a

young European designer who could be made into a fashion celebrity. After scouring Europe without success, Young went to London where he landed on Quant as being just the thing [98].[25]

JC Penney launched its Young International Designer Collection with trial designs by Quant in autumn 1962.[26] A line of 'Chelsea Girl' apparel – named after Chelsea, the area of London where Bazaar, Quant's flagship boutique, was located – was created for the press launch at the British Embassy and for test marketing by 63 JC Penney suburban stores.[27] This youthful wardrobe consisted of colour-coordinated, mix-and-match sportswear, all produced in Steinbergs' factories under Quant's supervision. The garments were made in American 'junior' sizes – 7, 9, 11, 13 and 15 –

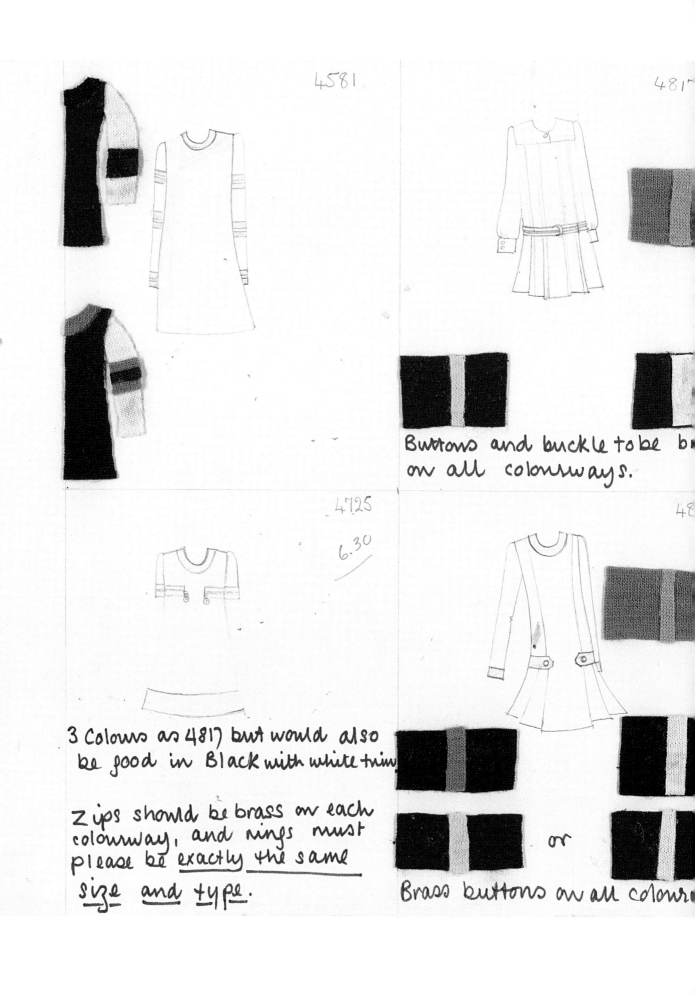

4581.

481

Buttons and buckle to be b
on all colourways.

4725

6.30

3 Colours as 4817 but would also
be good in Black with white trim.

Zips should be brass on each
colourway, and rings must
please be exactly the same
size and type.

48

or

Brass buttons on all colour

8.10

4809

Zip to match bodice colour.
Inset in contrast band. .

3412

100 Sketches and colourways for 'skimmer-plus-shorts' outfits, made from a blend of wool, Orlon acrylic and acetate tricot, for JC Penney, 1967
Museum of the City of New York: 67.73.6
Illustrations by Suzanne Isaacs

which were designed to fit a slender, short-waisted and youthfully proportioned figure, either the still-developing body of a teenager or the svelte figure of an adult with a slim build.[28] Following the British Embassy launch, Quant went on a cross-country tour to promote the line and generate interest in her persona.

When the London fashions became best sellers, JC Penney expanded the promotion, but to ensure further success, the store asked Quant to tweak her designs to suit American tastes. In April 1963, JC Penney stocked its second 'Chelsea Girl' line in 80 suburban stores; Quant made personal appearances at three Long Island and New Jersey stores, accompanied by Young who commented on a televized fashion show.[29] In the spring of 1964, the fourth Quant collection appeared both in stores and in the JC Penney mail-order catalogue, which showed 'the casual new Chelsea Look' on British supermodel Jean Shrimpton photographed by David Bailey against Big Ben and the Houses of Parliament.[30] By that autumn, the clothes were being sewn in America. The 1965 catalogue explained why: 'Designed in England and made in America, for the "import" look plus "American" fit!'.[31] American garment makers not only had a good handle on junior sizing, but their New York factories could experiment with colours and fabrics for Quant as she made samples to show the sportswear buyers at JC Penney Manhattan headquarters [100].[32] JC Penney eventually expanded the Young International Designer Collection to include Micheline Izquierdo or Mitzou of Madrid; Caroline Charles and John Michael Ingram from London; two French designers, Ariel and Victoire, both from Paris; and Susie of New York [99].[33]

Meanwhile, Quant sold a lower-priced ready-to-wear line through a new firm called the Mary Quant's Ginger Group Ltd. The name was a pun on the British political term 'ginger group', which refers to an activist faction within a party or movement that advocates stronger action on a particular issue. In this instance, the aim was to produce edgy fashion at low prices to enable wider consumption. In February 1963, the *Financial*

Times reported that Quant and Steinbergs, the maker-up, had formed a partnership 'to manufacture and market high-fashion ready-to-wear clothes at budget prices'. Each partner subscribed to half the shares.[34] The first show of Ginger Group fashions took place in London in May 1963.[35] The collection, which was sold at home and abroad, featured sizes 7, 9, 11 and 13, unusual colour combinations and countless mix-and-match possibilities. The use of American elements – the 'junior' sizing system favoured by teenagers and the practical separates concept – may have been the direct influence of Quant's recent collaboration with JC Penney in America.[36]

Women's Wear Daily published some sales figures: initial orders for the new Ginger Group fashions totaled 30,000 items; while shipments went to 110 British stores that had special 'Mary Quant departments' and to some 20 American stores other than JC Penney, which had its exclusive Quant line.[37] Simple elegance and modern practicality were featured in models such as the 'Lazy Bones' evening dress, which had a snow-white bodice, an empire waist accented by a pink bow, and a long black skirt in Dycel synthetic fabric.[38] At its 1964 annual meeting, Steinbergs remarked that Mary Quant's Ginger Group was stirring up interest, 'particularly from America'.[39]

Quant's success with JC Penney led to another American business deal, this one with the Puritan Fashions Corporation. As one of the largest American apparel makers, Puritan had corporate offices on Broadway in New York; 15 subsidiaries and divisions; 20 factories; and 14 shipping centres in the Eastern part of the country. Puritan had mainly focused on traditional styles until 1964, when it obtained the license to make a few Beatle-themed products – and was swept away by the 'swinging youth market'. When $3 million in Beatles merchandise sold in a few short weeks, Puritan chief Carl Rosen acknowledged the buying power of consumers aged under 25. By April 1965, Paul Young from JC Penney was recruited to Puritan as a vice president, and shortly there-after, the firm launched a novel promotion called Youthquake. The title was a nod to the American fashion editor Diana Vreeland who had coined the term to describe the Baby Boomer market in the January 1965 issue of *Vogue*.[40]

Youthquake was a marketing extravaganza built around up-to-the-minute fashion, a boutique shopping experience and celebrity designer endorsements [101]. Paul Young turned to young designers for fresh ideas, tapping Mary Quant, Foale and Tuffin, Veronica Marsh, and Emmanuelle Khanh from Europe and their counterparts Deanna Littell, Joel Schumacher and Betsey Johnson from America. He created a special boutique called Paraphernalia to showcase the clothes. The flagship was at 799 Madison Avenue and, starting in 1966, franchised shops were located in department stores around the country. The investment in marketing and youthful styles paid off. Puritan sales grew from $38 million in 1963, to $84 million in 1965, and to $100 million in 1968.[41]

Beatlemania had turned the eyes of American teens towards Britain, making the London designers a real asset to Youthquake. Quant and Foale and Tuffin each signed three-year contracts to provide Puritan with exclusive collections. Quant designed for two Puritan divisions – Barnesville U.S.A. and Young Naturals – while Foale and Tuffin designed for a division called JP's Only. Quant agreed to create 25 designs per season for young misses dresses and sportswear. The autumn 1965 collection was priced to retail from between $20 to $30, placing the designs at the upper end of the mass market.[42] Under Puritan's sponsorship, Quant promoted the line and developed her celebrity profile in personal appearances at major department stores such as Dayton's in Minneapolis.[43] A new generation of Anglophiles relished her British accent, manners and looks, perhaps unaware that Quant was quite shy and somewhat uncomfortable with all of the attention.

While the mainstream press reported that Americans were mad for Mod, the circumspect British weekly, *The Economist*, looked beyond the

hype to see how the London Look really stacked up. The magazine noted that of the £40 million of British clothing exported each year, a full 75 per cent consisted of 'classics' such as twin-sets, tartans, tweeds and raincoats. Companies like Braemar, Burberry and Pringle all exported traditional designs. Burberry had adapted British heritage to modern times, producing its familiar beige trench coat in the hemline of the moment: the thigh-high mini.[44] At Steinbergs, the Alexon division made 25,000 coats and suits per week, mostly for export to America; a large portion of this merchandise relied on 'British classicism for the over-all look'.[45]

No business deal or fashion trend is meant to last forever. Fashion thrives on ceaseless change, as Quant well knew. She wisely diversi-fied into cosmetics and accessories, advancing the idea of a head-to-toe look while expanding the reach of her brand.[46] By mid-decade, change was afoot at Steinbergs.[47] Mod styling was running its course, and new talent was generating fresh ideas. By 1965, Steinbergs was collaborating with the designer Jean-Claude Gaubert on a Paris-inspired export line, and by 1967, the Alexon division touted the 'pretty young designer' Alannah Tandy as the creative force behind the Youngset brand.[48] In March 1970, the newspapers announced that Quant acquired Steinbergs' interest in Mary Quant's Ginger Group, making her the sole shareholder. The former partners continued to collaborate, however.[49] The maker-up and exporter, which changed its name to the Steinberg Group in 1973, continued to produce Quant's clothing designs through the mid-1970s, although the historical record is silent on the details.[50]

Puritan president Carl Rosen attributed the American turn away from Mod to basic demographics. By 1971, the consumers of 'young, kooky fashions' were new adults who shopped for styles that were contemporary and youthful, rather than edgy and defiant.[51] The tastes of the new high-school and college cohort were shaped by a curious blend of *Bonnie and Clyde* nostalgia, Woodstock hippie-dom, and Yves Saint Laurent tailoring. It comes as no surprise that Quant last appeared in the JC Penney catalogue in the autumn–winter edition for 1971, alongside the emerging American designers Erika Elias, Betsey Johnson and Wayne Rogers whose colourful eclectic styles in part took inspiration from show business, bohemia, and an imagined prairie past.[52] By 1972, the Young International Designer Collection was old hat. Synthetics had supplanted natural fibres, separates were mainstream, and British tweeds were part of a nascent preppy look. The 'kooky' styles of Mod were 'out,' and mix-and-match separates were 'in'.[53]

What's in a Name?

During the 1960s, the ready-to-wear industry overturned the French tradition of fashion as the purview of the wealthy few. A new generation of young British designers played a pivotal role in this reorientation. They created street-inspired practical fashion for everyone. Quant was instrumental in this sea change with her London boutiques, the Ginger Group, and her collaborations with American retailers and manufacturers.

Like other promoters of the Mod look, the trio behind the Mary Quant business – designer Quant, husband and marketer Alexander Plunket Greene, and lawyer Archie McNair – came to understand that exporting British-made garments was a costly, cumbersome process, and that greater gain was to be had by licensing product designs and brands. With the Young International Designer Collection and Youthquake, the identity of the designer and the cultural cachet of London were major selling points. The Mary Quant name, reputation, and iconic daisy symbol had greater commercial value than the hundreds of sketches the designer created every season.[54] This was one of the main takeaways from the long-distance collaborations with JC Penney and Puritan.

The old French haute couture business model had pivoted on an eccentric personality, a label, an image, fame in the press, and a perfume.[55] During the 1960s and 1970s, the French couture industry reoriented its priorities away from luxury dressmaking to branding. In 1984, *The Economist* reported that the Paris fashion business was kept afloat by income from prêt-à-porter (high-end ready-to-wear) and from licensing fees, the latter a strategy pioneered by Coco Chanel with fragrances in 1924. In licensing, the fashion houses created the product prototypes, but left the manufacturing and the marketing to others in exchange for royalties. The brand and the creative personality behind it were the most valuable assets of the business. The story was much the same with popular-priced designs. Quant, the mother of youthful everyday fashion, had 'practically given up making her own products, preferring to market her talents as a "design studio" bringing in around $35m a year in royalties'.[56]

Over the course of the 1960s and 1970s, consumers learned to associate a particular designer's name with a particular look and particular level of quality. *Women's Wear Daily* noted that designer licensing was 'born in France, refined in the United States and exploited in Japan'.[57] This new model for fashion enterprise owed much to French and American entrepreneurs like Yves Saint Laurent, Pierre Cardin, Daniel Hechter, Oscar de la Renta and Ralph Lauren, but Quant also contributed to the transition as a design innovator, an early brand promoter, and an international celebrity. Her precocious rise as a creative superstar in the early 1960s and her seminal role in the British fashion invasion of the United States (which predated the better-known British music invasion) provided Quant with a platform for advocating easy-going, moderately priced fashion. In her own way, Mary Quant – one of the world's first celebrity designers of affordable fashion – helped to launch the fashion brand revolution that is still with us today.

PART FOUR

1965–1967

The Shock of the Knee

With a *trompe l'oeil* romper suit effect, 'Peter Pan' collar and patch pocket, this 1966 mini dress, worn a good three inches above the knee by art historian Deborah Cherry, demonstrates how Quant injected youth and fun into grown-up fashion. Designed to be worn with flat shoes, its comfortable, sporty silhouette enabled free movement and was a complete contrast to the waisted, high-heeled fashions of the 1950s [104].

The apparent invention or introduction of the mini skirt was a gradual process, evolving from the late 1950s. As early as 1958, a BBC deputy director complained about the girls in the audience of the live music show 'Six-Five Special' who wore 'very abbreviated skirts'.[1] In subsequent years, Quant, with a growing presence in visual media, played a central role in its wider adoption by contemporary women. Her knee-skimming skirts were noted in the press as early as her 1960 visit to New York [4].[2] Quant customers such as Nicky Hessenberg (see also p.42) who wore short skirts in the first half of the decade provoked scandalized comment on the streets of New York where fashion was more traditional.[3] Nevertheless, contemporary photographs and some surviving dresses (those which were not shortened by their owners later), show that very short skirts revealing more than an inch or so of the lower thigh, were not often worn until 1966.

The origins of the word 'mini' (as a prefix derived from 'miniature') have been traced to 1934, when it was used to describe a three-wheeled car.[4] The Mini-Minor car was first made in 1959, and in 1961 this was shortened to the Mini. Four years later, the terms 'mini dresses' and 'mini skirts' were first seen in print, although they were perhaps not widely used: Quant completed *Quant by Quant* in 1965 (published by Cassell on 14 April 1966) without mentioning either. However, 'Short, short skirts' do feature, particularly with reference to the reaction they created for the 'Youthquake' tour of America in 1965.[5] In the

closing chapter of her follow-up *Autobiography* of 2012, Quant takes the idea of the 'sixties mini' and celebrates it as 'the most self-indulgent, optimistic "look at me, isn't life wonderful" fashion ever devised … the beginning of women's lib', anticipating the 'fashion freedom' of the early twenty-first century.[6]

In 2018, Toyah Willcox recalled the impact of Mary Quant and her short dresses on her awareness of fashion, as an eight year old in 1966, living in Birmingham:

> Coming from a very strict background and going to an all girls school with steadfast rules on school uniform I found the flair of Mary Quant's designs exciting and liberating, especially the way at this particular time the designs seemed to influence music and dance culture too. Watching *Top of the Pops* it appeared if you wore a Mary Quant dress there was only one way you could dance and that was with your legs tightly together and your elbows tucked into your waist.
>
> My sister Nicola was 17 at the time. One day she came home with a Mary Quant dress she had bought with her first wage packet and my mother hit the roof and made her take the dress straight back to Rackham's department store and swap it with something more modest. My sister cried and cried about this but there was no way my mother would allow her to be so immodest in public … mini skirts were completely outrageous when they first hit the street.[7]

In the rarified world of Parisian couture, where designers showed luxurious, cutting edge designs which were custom made to fit clients, very early signs of the mini could also be detected in the late 1950s, when Balenciaga introduced simple, semi-fitted shapes such as the sack dress, anticipating a different

PREVIOUS PAGE
103 'The Quant Formula in Fashion'
Honey, special issue, 1967
V&A: NAL 607.AT.0015

104 Mary Quant's Ginger Group
Dress with *trompe l'oeil* design, 1967
Cotton drill
Worn and given by Deborah Cherry
V&A: T.61–2018

105 Simone d'Aillemont modelling dress and jacket by André Courrèges, 1965
Photograph by John French

106 Celia Hammond modelling 'Cad' pinafore dress, 1963
Photograph by Terence Donovan
Mary Quant Archive

emphasis in the fashionable silhouette, away from the wearer's waist. Yves Saint Laurent's 1959 Trapeze line for Dior offered another alternative, with some skirts starting to show more leg, or even some knee. But it was Courrèges who achieved the most international publicity for a couture collection including short skirts in 1964 as reported in the *New York Times*: 'his controversial pants suits, above-the-knee skirts and sleek mid-calf boots have aroused much excitement since they were introduced last season. They made sense and, at the same time, gave women a bold new perspective about their lives.'[8] Another distinctive Paris accessory included bonnets that fastened under the chin, and these were also seen in Quant fashion photographs at about the same time [105, 106]. The younger Paris names such as Pierre Cardin and Paco Rabanne, following the lead shown by Quant in London, fuelled the shift towards youthfulness and ease of movement in fashion. French designer Emmanuelle Khanh and the Parisian Dorothée Bis were also significant in articulating a response to the demand for young and different styles. In Britain, John Bates received attention for his revealing designs and short skirts, particularly for 'Casbah', which won Dress of the Year in 1965, and is now in the collection of the Fashion Museum, Bath.[9] Yet in reality, as Quant perceived, it was young women like her, and schoolgirls on the streets, who improvised short skirts; Quant's designs amplified the effect and brought the designer mini to the mass market. As Alexander Fury wrote in response to news of the death of Courrèges in 2016, legs came first:

> ... because the permissive 1960s encouraged provocative experimentation, not least in attire, and doubtless young women on the street began to raise their hemlines high before couture determined it was chic, or even before Quant offered her ready-to-wear versions. That's the issue with so much in fashion: I'm not sure anyone can really claim ownership. Fashion belongs to everyone.[10]

Given her views on democratizing fashion in *Quant by Quant*, this is a sentiment that the designer would share.[11] History however is written from the visual stories that hit the headlines; a key moment in the popularizing of shorter skirts beyond Britain was 30 October 1965, when Jean Shrimpton appeared at the Melbourne races wearing a simple white shift dress, no hat, no stockings and no gloves. She shocked conservative Melbourne, generating pages of news coverage around the world.[12] Clothes designed by Mary Quant were widely available in Australia, as shops initially imported the Ginger Group collection, and designs were later manufactured under license by the company Taffs, with a large factory in St Mary's, New South Wales.[13] However, Shrimpton's dress was apparently made by dressmaker Colin Rolfe, with a shorter length than normal because of a lack of material. Certainly by 1966, young women in short skirts were a common sight in London: Felicity Green's *Daily Mirror* feature, entitled 'Have skirts now reached fail safe?' showed this perfectly, including photographs of secretaries, students and shop assistants aged between 15 and 20, all wearing dresses and skirts with hems 'only just' below the bottom.[14]

Mary Quant's designs for her wholesale Ginger Group range were instrumental in

107 Grace Coddington and Sue Aylwin modelling
skirt and dress with halter-neck straps
Photograph by Terence Donovan

108 Showcard for Mary Quant's Ginger Group, c.1963
Mary Quant Archive

promoting the simple lines of the mini skirt.
Two striking Ginger Group designs were
reproduced as cartoon-like fashion drawings
by Maureen Roffey for display in shops
stocking the Ginger Group range [108]. One
is essentially a skirt made of buff coloured
linen attached to a halter neck strap, worn
over a skinny rib sweater. The architect
Alison Smithson, known for designing 'New
Brutalist' buildings with her husband Peter,
owned one of these, and later gave it to the
Fashion Museum, Bath, and a slightly shorter
version, now at the V&A was specially made
for the 1973 London Museum exhibition.[15] It
is now a challenge to find original surviving
examples of dresses from 1964 and 1965 that
don't have altered hemlines, as women often
shortened skirts themselves as skirts rose
extreme heights towards the end of the 1960s.

The other design on the Ginger Group
showcard, a simple pinafore style dress with
visible zip and centre front pleated skirt, was
modelled by Grace Coddington photographed
by Terence Donovan [110]. The original
design for this dress, or a very similar dress
entitled 'Heather', survives in a private collection [109]. The drawing is annotated with
instructions for the sample maker emphasizing
key Quant elements of this 'rather short'
dress, such as contrasting top-stitching, patch
pockets with 'zips to show' and long darts
from hip to bust. These designs, completed
with a Vidal Sassoon bob, dark eyes and
pale lips show the development of Quant's
style towards an increasingly 'mod' and
minimalist look, in plain fabrics, devoid of the
historic referencing of the earlier 1960s.

Quant's sketching style was necessarily
speedy and pragmatic: by spring 1965 she was
generating 200 designs a year for mass production (four collections of 50 garments each) for
Ginger Group, along with a further 80 designs
for JC Penney and 100 for Puritan Fashions.
Ernestine Carter calculated the total number of
designs required that year as 528, once the two
collections a year for Butterick paper patterns,

fur coats for Debenham & Freebody, coats for
Alexon, undergarments for Youthlines, and
Courtelle knitting patterns for Courtaulds were
considered (although accessories for Puritan,
including hats, sweaters, handbags and stockings were not included in this total).[16] This
compares with couturiers like Norman Hartnell
who in the 1950s showed about 200 models
each year, or 100 per season, which might
translate into about 2,000 orders.[17] Quant
would often be inspired by fabrics, which were
sourced at international fairs, often with the
help of her assistants, such as Shirley Shurville,
or from 1965, Suzanne Isaacs. The first stage
of putting one of Quant's annotated pencil
sketches into production, was for a pattern to be
made by a sample pattern cutter, and a sample
then constructed in the workroom by one of the
small team of seamstresses. This process was
described in 2015 by Gerald Farraday, who was
in charge of sample making from 1972 to 1982:

109 Mary Quant
Design for 'Heather' dress with top stitching
and brass zips, 1965
Heather Tilbury Phillips

110 Grace Coddington modelling 'Heather', 1965
Photograph by Terence Donovan

When I started, the Ginger Group was still operating and the sample workroom would develop the design range through sample patterns and sample garments. The patterns for the selected designs would then be developed into card production patterns (the originals being made in paper), different coloured card was used for contrasting fabric, interlinings and sizes and then garment samples for the manufacturing range were made using the production patterns. These patterns and samples would then be handed over to Ginger Group for further development as necessary for their production processes. The original paper patterns were kept in large manila envelopes with a line drawing of the design and style number and name on the cover and stored at Ives Street.

The sample workroom was quite large. There were three or sometimes four sample pattern cutters, a sample fabric cutter, eight sample machinists and a finisher. Initially, the main task of the workroom was the development of the prototype designs, sample patterns, sample garments and the repeat samples for fashion shows and sales. Later we went on to produce the semi-couture collections.

Mary created her own designs and also employed an assistant designer (by the 1970s) but all design work was approved by Mary. She would discuss them, make her own adjustments and fabric selection and always had the final say. The sample workshop was part of the creative team. Mary would bring in sketches of the designs or sometimes just a note about adjusting a previous design. We would talk through anything that needed clarification but you understood exactly what Mary wanted because of the closeness and intimacy of the working environment. She was adamant about what she wanted and

the workroom would have to find a way of doing it. She was always popping in to see how things were going; she'd be eager to see who was working on which design and how things were progressing.

Mary was very precise when looking at something and immediately she would spot where she wanted any change to take place. She might want a design detail altered by an eighth or sixteen of an inch, even if it was in a difficult fabric to handle such as a jersey or satin and might entail taking the garment apart. It was always done. Her passion and energy were contagious and inspiring.

We had house models to see and fit the garments on. There was Sarah Dawson, Carina [Frost], Amanda Lear and Sara Hollamby who also doubled as Mary and Pam's secretary. They were quite slim but not emaciated. I've got a note in one of my diaries of some of the sizes, 34 hips were quite normal.

Coming up to collection show dates was always a busy time for the sample room and it often meant coming in at weekends or working late into the evenings, but it was a buzzy atmosphere and exciting time. Mary always appreciated this and would send in teas and lunches. We made several collections a year including for Spain and

the USA but we didn't sell at trade fairs.
The UK collections were always launched
with a breakfast show at 9.30a.m. We put
on press shows at the Terrazza Est in
Chancery Lane or often at the Savoy Hotel.
Some of us from the sample room would
go along to help as dressers or deal with
any last minute fittings back stage. Mary
liked to work with a wide variety of

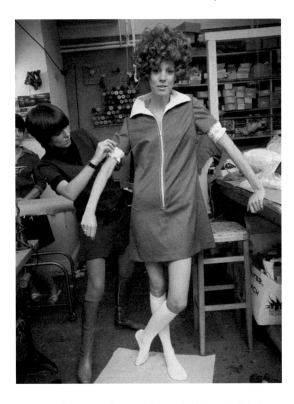

fabrics. Sales people would bring in fabric
swatches from companies such as Liberty
and Bernard Nevill and would sometimes
arrange to re-colour them to Mary's
requirements. This was often at least a year
in advance. She liked co-ordinating colours
or indeed, mismatching them. When the
fabric lengths for sampling arrived they
were kept in the fabric stock room,
managed by Tony. Sometimes these were
small sample lengths of just a couple of
metres, sometimes half a piece or a whole

piece, ('a piece' is a standard length of
fabric as supplied by the manufacturer).
Tony would attach a docket to the piece
or roll of fabric so that we had a record
of usage. Trimmings were sourced from
wholesalers but on occasion, if needed in
a hurry, we would buy from retailers like
Peter Jones and then find a wholesale
supplier later.

The quality of the garments produced
in the sample workroom was really high.
Mary was absolutely adamant. Quality
of make and quality of fabric. Mary
trained with Erik as a milliner. That was
couture so she was seeing superb
attention to detail and hand finishing.
She always had that in her mind's eye.
She wouldn't accept second best.

The sample machinists were very skilled
and knowledgeable, you'd work hand in
hand with them, they could do fittings as
well. We'd fit on the dress stand or the
house model. Any adjustments were noted
and made to the patterns and, if necessary,
another sample would be made. Tailoring
was outsourced but a first prototype
would be made in the workroom.[18]

Once approved for production, samples
and a completed pattern were passed to a
Steinberg pattern cutter for grading into
four different American teen sizes – 7 to
13 for manufacturing.

Jack Isenberg, a fashion industry manager
at the time, began his career working for
Steinbergs, and he provides perspectives on
the production process and marketing Quant's
designs, as well as her wider impact on business.

It was 1966 and I had graduated from
the Fashion Institute of Technology in
New York City with a degree in business
administration for the apparel industry.

I began my 'career' in fashion working for Steinbergs, a multi divisional clothing company mostly manufacturing tailored clothing under the Alexon Label. One of their divisions, Horrockses, manufactured dresses and had formed a joint venture with Mary Quant to produce her designs using the 'Mary Quant's Ginger Group' label. The company was headed jointly by Leon Rapkin (Horrockses) and Archie McNair (Quant). Reflecting now, I have no idea how these totally cultural opposites found themselves in business together but it was not a marriage made in heaven. Before I go further let's go back to the cultural difference of the partnership of Quant and Steinbergs because I think it's important to reflect on the differences that the 1960s brought about. Quant represented the 'new society' – a total revolution in clothing that was one of the vehicles that changed the norms and mores of British society – Terence Conran was doing it with furniture and the Beatles/Rolling Stones with music – every aspect of everyday life was being questioned. Quant's introduction of the mini skirt was a catalyst in what became the very thing that British society had never previously allowed 'MOBILITY' (the ability to move from one class to another) – the shackles were finally removed from the class system.

Steinbergs/Horrockses represented the previous value system – they had a warrant for supplying dresses to royalty. The Managing Director (Jack Steinberg) had married into the Wolfson family. The company was headquartered in a multi storey modern office building which they owned. Afternoon tea was served to the executives by a person wearing a black jacket and stripe pants. A Rolls Royce was the auto of choice with a chauffeur of course. It was the epitome of Britain BMQ (Before Mary Quant). So you can see that

it was a tough assignment to accept the refreshing approach that Quant brought to the table. They had done it this way for years, Quant said 'No' this is the way to do it. They must have felt very threatened. Clashes were inevitable between the two groups and there were many. It was to be proven that Britain and maybe the world would never be the same – could it be, that the Victorian value system had finally been superseded by a force of creativity never seen before. It was all British, the Empire was gone but look what we had replaced it with; 'The Mini Skirt', 'She Loves You', and 'Jumping Jack Flash'. My job was twofold – I was assistant to Leon Rapkin and was responsible (under his guidance) for coordinating the sales to production. It was an expansive position which covered a lot of territory. It began with the approval of the design sample being put into the line and collecting all the information required to produce the garments that were sold – more about that as my story progresses.

Line selection was a very tense time with the powers that be scoring points and trying to prove who was the leader of the pack. The meetings were held first at Ives St (Mary's HQ) and as the line progressed it moved to the showroom in South Molton Street. The climax was the naming of the accepted styles – each garment was given a name – 'Woof Woof', 'Banana Split' (a dress with a very long zipper in the front) and my favourite, 'Inside Job' which were a pair of flannel pants, the inside leg being light the outside leg being dark.

As the line was being developed I and the Steinbergs/Horrockses production team with the help of Mary's team gathered the information regarding fabric and trim sources, collected the paper patterns (so that production patterns could be made). Simultaneously, Leon Rapkin aided and abetted by myself with much input from

113 Mary Quant in her fabric stockroom, 1967

Sidney Cherfas (sales manager) would project the sales of each garment so that a fabric purchase could be made. This was very fluid as the selling season progressed this was apt to change often.

Back to Jack Isenberg and Mary Quant's Ginger Group – we have looked at putting the line together and all that peripheral stuff, now comes the really interesting part – the selling of the line. The initial effort started at the prêt-à-porter in Paris. It was usual that the stands of exhibitors were open for all to see their products – the decision was made to enclose the Quant stand, much to the horror of the French organizers. Jon Bannenberg (one of the interior designers of *Queen Elizabeth II* – the ship) designed the stand. A pitch battle ensued over the enclosure (the French versus the English) but Quant came out the winner. The stand was enclosed.

With Leon Rapkin giving the commentary in French (with an accent even the French admired), a bevy of top models such as Jan DeSouza, Kari Ann Moller strutting down the runway – not only did each performance play to a full house but the audience were leaving orders – the show became the talk of the town. Quant had taken Paris by storm in no uncertain terms.

Not only was the excitement exclusively at the prêt-à-porter. It extended into Paris as well. There was dinner at Maxims where a large party including the model contingent, who were wearing mini skirts were walking

to the table. A deathly hush came over the entire restaurant. They were stared at by every diner in the place. I have never been sure if it was disgust, disbelief or shock, but it certainly caused a major reaction.

Next stop was 'if you make there, you can make it any where' otherwise known as the Big Apple or New York City. Mary's choice of hotels was the Algonquin, famous for its hosting of literary and theatrical notables, most prominently the members of the Algonquin Round Table. The round table room became the Ginger Group's war room – future customers were shown the line there, strategy sessions were held there – it became the home away from home. It was the scene of a titan battle between Bloomingdale's and Macy's as to who should have exclusive selling rights in New York. Bloomingdale's won. The Ginger Group was with the elite suppliers having its own department or shop 'n' shop. With all the interest from newspapers, magazines and broadcasters, all the purchase orders taken from retailers, the New York visit was a smashing success. The Ginger Group was on its way to becoming a major resource, as long as the politics could be contained and the production team did their job.

For a while it worked but I am not too sure as to why the partnership fell apart. I had left prior to that happening. I have been involved in the garment business for a considerable length of time but I never witnessed the extent of excitement and the height of originality that Mary Quant created and brought to clothing. Quant, the lady from King's Road, is a very important cog in writing the history of the modernization of Britain's norms and mores. I really appreciated my inside view of what in hindsight was an important time in the twentieth century.[19]

114 Mary Quant
'Highball' glitter stockings, 1967
Lurex: 72 per cent metallic yarn,
28 per cent nylon
V&A: T.86:1 to 2–2018

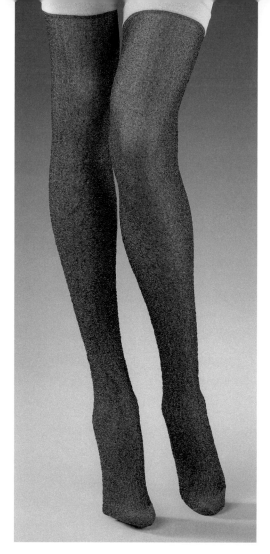

The shorter hemlines of the Ginger Group styles reflected these changing social codes, and developed in tandem with the increasing popularity of tights, which dispensed completely with the need for separate suspender belts and stockings. In the 1950s, tights were not widely worn, apart from thick woollen ones for winter. Balenciaga was reputedly responsible for introducing tights to the couture market, while Marks and Spencer first produced tights from 1963, the same year as Mary Quant's Ginger Group.[20] Stockings and tights, were manufactured for Mary Quant's from 1964, by the Nylon Hosiery Company.[21] This company was established in 1954, when Nirvair Curry, having emigrated from India with her husband Swaren and his brother Derry, began selling fully fashioned seamed stockings from a market stall near St Paul's. Initially she monogrammed seamed stockings with diamanté and flock using an iron at home. By the 1960s, the company operated from addresses at 3–5 Cavendish Place and 214 Oxford Street, selling through trade fairs, sometimes connecting with agents selling the Mary Quant cosmetics ranges, in 'New York, Paris, Milan, Copenhagen, Helsinki, Brazil and the Middle East'. The Currys worked with various manufacturers to produce a wide range of hosiery, some made with old fashioned frame knitting machines in Leicestershire, and also at their factory in Mansfield, Nottinghamshire.

Derry Curry, who was responsible for most of the day-to-day running and development of Quant hosiery, had explored the possibility of manufacturing for other designers but found that while many were interested in receiving royalties they were 'not really interested in designing … Mary was very keen; she was just the opposite. She wouldn't let us use her name unless she had input, which in the beginning we thought was going to be a nuisance but it was great because she is very good.'[22]

Once their partnership with Mary Quant was established, the Curry brothers developed a technique of making long stockings which

were joined together at the top, and they were produced as well as stockings in specially dyed bright colours to contrast and co-ordinate with Mary Quant separates. The range expanded with new colours and patterned knits, and from 1966, the effervescent 'Highball' glitter stockings in silver, gold, green blue and red [114, 115].[23] The distinctive Mary Quant packaging, initially in dark green or brown, but later in black, with the daisy logo, continued the consistent brand identity, helping the products to stand out amongst competitors such as Dior and Pretty Polly. The Mary Quant tights were made under license into the 1980s and proved to be a most enduring product line, with stockings, tights and socks in every length and every possible colour and pattern permutation featured in magazines and available to buy in high streets and department stores.

The introduction of Lycra in the mid-1960s helped to transform underwear, freeing women from the corset-like garments previously required. This coincided with Quant realizing

MARY QUANT

STOCKINGS

MARY QUANT

SEAMFREE MICRO-MESH STOCKINGS

MARY QUANT

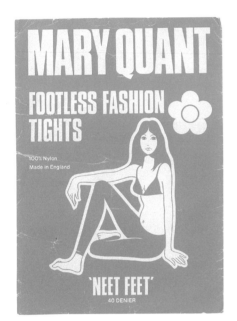

MARY QUANT

FOOTLESS FASHION TIGHTS

100% Nylon
Made in England

'NEET FEET'
40 DENIER

MaryQuant Tights

MaryQuant Tights

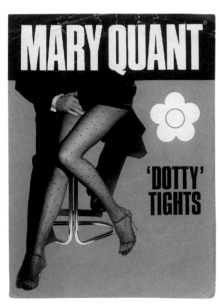

MARY QUANT

'DOTTY' TIGHTS

MARY QUANT TIGHTS

STARKERS

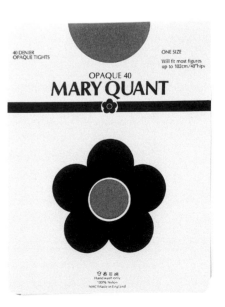

40 DENIER
OPAQUE TIGHTS

ONE SIZE
Will fit most figures
up to 102cm/40"hips

OPAQUE 40
MARY QUANT

Hand wash only
100% Nylon
NHE Made in England

the need for new support garments to suit
the natural, although slim, shape her clothes
implied. These Quant undergarments were
produced by Weingarten Brothers in
Portsmouth, under the name of 'Q-form' for
their Youthlines brand, with the now recognizable Quant daisy logo. This was woven
with six petals rather than five. Weingarten
Brothers made corsetry in New York from the
late nineteenth century, opening a factory in All
Saints Road in Portsmouth in 1905 that appears
to have closed or moved in 1972.[24] The Q-form
range included bras, girdles, pant and suspender belts, and later, body stockings, initially in
white on black and black on white, with 'natural' skin tones added in 1966. Advertisements
in new magazines like *Honey* (published from
1960), *Nova* (1965) addressed the appropriately youthful market sector, and emphasized
comfort and movement. A feature in *Petticoat*
(first published in 1966) focused on the Mary
Quant body stocking, which was designed to be
worn with suspenders, indicating that stockings
were still the norm. The model, Gay, 'likes the

smooth line, the concealed suspenders that stop the
mid-thigh bump and holds stockings above mini
skirt level, and the way it holds her shape, naturally'
[116, 117].[25] Also in 1965 a further licensing deal,
for swimwear, was made with Abella International.

Designing garments remained Quant's
main focus alongside these products made under
license. Her designs during this prolific year
included functional and fashionable trousers
and dungarees, in woven wools and for summer,
trouser suits in Art Nouveau style Liberty furnishing fabric. These were a useful alternative for those
who felt uncomfortable in increasingly short skirts,
although also represented a challenge to tradition:
as previously seen, trousers were generally only
worn by women informally, at home. This was
perhaps one of the most significant sartorial
changes for women of the period, and Quant helped
to make trousers a viable option for women to wear
to different occasions. By the 1970s, from the
evidence of publicity photographs, Quant preferred
to wear trousers herself, and so helped to popularize
an increasingly informal and unisex approach
to style.

With the customary formality of London's social life changing, for its younger residents at least, the demand for fur coats, the most expensive element of any 'deb's' wardrobe, was declining. Quant's designs for this sector of the market were sought after by different manufacturers and retailers, and in 1965 she was designing fur coats for the venerable department store Debenham & Freebody. These designs may have been made by the specialist London furriers Roat, as additional labels bearing this name can be found in some surviving garments.[26] An astrakhan or Persian lamb coat in the V&A collection is featured in a *Tatler*, described as having 'typical originality.... Its 'strict little stand-up collar, long sleeves and plain tailor's buttons make it equally right for daytime formality'.[27] Fur coats (Quant-designed or not) were beyond the reach of the average consumer, this example costing 220 guineas, or £231 (about £4,070 today).[28] Fur coats remained the ultimate status symbol for the newly fashionable elite such as Beatle George Harrison and model Pattie Boyd, who were

married in Mary Quant fur coats. Leather coats and other garments were also an important element of the fashionable wardrobe, while a fake pony-fur coat (by an un-named designer) could be bought as a kit to make up at home from *Honey* magazine in 1966, costing just £6 12s, or £116 today.[29] From 1965, there was also the option of Alligator raincoats designed by Quant, using the PVC Quant delighted in, some even designed with belts fastening with giant safety pins, predating punk by a decade.[30] Quant also designed coats using other new fabrics such as Celon, a type of Nylon marketed by Courtaulds. A design for this coat survives, complete with instructions written by Quant, addressed to a Mr Gouldman, who presumably worked for Alligator [119, 120]. The handwritten note reveals Quant's ability to influence traditional manufacturers to try new ideas, reading 'I would like to persuade you to try this sketch (1) Nylon white and ciré which is the most sharp & exciting & saleable'. Quant goes on to suggest a second trial in white and black padded nylon.[31]

118 Mary Quant Design for 'Celon' nylon coat by Alligator, with instructions on the reverse addressed to a Mr Gouldman, *c.*1966
Heather Tilbury Phillips

119 Advertisement for 'Celon' coat by Alligator, *c.*1966

120 Mary Quant for Alligator Raincoat, 1966–7 PVC
Worn and given by Beryl Davies
V&A: T.95–2018

121 Mary Quant tights and shoes, c.1965

Mary Quant Archive

From 1964 Quant collaborated with an increasing number of manufacturers to diversify into new product areas at more accessible price brackets, including paper patterns, rainwear, underwear, stockings and tights, to achieve her aim of being a democratizing force in fashion. A pair of 'sparkle stockings' cost just under a pound at 19sh 11.d (approximately £16 today) in 1966.[32] However, these represented a special purchase; two pairs given to the V&A in 2017 by Diane Harris were originally a Christmas present from her husband.[33]

Creating knitting patterns also increased Quant's accessibility, enabling clever home knitters to wear her designs; Sue Robertson's mother Rose made a dress, now in the V&A collection, to the tee shirt dress-style pattern illustrated on p.67 – a design well suited to jersey, whether the bonded jersey Ginger Group styles, or a thicker effect achieved with the hand-knitted synthetic yarn it was intended to promote.[34]

In 1966, Quant was also preoccupied with ambitious plans to launch a Mary Quant range of cosmetics (see p.154). In addition, a range of PVC clothes and bags, some complete with daisy logo, registered as a trademark the same year helped to complete the total Quant look [121].

The hard work of the preceding decade was recognized with an OBE, which Quant received from the Queen in November 1966, together with Plunket Greene and McNair, in a ceremony that provided a compelling photo opportunity, and was reported around the world. Opting for the comfort and informality of one of her signature wool zipped jersey dresses and matching beret, tights and shoes, finished with the dapper touch of backless gloves, probably made to her designs by Dents.[35] Quant chose this practical outfit for the ceremony to suit both weather and protocol, cleverly solving the question of formal headwear and avoiding the need for a traditional tailored coat.

Quant designed jersey dresses such as these in hundreds of colours and permutations, demonstrating the perfect look for the new confident young woman, enjoying spending power and increased choice when shopping on the high street. As previously seen, Quant originally discovered the bonded jersey fabric in America, and her assistant Shirley Shurville (see p.97) found a British supplier, Ames Mill, through a rep for the textiles agency Standard International, which could match the American sample. The bright colours and

sculptural qualities of this fabric were perfectly
suited to the development and flourishing
of the simple mini dress, with contrasting
borders, trimmings and pocket logos. Most
examples in the V&A collection are 100 per
cent wool, heat-bonded to a synthetic backing
fabric [123–130].[36] Variations of the jersey
dresses were designed especially for the
American market: a series of swatch boards
now in the collection of the Museum of the
City of New York show the materials, trims and
colourways for different styles made in the US
for the JC Penney stores [100]. These boards
were put together by Quant's assistant,
Suzanne Isaacs.[37]

Another version of this colourful jersey style
can be seen in the portrait on the cover of the
first edition of *Quant by Quant* [5]. The designer is posed seated on the floor, with a large
swatch book showing striped jersey samples
from the firm Stevcoknit, which was based in
North Carolina.[38] According to Shirley
Shurville, this style was actually a long jersey
top, bought by Quant from the 'Intimate
Apparel' or sleepwear department in Lord and
Taylor in New York. This concept of housewear
encouraged Quant to design a series of match-

ing jersey clothes with bras, pants, socks and
mini skirts, promoted as 'underwear as
outerwear'.[39]

A typical Quant jersey dress was chosen
by fashion editor Clare Rendlesham for Audrey
Hepburn to wear in the 1967 film *Two for the
Road*, giving the actress, usually associated
with French couturier Givenchy, an entirely
new look. Quant's clothes had also been worn
on screen by Claire Bloom in *The Haunting*
(1963), Nancy Kwan in *The Wild Affair* (1965)
and Charlotte Rampling in *Georgy Girl*
(1967).[40] With Quant as the celebrity face of
her own brand, endorsement by movie stars
was not a priority, although of course her
designs were worn by many actresses and
singers often in the public eye, such as Cilla
Black. The shy, but widely travelled Quant had
become accustomed to crowds wherever she
went, not only for her collaborations in America
(see Regina Lee Blazszcyck's essay on p.110);
the photograph here shows her with menswear
designer and retailer John Stephen on a promotional trip to Rome where a 'Carnaby Street'
boutique was opened on the Via Margutta [122].

While her Ginger Group designs still
appeared often in high fashion magazines,

123 Mary Quant
Dress with pocket, 1967
Jersey
Mary Quant Archive

124 Mary Quant
V-necked dress, 1966
Jersey
Mary Quant Archive

125 Grace Coddington
modelling 'Footer' dress,
1967

126 Mary Quant
'Footer' dress, 1967
Jersey
Mary Quant Archive

FOLLOWING PAGES
127 Mary Quant
Dress with hood, 1967
Jersey
Mary Quant Archive

128 Mary Quant
'Footer' dress, 1967
Jersey
Mary Quant Archive

129 Dress with pocket, 1966
Jersey
V&A: T.86–1982

130 Mary Quant
Skater dress, 1967
Jersey
Given by Janette Flood
V&A: T.79–2018

Quant's products found even more support in
the new magazines focusing on the interests
and outlook of younger women, from a broad
social background. A *Honey* feature of 1967
explored every aspect of Quant, from her ideas
on make up to her personal taste in home decorating and cooking – her whole approach
to organizing life was summed up as a belief
that:

> Each girl must be essentially herself.
> To me the *Honey* reader personifies the
> adventurous young spirit, restless, soon
> tiring of ideas ... the clothes I design
> must be a perfect foil for her, strong
> enough to echo her personality, but
> never dominating or inhibiting it. They
> must live and work for her – to be used
> or abused at will – and have the throw-
> away comfort of blue-jeans.[41]

This special booklet traced the story of
four 'ordinary' girls – now the target market
for the brand – who were given a Quant make
over, and allowed to interview the designer
afterwards. It portrays the designer at ease
with herself as the embodiment of her brand:
her husband and business partner are back
room boys now, and she was at the height of
her productivity, although at 36, much older
than the 20-year-olds she dressed in the make-
over. Naturally, the Ginger Group clothes were
promoted alongside the other products – the
pages showing a range of baby pink and pretty

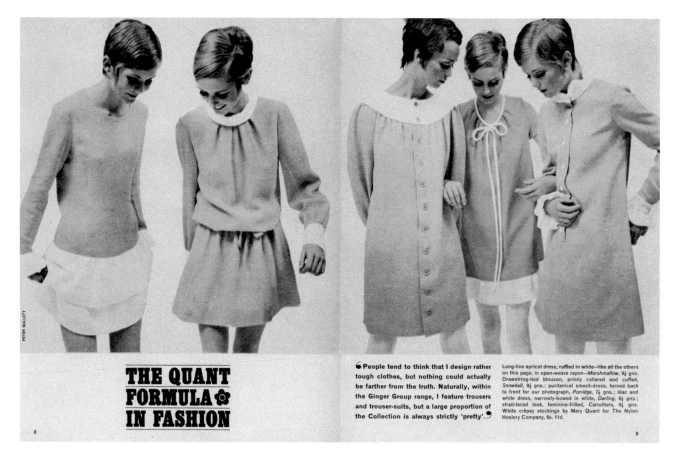

THE QUANT
FORMULA ⚙
IN FASHION

❝People tend to think that I design rather tough clothes, but nothing could actually be farther from the truth. Naturally, within the Ginger Group range, I feature trousers and trouser-suits, but a large proportion of the Collection is always strictly 'pretty'.❞

Long-line apricot dress, ruffled in white—like all the others on this page, in open-weave rayon—*Marshmallow*, 9½ gns. Drawstring-tied blouson, primly collared and cuffed, *Snowball*, 9½ gns.; puritanical smock-dress, turned back to front for our photograph, *Porridge*, 7½ gns.; lilac and white dress, narrowly-bowed in white, *Darling*, 9½ gns.; strait-laced look, feminine-frilled, *Carruthers*, 9½ gns. White crêpey stockings by Mary Quant for The Nylon Hosiery Company, 6s. 11d.

8   9

134 Mary Quant's Ginger Group Dress with 'Puritan' collar 1967 Cotton
Worn by Patricia Lowe

135 'The Quant Formula in Fashion'
Honey, special issue, 1967
V&A: NAL 607.AT.0015

peach coloured dresses, as worn by Twiggy and other blonde Quant models, contrasting with pages of more robust overcoats made by Alligator and masculine inspired tailoring [124 and 125]. Another spread celebrates her new discovery of velour, celebrated for its richness and ability to take dyed colours like 'boiled sweets'. Stretch towelling was used for a new range of loungewear, manufactured in Germany, which included full-length body suits and short all-in-ones [135].

Mary Quant was often photographed at work at her vast drawing board in the drawing room of her home in Draycott Place [132]. This photograph shows her with a sample from her 'Quant Afoot' range of plastic shoes and boots, made by G. B. Britton & Sons of Kingswood, Bristol (also the manufacturers of 'Tuf' work shoes). This project was launched in August 1967, amidst much press interest in this novel approach to footwear. Made out of extruded plastic in bright colours, in 'scarlet, chestnut, citrus, green, burgundy and black', they were available as ankle-height 'shoe boots', and some with zipped, removable knee high extensions. The soles were see-through and had a Quant

daisy shape moulded into the sole, which made daisy shaped footprints in snow and mud. As the colours co-ordinated with Mary Quant tights and Ginger Group dresses, they helped to create a total look at an affordable price.[42] The manufacturers planned to make half a million pairs, and they certainly were popular, but although fun to wear, and despite a soft lining, the plastic was not breathable so they were impractical for frequent use.

The project reflected Quant's continuing quest for new materials and new manufacturing methods, which she discussed in an interview with *Guardian* journalist Alison Adburgham, describing tights with built in shoes to be launched that year, and body stockings with plastic feet.[43] The interview reveals Quant's struggle to accept the shift in fashion back to inspiration from the past. 'It can't be called a fashion, because it's old clothes, and it's always depressing to wear clothes of the past. Whenever I see that happening I feel we designers have failed to supply the answer.' At the same time however, the mood of fashion was insistently turning back, and some of her designs for Ginger Group incorporated

IS THIS JUST ANOTHER FAD?

The big beret.

12s 6d.

12 Quant colours.

Enquiries
for Quant berets
to
39 Fitzroy
Square,
London W1.

MARY QUANT

136 Twiggy modelling pinstripe suit
'Young Idea's Dandy Look'
Vogue, 15 September 1967
Photograph by Helmut Newton

137 *Is this just another fad?*
Advertisement for Mary Quant berets, 1967

worn by hip-hop artists, the Kangol beret was first manufactured in Cumbria in 1939 by Jacques Spreiregen, who came to Britain as a refugee from Poland. Initially importing berets from France, for military use and workwear, the name Kangol apparently came from K (for silk or knitted), 'ang' from angora and 'ol' from wool. The beret, and other hats were successfully marketed as fashion essentials in the post-war period, and Kangol developed a line of hats endorsed by the Beatles in 1964.[45] Three years later, the Mary Quant berets were available in 12 colours, and cost 12 shillings and 6 pence. They were stamped inside with both the daisy logo and the Kangol crossed knitting needles, and worked well to create Quant's head to toe co-ordinated look, as the advertisements placed in magazines such as *Vogue* demonstrate.[46] The adverts with slogans such as 'Is this just another fad?' continued the distinctive satirical, self-aware tone of the Quant brand seen in advertising for her cosmetics, playing on her reputation for generating innovative and commercial products. Kangol's public relations officer Heather Tilbury noted that the berets were an inexpensive way of updating an outfit, and they were widely featured in younger magazines including *Petticoat*, *Flair*, *Jackie* and *19*, generating additional business for both Kangol and Quant.[47]

The fashion magazines, from *Vogue* to *Petticoat*, all reflect the shifting mood in 1967, away from mod, minimal hard edges and baby doll shapes towards a longer, flowing, more grown up elegance, like the Ginger Group charcoal and white jacket and trousers shown in the 'Dandy Look' spread in *Vogue*'s Young Idea pages in September 1967 [136]. Mary Quant was still a leading force in fashion, with a recently opened flagship store in the heart of Mayfair, at 113 New Bond Street, and her designs and name appearing in many pages; but increasingly, it was her mass produced designs, like the coloured tights and cosmetics, that reinforced this presence in fashion media towards the end of the decade.

and welcomed this trend, as shown by the V&A's skirt and jacket made out of William Morris 'Marigold' furnishing cotton, revived by Sanderson in the 1960s. Antique style broderie anglaise trim and delicate laces were used on some mini dresses [134], particularly from the 'Calico Collection' of 1966, which was apparently inspired by Edwardian dustcoats and over-dresses found in cupboards at the Plunket Greene country house in Surrey. Quant described how the resulting 'smock dresses, low-waisted frocks with gathered, flounced skirts, and, best of all, provocative hot pants with matching broderie anglaise frills … all very short … sold faster than we could make them.'[44]

A further collaboration was announced in the autumn of 1967, with the British beret makers Kangol, perhaps as a result of Quant's choice of a cream beret for her OBE ceremony in 1966 [137]. Still a heritage British brand, and known now for the bucket and casual hats

Quant and Cosmetics

Beatrice Behlen

In March 1966, cosmetic buyers and journalists received five pieces of a jigsaw puzzle [138]. They assembled into a photograph showing 22 models wearing mini dresses, including Celia Hammond, Grace Coddington and Peggy Moffitt, beneath the words: '"Make-up ideas all mixed up!" said Mary Quant watching top models floundering in the beauty jungle. Result: MARY QUANT make-up. Cut out for a big new swinging market! It's the missing link in make-up.' This confident announcement indicated the concept behind the new range: young, no nonsense, problem-solving and easy to use. The following day, the final piece of the jigsaw delivered an invitation to a champagne launch party at a club in London's Mayfair.

In 1968, Quant summarized why she had got involved 'with the make-up bit': 'now that the clothes were different the face was wrong.'[1] Fashion had changed dramatically, but make-up had been left behind. This applied not only to the kind of products available, but also to the colours, packaging, advertising and the way in which cosmetics were sold. Quant recalled that:

> Nobody had considered a colour other than red, pink or vaguely orange for lipstick or that there was colour other than blue and green and possibly purple for eye-shadow, so there was no flexibility and no fun with make-up ... and the people who sold make-up in stores were always the most dragon-like women – terrifying – who'd come after customers and grab their customers ... make-up was stuck back in war time ideas.[2]

According to Archie McNair, the trio had initially approached Marjorie Goodwin, née Cussons, marketing director of Cussons Sons & Co, best known for Imperial Leather soap, who wanted to branch into the beauty market.[3] No deal was reached but Quant soon signed a contract with Stanley Picker, the American owner and chairman of Gala Cosmetics, part of the Myram Picker Group. At Picker's factory in Surbiton, just outside London, economy brands were produced, such as Miners and Outdoor Girl aimed at a younger customer, as well as the medium-priced Gala range. The Quant make-up launch was preceded by 18 months of development, which the designer later remembered as 'the most thrilling time':

> I had no doubts at all about my concept of the colours and products, as to me the need of the new was so glaringly obvious, but when the packaging and testing also went so smoothly and looked so terrific, it was the one time in my life I had total, total confidence in a venture's success.[4]

Quant was influenced by her own experiments with make-up – she claimed to have used artists' materials such as paint brushes, water-colour paint boxes and crayons, foreshadowing later products and their names.[5] On photo shoots Quant had observed models applying their own make-up using products, brushes and techniques developed for the theatre: 'They brush on *shadow* to create bones, slim noses and apply *light* to bring out eyes, illuminate cheek-bones.'[6] Quant wanted to streamline cosmetics, so that products worked well together, women spent less time applying them and had fewer items to carry around. In fashion, Quant had aimed to create a 'total look', built of interchangeable components that enhanced each other but allowed individual permutations.[7] She had persuaded manufacturers to make knitwear and tights in complementing colours and she now applied this formula to cosmetics:

> Everything co-ordinated out in the colours I wanted: the Colman's mustard and, you know, this prune-colour and putty, a putty-beige or an equivalent with a green in it and black and white. And that was something like '65, '66, I was working on the make-up already and used the same

'Make-up ideas all mixed up!' said Mary Quant watching top models floundering in the beauty jungle. Result: **MARY QUANT** make-up. Cut out for a big new swinging market! It's the missing link in make-up! Wait for it! Pièce de resistance tomorrow!

Message from Mary Quant: Please come to my champagne party to see my new make-up on March 28th, at 12 noon at The Garrison, 5 Hamilton Place, London W1. RSVP 48 Burlington Arcade, London W1. Telephone Hyd 4965

138 Invitation to Mary Quant make-up press launch, 28 March 1966
Photograph by Terence Donovan
Joy Debenham-Burton

139 *Mary Quant gives you the bare essentials*
Advertisement for Mary Quant make-up, 1966

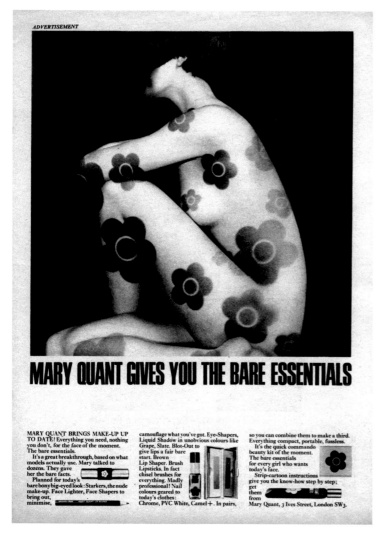

ADVERTISEMENT

MARY QUANT GIVES YOU THE BARE ESSENTIALS

MARY QUANT BRINGS MAKE-UP UP TO DATE! Everything you need, nothing you don't, for the face of the moment. The bare essentials.
It's a great breakthrough, based on what models actually use. Mary talked to dozens. They gave her the bare facts.
Planned for today's bare bony big-eyed look: Starkers, the nude make-up. Face Lighter, Face Shapers to bring out, minimise,

camouflage what you've got. Eye-Shapers, Liquid Shadow in unobvious colours like Grape, Slate. Blot-Out to give lips a fair bare start. Brown Lip Shaper. Brush Lipsticks. In fact chisel brushes for everything. Madly professional! Nail colours geared to today's clothes: Chrome, PVC White, Camel +. In pairs,

so you can combine them to make a third. Everything compact, portable, fussless.
It's the quick commando beauty kit of the moment. The bare essentials for every girl who wants today's face.
Strip-cartoon instructions give you the know-how step by step; get them from Mary Quant, 3 Ives Street, London SW3.

colours ... I brought in those colours to the nail polish which, of course nobody had ever seen nail polish in colours like that. And lipstick and eye shadows, and so the colours worked with all that. So there was a unity of course....[8]

The journalists, buyers and sales representatives who attended the first launch on 28 March 1966, or the second a week later at Mary Quant's home, witnessed a make-up revolution: an entirely new packaging concept. In the mid-1960s, many, albeit not all, beauty products were sold in plastic containers designed to imitate more valuable materials such as horn or were 'all pale pink quilting and bogus gold', as Quant remarked.[9] Declaring her love of the humble material – including its smell – Quant announced that her packaging was to be honest, 'hundred karat good plastic'.[10]

When designing clothes, Quant drew a daisy to indicate where a garment needed something extra without yet knowing exactly what: 'I used to doodle these daisies everywhere, I'm nervous, you know, and then they've gone onto clothes and then became formalized and became that daisy.'[11] In January 1966, the now formalized five-petalled black daisy was first registered as a trademark. It was to feature heavily on cosmetic containers and also on the body of a naked model in an early advertisement [211].[12] David McMekin, consultant designer to Gala Cosmetics, who worked with Quant on the packaging, noted her 'purist choice of Bauhaus chairs, silver dining-room and "no messing about" attitude which he translated into a five-petalled silver daisy on black or white shiny board.'[13] Reflecting Quant's desire for honesty and efficiency, lipsticks were sheathed in a brushed metal tube. Quant wanted something 'you could pull out of your pocket, or your bag without it looking as though it belonged in a boudoir. I thought, why can't lipsticks look like a cigarette lighter?'[14]

The products' tongue-in-cheek but matter-of-fact names hinted at their intended effect or purpose. There was 'Starkers' – abroad it was

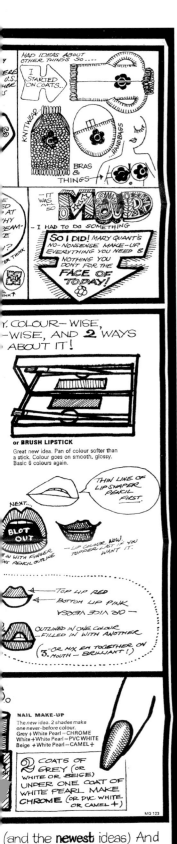

HAD IDEAS ABOUT OTHER THINGS SO.... I STARTED ON COATS...

KNITWEAR HANDBAGS

BRAS & THINGS

—IT WAS SO MOD — I HAD TO DO SOMETHING

SO I DID! MARY QUANT'S NO-NONSENSE MAKE-UP. EVERYTHING YOU NEED & NOTHING YOU DON'T FOR THE FACE OF TODAY!

Y. COLOUR—WISE, —WISE, AND 2 WAYS ABOUT IT!

or BRUSH LIPSTICK
Great new idea. Pan of colour softer than a stick. Colour goes on smooth, glossy. Basic 6 colours again.

THIN LINE OF LIP SHAPER PENCIL FIRST.

NEXT...

BLOT OUT

—LIP COLOUR NOW, THICKER LAST IF YOU WANT IT.

— TOP LIP RED

— BOTTOM LIP PINK

— OR VICE VERSA

— OUTLINED IN ONE COLOUR — FILLED IN WITH ANOTHER

(3. — OR MIX 'EM TOGETHER, ON MOUTH — BRILLIANT!)

NAIL MAKE-UP
The new idea. 2 shades make one never-before colour.
Grey + White Pearl = CHROME
White + White Pearl = PVC WHITE
Beige + White Pearl = CAMEL +

2 COATS OF GREY (OR WHITE OR BEIGE) UNDER ONE COAT OF WHITE PEARL MAKE CHROME (OR PVC WHITE OR CAMEL +)

MQ 123

(and the newest ideas) And Chelsea London England

explained that this was 'British slang for naked' – a foundation available in fair, medium and dark.[15] 'Face Shapers' were for contouring: 'mushroom beige' to create shadow and 'ivory' to highlight, complimented by 'Face Lighter', a cream-based product in a small tube. Translucent 'Face Final' powder was sold with sponge puff in a compact. The lighter colours of 'Eye Gloss', a pearlized cream eye shadow, formed the base for liquid 'Eye Shapers' or powder-based 'Brush Eye Shapers', eye shadows in three coordinated shades – Moody Blues, Greens or Ochres, assembled in a mirrored compact. Quant frequently offered products in two formulations: clients could choose between cake mascara or mascara in a tube with wand, both in black, brown and blue. Lips could be tinted in six shades, available as a tube or as 'Brush Lipstick' in a pan, all with matching nail varnish.

'To appear *natural*' was the desired effect for 'the new type of woman' and to get away from the masks created by pancake foundation.[16] Journalist Margaret Allen writing in 1981 called this 'pale unmade-up look on the face and lips with all the focus on the eyes', the 'British' or 'London' look, which soon spread across the world.[17]

Mary Quant was the best ambassador for her brand and in 1967 described her own make-up routine for a *Honey* magazine special:

FACE: An 'under' cover like *Starkers*, a nude make-up, semi-matt, just like skin!

EYES: Brown behind the eye-socket, white on the eyebrow bone, from twin pots of *Brown* and *Pearl White* pressed shadow. LIPS: Two out of the six basic lipsticks: the palest, plus one of the brightest pinks – either Q.1 or Q.6 (Then I can make the colour either stronger or darker.) Highlighting these three features makes an interesting enough face to go on with. Extra make-up can be applied at the same time or later. You could try FRECKLES, pin-pointed with *Brown Eye Shaper*....

More trickery comes with *Face Shapers* contour powders. The pearlized one pitches up the shine on cheek-bones. I also mop it under my brow and on my chin. And I stipple the darker shadow on my chin, to make my jaw look shorter.

Face Final holds that lot firm. Then the dark shaper is used again, to define the outer edge of my lipstick. Throw in a *Liquid Liner* for making the obvious eye lines ... [sic] also vital for faking lashes on the lower lids. I dip in the brush, fluff it on a tissue, then lightly flick in the lashes. Next comes mascara and, of course, wads of tissue. Total: only seven items![18]

The cosmetic revolution also extended to the sales force: to replace the intimidating 'dragon-like women', six young cosmetic consultants had been recruited prior to the launch. Joy Ingram (now Debenham-Burton) who became their supervisor in March 1966, remembered that they had been employed: 'not only because they looked good, but because they had strong personalities.'[19] Dressed in black jersey mini dresses, with white trimming and daisy on the breast pocket, the sales consultants' role as representatives of the brand was to inspire customers to want 'to look like that girl' [140].[20] The situation was more complicated for the predominantly male sales representatives, who had to sell a radically new concept they might not themselves

142 Mary Quant Beauty Bus, 1971

Holding onto the Mary Quant Beauty bus are Gala
employees (from left to right): Vicki Bedford, International
Demonstrator; Rowena Honey-Will, PR Secretary;
Sylvia Titterington and Sally Compton, International
Demonstrators; David Notermans, Bus Driver and Display
Artist; Pat Mash, International PR Executive; Trevor Henzell,
Mary Quant International Sales and Marketing manager.

have entirely grasped to often conservative
department store buyers who 'were all still
wearing hats'.[21]

After the launch, reps and sales girls
embarked on a promotional tour taking in
several UK cities. At pop-up counters in department stores, customers were introduced to the
new products by having half their face made-up
by a consultant who would finish with dotting
a small daisy near one eye. To help make sense
of the new line, how and in which order it
should be applied, a cartoon strip was developed,
printed on fine paper so it could fold up into
a small rectangle [141]. Patricia (Pat) Mash
(now Gahan) who started to work as a Quant
consultant in July 1966, remembered the
strip as a brilliant marketing tool: a woman
might dip her toe into being modern by
buying a Mary Quant lipstick 'but they get
this cartoon strip, and they look at it when
they go home, and then the next week they'd
come back for Starkers, and the next week
they come up for something else. And so they
built up the whole collection of Quant'.[22]

The original six-woman sales force was
soon expanded to staff the permanent counters
established in many department stores. In
London, Mary Quant cosmetics were available
in Miss Selfridge, Fenwicks, Harrods' Way In
boutique, Dickins & Jones, DH Evans, John
Lewis and Peter Robinson, the Regent Street
branch of Boots, but, maybe surprisingly, not
in any of the Quant shops.

Between April and July 1966, the cosmetics
were introduced in several European countries
and in August, Pat Mash and two colleagues were
sent on a tour of America. *Women's Wear Daily*
reported that as in Britain, the 'Quant collection'
was to be sold in the ready-to-wear rather
than beauty departments of American stores.[23]
Possibly the most spectacular means of driving
sales abroad was the Quant beauty bus: a bright
red Routemaster, one of the distinctive London
double-deckers which was internally stripped
and custom fitted with long make-up tables,
mirrors and swivel stools for make-up training

and makeovers [142]. Between 1970 and 1975,
the original bus and its white successor toured
around Europe, Canada, America and Venezuela.
Once it was stationed opposite a major stockist
of the brand, make-up artists sent out from
London and trained local consultants, set to
work. At any one time as many as 24 clients
could enjoy the Mary Quant make-up experience.
Pat Mash, by 1970 responsible for International
Public Relations, remembered that 'sales were
not made on the bus, but the young clients were
each given a MQ cartoon strip showing how
to use the products with a list of those suitable
for each individual. The products were then
purchased in the adjacent store or pharmacy.'[24]

Advertising

The striking advertising for Mary Quant cosmetics, which was very different to that of most other
make-up brands, was developed with Tom
Wolsey, who had become art director of a men's
quarterly consumer magazine at its relaunch in
1960. Under Wolsey, the design of *Man about
Town* – soon shortened to *About Town*, then just
Town – became highly influential with its focus
on photography from emerging talent such as
David Bailey and Terence Donovan, who was
to photograph the 22 models for the jigsaw
puzzle.[25] Wolsey advised via several advertising
agencies he formed and worked with, but also
on a personal basis, having become a friend of
Quant and Plunket Greene.[26]

Wolsey's approach was similar to the one he
had pioneered at *Town*: an arresting image, often
a crop or close-up, paired with a bold, confronta-

143 *Cry, baby.*
Advertisement for Mary
Quant tearproof mascara,
1967

tional, headline, frequently employing puns, and witty text in an informal tone. The 1967 advertisement for 'Starkers' and 'Face Lighter', is a case in point: 'Bare-faced liar' is written across the close-up of a model staring straight into the camera, one gold front tooth just visible behind her slightly open lips. She is: 'Bare, bony, beautiful. Fresh. Natural. Liar! Yes and No.', her natural beauty entirely due to Mary Quant cosmetics. More startling is an advertisement of the same year for waterproof mascara [143]. Half the magazine's page is filled by a model's blonde, side-swept fringe that touches the dark lashes of her left eye, from which a tear has just fallen. She can be a 'Cry, baby.' because she is wearing 'Mary Quant new tearproof mascara'. After Wolsey's move to America in 1972, other agencies continued to produce arresting advertising for the brand (see pp.164–71).

New Products and Perfume

Perfume was the first product added to the range. Mary Quant described her difficulties convincing the conservative male perfumers of Grasse, the traditional French home of perfume, of her vision for a new scent. Admittedly, this was somewhat contradictory: her offerings were meant to be 'open and confident like men's scents, but also female, sexy, daring and complex', as well as evoking 'an erotic feel coupled with a kind of cleanliness'.[27] Eventually a satisfactory result was achieved and in October 1966 the perfume pair A.M. and P.M. was launched [145]. According to Pat Mash the 'piece de resistance' were 'great big knuckle duster rings in the MQ five petal daisy shape, the centre circle covered by a coloured glass "Jewel"'. The ring's lid flipped open to reveal a base holding perfume wax in either of the scents.[28] One of the Tom Wolsey-designed advertisements featured a front and side shot of one model's face, holding a facetted jewel and flower between her lips. She is a 'Two-Timer', who in daytime is 'guileless as a marguerite' but turning to 'smoulder, tempt, threat' at night.[29] In 1974 Mary Quant launched another scent, Havoc, a perfume and cologne 'for girls who like to play it'.
    Surprisingly perhaps, the original product

range did not include false eyelashes, which were such a major feature of the look of the 1960s. Subsequently, in March 1967, not one but three false eyelash products were introduced: 'Lashings' – lashes for upper and lower lids, the latter 'single hairs you fix individually'; 'Natural Lashes' giving 'just a hint of falseness' and – on the other end of the scale – 'Vamps'.[30] Later that year one of the most well-known Quant cosmetic products, 'Loads of Lash!', was launched: a single 8-inch-long (20.3 cm) strip of real hair lashes.[31] 'Lower Lidders Lashes', added in 1968, reflected the move towards a new type of natural look: 'feather light' lashes were attached to a transparent, instead of the usual black strip.[32] Other lash products continued to be developed, including reusable 'Wash 'n Wear' lashes, on sale from 1972.[33]

Quant's first foray into skincare was 'Skin Think' in late 1968, which followed the 'functional and fun'[34] concept of her cosmetics. The range included 'Come Clean' cleanser, 'Get Fresh' toner, 'Skin Drink' under make-up moisturiser and 'Skin Saver' 'maxi-moisturiser', as well as a small round box with 'sunshine-yellow pills' containing B and C vitamins, reflecting Quant's belief that 'the future of cosmetics is working on the body from the inside as well as from without'.[35] Plunket Greene thought the addition of the 'brilliant yellow' pills 'God's gift to a marketing man' but did not enjoy his wife trying out 'cream after cream after cream'. Quant told journalist Sheila Black: 'I used to sit there for hours, taking creams on and off. The housekeeper thought I'd gone mad.'[36] In the late 1960s and early 1970s, Quant brought out 'Topspeed Tan', a staining cream with sunscreen, 'Sunshine Oil', a spray-on product preparing the skin for tanning and 'Redskin Relief', an 'aerosol foam to sooth sunburnt skin'.[37]

Already in October 1966, Quant had introduced her first 'paint box' – an efficient means of presenting products in one container: a flat white box with a large mirror inside the lid held three eye shapers (or shadows), black cake liner, block mascara, two brush lipsticks,

two brushes for eyes and a broader 'chisel' for lips.[38] Unlike *minaudieres*, small jewel-like cases with make-up compartments that were popular in the 1930s, Quant's container was not made of precious materials but of plastic, decorated with a silver daisy. Other articles along the same principle followed: a rectangular box covered with easy-wipe yellow plastic contained everything for an overnight stay. One of its two stackable internal trays held sample size skincare products, the other cosmetics. The Mary Quant *Toolkit* was a smaller version assembling lipstick, 'Starkers', eye gloss, eyebrow pencil and mascara – 'all the basics' – in a yellow plastic pouch.[39]

The names and packaging of Quant cosmetic products continued to amuse and delight: 'Cheeky' was a liquid 'non-greasy blush-rouge' and 'Blushbaby' a powder-based blusher, while 'Jeepers Peepers' referred to powder eyeshadows.[40] Initially, colours were designated by numbers but soon these were replaced by names such as 'Ginger Pop', 'Cherry Pop' and 'Banana Shine' (1972) and the four shades of the 'Naughty Nails' polishes brought out in 1973: 'Sultry Sapphire', 'Evil Emerald', 'Forever Amber' and 'Tempting Turquoise'.[41] The colours remained one of the brand's most memorable and outstanding features. The later singer Toyah Willcox was only eight

145 *My analyst says:…my a.m. self is fresh, guileless, totally disarming…my p.m. self is smouldering, sexy, totally dangerous*
Advertisement for Mary Quant a.m. and p.m. perfume, 1966

years old and living in Birmingham when Quant's cosmetics hit the market. Perhaps unsurprisingly she was not allowed to wear make-up during the 1960s, but her older sister:

> … would bring home beautiful round Mary Quant bottles of nail varnish in amazing colours such as canary yellow, shimmery green and night time black. i [sic] could stare at these beautiful bottles for hours, the design was one of the best things i [sic] have ever seen. Mary Quant celebrated colour in all its spectrum and this had a huge influence on how i [sic] saw make up as an instrument of self-discovery and self-expression.[42]

Make-up To Make Love In

Towards the end of the decade, beauty ideals changed to match the growing popularity of an inter-war aesthetic. Twiggy recalled wanting to look 'thirties and glamorous', growing her hair, ditching false eyelashes and experimenting with 'smudgy colours'.[43] This trend was picked up by fashion store Biba, established by Barbara Hulanicki, who launched her cosmetic line in 1969, competing for the cheaper and younger end of the market.

Quant incited another revolution: a gel-based cosmetic range that was less likely to irritate, required less dye and had superior staying powder. Gala creative manager Jill Lauderdale, who worked with Quant on the new line, described it as 'the perfect product. It was avantgarde. It was transparent. It lasted 24 hours.'[44] Sue Steward who took over from Lauderdale recalled in 1971: 'We wanted to produce a range in which a girl could kiss and cuddle without looking smudged and frightful. Normally if a girl goes to bed in her make-up, she gets up looking a hideous mess.'[45] This thinking inspired the name: *Make-up To Make Love In* which 'even in the Quant organisation' was thought by some to be 'too risqué'.[46] Before arriving in the shops in June 1970, the new line was introduced to Quant consultants at a conference in London and to the press 'at a luncheon in Dell'Aretusa' – a private club on King's Road, apparently one of Mary's favourite places.[47]

The newly appointed agency Aalders, Marchant, Weinreich produced advertisements and promotional material with the photographer Barry Lategan.[48] One leaflet featured a slightly dishevelled looking model on the cover under the headline: 'Love is the great destroyer of the beautiful face.' Inside, now looking perfect, the model leaned against a turtleneck-clad young man and the 'incredible new cosmetics that love can't shift' were explained: 'Colour Stick' foundation and 'Blush Stick' 'look dark, but they smooth on light', providing colour, rather than cover. There were also *Eye Tint*s in 'blue, aqua, soft green, violet, yellow and bronze' and smudge-proof 'Lash Colour' mascara in black and brown/black. The perfume duo A.M. and P.M. (now without the dots) was re-invented in *Potion* form with 'an oil base to stay longer'. Quant had thought of everything and included a pretty little box with 'Breathalysers' – 'tiny perfumed pills to keep your mouth fresh'.[49] Margaret Allen, writing about the beauty industry in 1981, recalled that 'the range was one of the marketing successes of the year and established the Quant line as a serious producer in the British market'.[50]

Special Recipe

In May 1972, Quant launched the 'Special Recipe' range, initially focusing on cosmetics. The product and colour names were very different from six years earlier: they emphasized the naturalness of the product while the packaging reflected the fashion for Victoriana, albeit in Quant's beloved plastic. Cream and liquid foundation were available 'in five natural skin-tone shades of Pale Putty, Middle Earth, Nut Brown, Country Clay and Natural Ochre'.[51] There was also cream rouge, mascara and 'Eyeshading' (liquid eye shadow), 'all in lovely sad colours and chock full of earth pigments and vegetable extracts, honey, wheatgerm and almond oil'.[52] Quant recalled: 'The whole concept was nostalgic and the packaging was old-fashioned and romantic. I wanted black and gold chunky pots and jars, with sympathetic rounded graphics, in black, mustard and gold'.[53] Labels featured an old-fashioned serif typeface, the drawing of a wheatsheaf and the words 'Guaranteed Pure', 'Genuine and Original'. Advertisements showed the products artfully arranged among vegetables on a rustic wooden table or strewn between real daisies and real grass. Further cosmetic as well as skincare products were added over the next few years, including cold cream, face masks, perfume essence and bath products.[54]

The main brand continued to develop as well. In September 1973, Quant stated that 'Crayon sticks in 20 colours – for colour everywhere' were 'the best idea I've ever had'. The crayons in white, grey, brown and brighter colours such as yellow and orange were thin and partially encased in metal. Two months later a set of 10 crayons in pastel colours were advertised. These were chunkier and, like artist's crayons, were sold in a metal box, albeit a bright yellow one adorned with a black daisy [146].[55] The same year saw the emergence of 'Jellybabies', a new range of gel-based products, including 'Gel Skin Colour', 'Gel Colour' eye shadow and 'Gel Mascara'. The packaging was another stroke of genius: the white containers were made in the shape of slim baby bottles complete with teat.

Possibly even more avant garde than 'Make-up To Make Love In' was 'Make-Up for Men', which, Quant remembered 'caused extraordinary shock' but also led to 'a staggering amount of publicity everywhere'.[56] One advertisement destined for the American issue of *Cosmopolitan* in 1974 showed a couple wearing the same make-up down to the Evil Emerald nail varnish. The text explained that to look as good as they can, both sexes should use 'A little black Stick smudged around the eyes. A brushful or two of Tear proof Mascara. Shaping with Mary's new Blushbaby in the Toffee colour, and a finger full of clear shining Glosspot on the mouth.' The result: 'a man still looks like a man, only better'.[57] The products were sold in a paint box in manly black which also contained moisturiser 'in either a colourless version or a "healthy" one', and two contour powders.[58] In the 1970s, the Liverpool teenager Holly Johnson, the future lead singer of Frankie Goes to Hollywood, was an avid user of 'Make-Up for Men': 'in the time-honoured tradition of teenagers, he would leave the house bare-faced then whip out his compact once round the first corner', transforming himself 'into an exotically painted aspirant to Merseyside's demimonde'.[59]

In 1977 Quant brought out 'Skin Programme', a new skincare line 'bang up to date with all the most effective ingredients

146 Mary Quant Crayons
Museum of London: 74.330/32kkb

built in'. With unusual candour for a beauty advertisement, Quant stated that her line was 'not the Fountain of Youth' and that she was 'not promising any miracles', but that following a routine using the new products 'you'll look younger than you would without it'.[60] To prove her point Quant did what she had so far avoided and appeared in the advertising campaign.

Later Years

By the time Quant launched 'Skin Programme', Gala Cosmetics had become part of the health-care company Smith & Nephew. In 1980 the company was acquired by the American cosmetics brand Max Factor, which in turn became part of the Proctor & Gamble Group in 1991.[61] Already in 1970, Mary Quant Cosmetics Japan had been established, a subsidiary of what was to be renamed Club Cosmetics, itself the successor of a company founded in 1903 to sell, and later to produce, cosmetics and aligned products.[62] Initially selling in fashion and department stores, in 1986 Quant Cosmetics Japan owned 75 shops, growing to 200 in 1996, the year Quant dedicated a book to Juichi Nakayama, the CEO of the company.[63]

Quant has often spoken of her love of Japan and its people. According to Archie McNair, the admiration was mutual: 'Japanese girls identified with Mary very well. They loved her.'[64] Nakayama persuaded Quant to endorse, rather than initiate herself, fashion accessories which were sold from the early 1980s.[65] McNair believed that the Japanese company reflected the 'Quant idiom' well and after initial reluctance Quant accepted this change and frequently went to Japan to work on new products. The designer particularly admired the high quality of the products produced in Japan, the attention to detail and Japanese aesthetics which mirrored her own. In an interview in 1990, Quant told Libby Purves: "You should see the shops: they're like sweetie-shops, full of delicious things, so small and pretty and nicely wrapped." She tosses me a pair of knickers, dainty in a daisy envelope, whips out a plastic rain-cape from a green daisy pouch. "See? Everything in something, nice and neat. Like little presents to yourself."[66]

While the Japanese business expanded, Mary Quant published several advice books. *Colour by Quant*, written with fashion journalist Felicity Green (at that point Managing Director, Europe of Vidal Sassoon) came out in 1984, guiding readers in the use of colour on face, hair and clothes. Somewhat surprisingly, no cosmetic brands are mentioned and products are photographed in such a way that they cannot be identified.[67] In 1986, *Quant on Make-up: A Complete Guide to Creative Make-Up* followed, co-authored by journalist Vicci Bentley, then beauty editor of *Woman's Journal*. The striking front image would not have looked out of place on *i-D* magazine. It featured the central part of 'The Graphic Face', a dramatic Kabuki-style, Piet Mondrian-influenced make-up, one of the 18 looks included in the book. The make-up products appearing in the images include Mary Quant 'Action Lash' mascara, 'Colourshine' lip gloss, kohl and eye pencils, as well as face powder.

In 1996 *Ultimate Make-up & Beauty* came out (republished in 1998 as *Classic Make-up & Beauty*). While fashions in make-up have changed, the step-by-step instructions of the book still hold strong. Clothes (not much are on show) and make-up were from the Mary Quant Colour Shop at 3 Ives Street.[68] The store was opened in 1994, selling cosmetics and accessories produced in Japan, following the acquisition of the worldwide rights of trademarks and licences by the Japanese company the previous year. Even without her input – Quant stopped being involved in 2000 – much of the original spirit behind her cosmetics lives on: their formulations might have changed but 'Eye Gloss' eyelid primer, 'Face Final' pressed powder and 'Blush Baby' blusher are still available, having been joined by 'Out of Sight' concealer, 'Billion Lashings' mascara and 'Talkative Eyes' eyeliner.[69]

Quant and Advertising: Collett Dickenson Pearce

Janine Sykes

Mary Quant and her brand came to public attention during the golden age of advertising. Flicking through the pages of *Vogue*, *Honey*, or any of the fashion magazines that promoted her designs, particularly in the 1960s, it is clear that manufacturers of textiles, stockings and cosmetics all had the budget to pay for expensive colour images. Moreover, they could afford to hire the agencies with the most creative artists as well as copywriters to enable them to capture the imagination of customers, and encourage them to buy their products. Initially, as a smaller, independent company, Quant and her business partners were skilled at creating marketing opportunities without the need for expensive advertising (although occasionally full-page adverts can be found for Bazaar in magazines, or when the label was rebranded as Mary Quant, in 1962).[1] They also received crucial support from fashion editors resulting in extensive coverage in magazines over three decades. From the early days, the Quant team also understood the great potential for strengthening their brand appeal with striking printed carrier bags and letterheads, and woven dress labels too, which helped to increase recognition of, and allegiance to, the brand. Once the business model was established for licensing manufacturers to create Quant designed products such as the Youthlines underwear, Alligator raincoats and Kangol berets, advertising in magazines became increasingly important for selling Quant's designs in shops. The licensees were responsible for paying for the advertising, to help ensure the biggest return for their investment in the Quant brand.

Quant and Plunket Greene were very much involved in creating and approving the different advertising campaigns, and worked closely with the different agencies involved. Some of the most innovative advertising was developed for Mary Quant's cosmetics (see also pp.154–63), including huge billboards showing the 48-sheet enlargements of models

demonstrating products such as 'Cry, baby.' and 'Bring back the Lash' posted on the King's Road, or 'Shadow Boxing' on the platform at South Kensington underground station. Quant recalled in 2012 how 'she crashed her Mini Minor' having first seen the 'Cry, baby.' billboard. She wrote that 'Pop Art was playing with scale and billboard-size images. And we were playing it back in the grossly enlarged dimensions of street advertising.'[2]

Throughout the late 1970s and 1980s, the cosmetics advertising account was held by the creatively-led London agency Collett Dickenson Pearce & Partners (CDP, founded in 1960). The two companies were the perfect match: both were pioneering in their respective fields, and together they redefined what fashion and advertising could achieve. This essay traces the influences on British advertising in the post-war period, including: the 'Mad Men' of Madison Avenue, the agitators of the so-called 'creative revolution';[3] developments in British art education; and enhanced printing technologies that enabled magazines and billboard adverts to be printed in higher definition. Making adverts the platforms from which new visions of life and style could be imagined.

CDP was one of the first British advertising agencies to experiment with teams of art directors and copywriters working together, following a model devised by the American agency, Doyle Dane Bernbach (DDB). Subsequently, combined art and copy teams became the norm within the industry, on both sides of the Atlantic. Before DDB, and particularly in British agencies, copywriting held primacy over art direction and often these roles were carried out by separate departments. The American copywriter Bill Bernbach co-founded DDB in 1949,[4] and had previously worked collaboratively with the commercial artist, Paul Rand: both men understood the importance of using art and copy in synthesis.[5] Bernbach re-structured his agency to include a creative department, where art and copy teams would work as one, which resulted in the

Luminous lids by Mary.

Mary's gone Hi-Tech.
She's come up with some-
thing that'll knock you straight
between the eyes.
Cocktail Sticks.
Soft creamy pencils that
glitter and flash in twelve blazing
colours.
Brilliant, Mary.

148 *Mary's Brave Face. Brave Faces from Quant*
Advertisement for Mary Quant make-up, c.1980

149 *Deadly Day and Night Shades by Mary*
Advertisement for Mary Quant make-up, c.1980

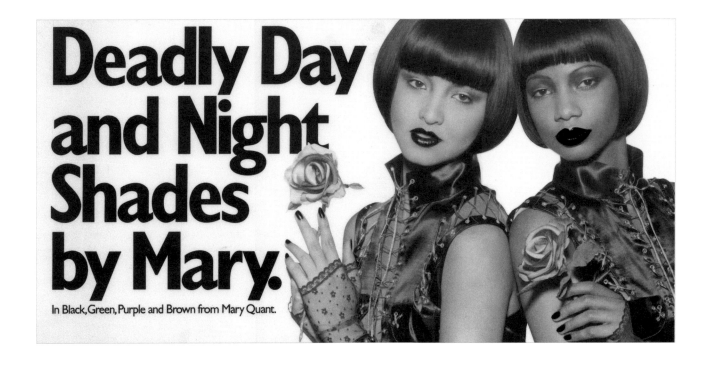

development of powerful advertising with a new emphasis on creativity – particularly 'the visual'. By adopting these new structures, CDP's work stood out from that of their competitors by communicating their clients' brand message more clearly and concisely than ever before.

The immense changes that DDB initiated in communications, was part of a wider socio-cultural creative revolution, which developed from the late 1950s. Great innovations in the industry sector are exemplified by CDP and Mary Quant Ltd – companies that placed creativity at the apex of their business model. Moreover, these organizations were to inspire and support the next generation of innovators, including the Saatchi brothers. As Maurice Saatchi explained: 'Mary Quant and Alexander Plunket Greene were the inspiration for Saatchi & Saatchi. They were the original backers and a role model for a creative and innovative organization.'[6]

Creative Advertising

In a review of *Not To Be Sold Separately*, an exhibition celebrating 50 years of the *Observer* magazine, John Hegarty explained how 1960s colour supplements and the advertisements contained within them, were not merely a window reflecting post-war affluence, but representative of the creative content which had broken away to visualize a new world which challenged and excited audiences.[7] This is because certain print advertisements, including 48-sheets (the largest street billboard) were enhanced by a new wave of highly creative work, such as the photography of Don McCullen and David Bailey, and art direction by Tom Wolsey.

Prior to CDP winning the Mary Quant account, the concept of Mary Quant the brand, representing radical fashion design for all, had already been created via extensive press coverage, reinforced by occasional advertising in fashion magazines. Quant and her husband were even recruited to advertise for other brands, as a celebrity couple, or 'people who set today's trends'. This can be seen in an advert for Long Life beer, published in *Harper's Bazaar* in May 1960, demonstrating a lifestyle that readers might aspire to.

A creative approach can be seen in a 1962 advert, featuring Celia Hammond, in which the diagonal composition suggests dynamism, while the copy (the words 'Mary Quant' are all that is required) doubles as an accessory or hand bag, placed below the model's left hand [40]. Likewise, in a 1967 advert for Kangol berets, the Quant logo replaces an earring and models' heads stand in for the letter 'o' in the copy: 'Mary Quant has just had an idea off the top of her head', exemplifying the emergence of a strategy celebrating Quant's creativity itself.[8] This approach was followed in a 1966 advert for the 'Mary Quant Inspired' Celon coat, where the model's androgynous pose displays an assertive attitude – a trait often found in the art direction of fashion photography of the time, as well as Quant adverts [119]. Perhaps the most consistent element of Quant cosmetic advertising is the slightly irreverent, direct gaze of the single eye in the iconic 1967 'Cry, baby.' poster, which also captured the 1960s Pop Art aesthetic [143]. Another striking example is the advert found in *Rave* in the summer of 1966, which provided instructions on how to achieve 'the face of the moment' and enabled readers to enjoy the surreal aesthetic of the elegant figure, clothed only in Quant's daisy logo [139]. Such adverts stood out from their competitors', demanding attention more immediately through the power of highly crafted art and copy. In doing so, they expertly communicated the Mary Quant brand.

Jill Saxton, the creative manager of Gala Cosmetics (the company that made Mary Quant make-up) noted that prior to CDP, a number of advertising agencies had held the Mary Quant make-up account, including Tom Wolsey's own company and Aalders Marchant Weinreich (AMW). By the mid-1970s however, Mary Quant was on CDP's client list. Over the 40 years that CDP existed, from 1960 to 2000, it won the most creative awards of any British advertising agency.[9] Ridley Scott, Alan Parker, David Puttnam and Charles Saatchi, are among the mass of creative talent once nurtured at CDP. The photographer David Bailey also collaborated with CDP on many campaigns.

Much of the creative work at the agency was undertaken by art director Ron Collins,[10] as well as copywriter Lynda McDonnell and art director Nigel Rose. The teams were overseen by creative director Colin Millward. From 1969, Millward was responsible for CDP's overall creative development while Collins worked directly on the Quant campaigns. Millward, Collins and Quant were all art graduates (albeit from different schools) who had experienced a particular type of education that perhaps informed the direction of the Mary Quant brand.

In 1946, as part of a series of peacetime developments in technical education, the Ministry of Education decreed that art schools should deliver service to industry. The British government's objectives for art education were concerned with achieving advances in the changing industrial base of the nation. The origins of this industrial strand of British art education can be traced back further, to the turn of the twentieth century, in the work of William Lethaby. As the first Professor of Design at the Central Government School of Design (which would become the RCA in 1896), Lethaby institutionalized the arts and crafts movement's philosophy, and followed the medieval workshop tradition as opposed to that of the fine art academy. By 1948, Robin Darwin had been inaugurated as Rector of the RCA, and Modernist ideas were seeping into British art schools from the New Bauhaus school in Chicago, which emphasized individual creativity in terms of (scientific) experimentation.

The major impact of Darwin's changes throughout the highest levels of the British art education system was the provision of courses of a thoroughly vocational nature in all industrial fields. Experiment, research and design replaced the fine art language used in pre-war art education. These new creative values, combined with the

151 *Quant by Quant, A new perfume by Mary*
Advertisement for Mary Quant perfume
Photograph by David Bailey

152 *Mary's lipstick dipstick*
Advertisement for Mary Quant lipgloss
Photograph by David Bailey

153 *Mary, we like your cheek. Mary Quant's Blush Baby*
Advertisement for Mary Quant blusher

Photograph by David Bailey

governmental reforms such as the introduction of the National Diploma in Design (NDD) in 1946, totally changed the focus of the British art education system towards a new liberalism which served emerging creative industries.[11]

Mary Quant, Colin Millward and Ron Collins all undertook the NDD: Millward and Quant trained in Illustration and Design, followed by a one-year diploma in art teaching; Millward graduated from Leeds College of Art (now Leeds Arts University) in 1949. Quant arrived at Goldsmiths in about 1949 – the year before Millward began his advertising career, subsequently joining CDP in 1960.[12] Collins gained his NDD in Graphic Design from Leeds in 1958, after which he entered the RCA. Millward and Collins not only went on to become part of the managerial sector within the creative industries, they became game-changers, like Mary Quant. It is in CDP's advertising for Mary Quant that their work collides.

Before we look more closely at a selection of the Mary Quant billboards, it is worth noting a common dominant theme – the

hairstyles. During the 1960s, the dark bob became a powerful sign of the new era, with Vidal Sassoon revolutionizing women's hairdressing. In creating Mary Quant's new short hairstyle in the autumn of 1960, Sassoon had reinvented the style of 1920s film actress, Louise Brooks, and in doing so, was projecting alongside his clients the original significance of this style as a symbol of women's liberation. According to Sassoon's 1968 autobiography, Quant had approached him with a problem: she wanted to find an alternative hairstyle for her models to the chignon in order to keep hair away from the clothes during her shows. Sassoon's solution was to cut it off, and use the bob style, already tried out on Quant, 'cutting her hair like she cut material. No fuss. No ornamentation. Just a neat swinging line'.[13] Thus her dark bob, and its permutations, became a strong identifier of Mary Quant herself, as well as her brand, stemming in part from her fashion aesthetic, but also signalling her independence [153]. Here the focal point of the composition is the attractive female subject, whose dark bob works together with the copy, to clearly communicate Mary Quant and all that she stands for. The inclusion of the word 'cheek' in the copy also connotes a touch of attitude, while the art direction provides a product demonstration of blusher. And here lies the difference – the distinctiveness of both the (Quant) brand and the (CDP) creative strategy. Unlike many make-up adverts, the art direction boldly places the act of applying make-up in the public arena, thereby subversively displaying an action that had hitherto been conventionally undertaken in private.

Another advertisement from around this time mirrors the name 'Quant' and apparently includes a visual reference to a historical image: the art direction echoes Man Ray's iconic photograph *Kiki with African Mask* (1926) depicting an ebony mask juxtaposed with the face of French model, Alice Prin [151]. This representation of the Parisian-centred avant-garde with which Ray's work is associated, transfers notions of radical art to the advert. In addition to French art, the copy 'Created in France' also tactically relocates Mary's perfume within the French perfume industry, which can trace back its roots to the Renaissance. Therefore, the art and copy combine to generate brand value, while positioning Quant as radical yet established as a commercial force. Moreover, in all six of the selected billboard make-up advertisements, the decision to use a model, as opposed to Mary Quant herself, provides the audience with not only an aspiration, but a realisable mode of becoming Quant-like.

All subsequent advertisements featured in this essay celebrate Mary Quant's creative approach to design – especially the concept of 'experimental' – using the make-up medium, materials and colour palettes to play with one's appearance. This is clearly communicated in the copy: 'Luminous lids by Mary' [147] and 'Deadly Day and Night Shades by Mary' [149]. Here the art and copy works inter-textually, transforming eye pencils into light sabres, which audiences had seen in the academy award-winning film *Star Wars* (1977). By the

1980s, the relevance of Mary Quant make-up was maintained through consistently innovative art direction, but the iconic bob was abandoned in favour of the antennae style developed by Simon Forbes.[14] Forbes' antennae hair and Vivienne Westwood's *Savage* collection of 1982 were the look of the time, and both are referenced in the art and in the copy 'Brave Faces from Quant. New eyes, cheeks, lips and nails for the civilized savage' [148]. The use of multi-racial models for the 'Deadly Day and Night Shades' billboard [149], not only works visually to advertise the contrasting colours of the make-up, but was a progressive and significant move for a fashion brand at the time. Although common in other areas of popular culture in the late 1970s, racially diverse models were generally under-represented in fashion photography and advertising. Not by Quant. Overall, these selected 48-sheet make-up advertisements reveal how the idea of Quant was to persist into the 1970s and 1980s – though hairstyles, or the use of models who looked like the younger Mary, achieving a timelessness for the brand.

The highest quality in graphics, art, copy and photography of the day ensured that the Quant brand retained its distinctiveness, delivering concepts such as 'brave' and 'powerful' to women who were eager for social change. These CDP make-up adverts continued to celebrate Mary Quant's creativity itself, inviting audiences to be Quant-like – to be bold and creative with luminous finishes and striking colour palettes. It is possible to trace the roots of the post-war art education received by Quant, Millward and Collins – their basic studies of form, line, colour and materials – and see what a profound effect this had on their creative practices.

By choosing CDP to handle the make-up account, Mary Quant Ltd ensured that the brand remained relevant. Each make-up advert created by this award-winning agency retained Quant's brave face, and in doing so, celebrated how Mary Quant had changed the world of fashion design and cosmetics.

PART FIVE

1968–1975
Liberated Fashion

The changed landscape of fashion in the later 1960s was described in a 1968 edition of *Vogue*, as the reign of 'a new quiet' after 'an explosion of energy and excitement'. Mary Quant had spearheaded the move towards space age clothes, but like her, the women she designed for were growing up, needing clothes for 'gardens, children, food, going out in the evening'.[1] At the same time, fashion was now more diverse, more wide-ranging and more inclusive, but less easy to define. Some designers emulated the movie star glamour of the 1930s. Designers like Ossie Clark and Biba in London, and in Paris, Yves Saint Laurent (who opened his boutique Rive Gauche in September 1966), were creating clothes which captured the mood of the moment and fulfilled the demand for designer ready-to-wear.

Mary Quant's designs became more fluid, often using lighter jersey fabrics [154]. Her mini skirts and dresses were still short, but often worn with long flowing maxi-jackets to break up the line of the figure. With a greater business focus on licensing, the Ginger Group clothes were often designed in conjunction with her assistants, who included Ruth Bartlett, Fiona Clark, Jane Marsh, Janie Ranger and later Liz Valenti.[2] Together they exploited the varied possibilities of synthetic and natural textiles with different colours and printed and woven patterns and textures [155]. Quant always retained final approval of each design.

Quant's own image changed to reflect the softer, fluid feel with jersey separates in plain colours. Increasingly she was photographed in trousers, sometimes wearing quite masculine styles, which reflected her own taste and the broader lean towards androgyny and informality in fashion. She chose to wear a longline waist-coat over a white tee shirt and jeans for her portrait painted by Bryan Organ in 1969. This was also the year that she was elected Royal Designer for Industry by the Royal Society of Arts.

Designs for the Ginger Group continued to offer bright and exuberant party clothes such as an empire line mini culotte dress, made from a rayon that was printed or flocked with velvet-like coloured spots [157]. The dress was worn by Nanna Bjornsdottir, who worked as a model for Mary Quant cosmetics. She wore the dress for special occasions, and more recently her daughters wore it for parties too.[3] By 1971, the Youthlines range had been replaced by very simple bra and pants sets knitted in the Midlands under the supervision of the Curry brothers, for Nylon Hosiery Company [158]. Often boldly striped and patterned, these modern undergarments show the complete rejection of any kind of shape and control-giving foundation, as the packaging images confirm.

Quant's interests in fabric for fashion was mirrored in her approach to interior decorating possibilities, as described by Heather Tilbury Phillips, who joined the Quant operation in 1970 from Kangol (see p.153):

PREVIOUS PAGE
154 Mary Quant, 1968
Photograph by John Adriaan
Mary Quant Archive

155 Mary Quant's Ginger Group 'Eclair' dress, 1969
Machine-woven synthetic lace
V&A: T.90–2018

156 Model wearing 'Gravy Train' dress and trousers, and Amanda Lear modelling 'Eclair' belted dress, 1969
Mary Quant Archive

If the 60s were celebrated for Mary's introduction of the mini skirt then her move towards home interiors was an integral part of her philosophy for the 70s. ICI Fibres had approached her to try and stimulate the domestic textiles market in the same way she had influenced fashion. Their previous introduction of nylon sheets and 'drip-dry' shirts for men had not been entirely successful despite the new concept of 'easy care'. Mary initially designed a range of co-ordinating bedwear in a mix of polyester and cotton. Sheets, pillowcases, and duvet covers were cleverly designed to combine pattern and colour and the introduction of deep dyes – purple, brown, navy, red, etc was quite revolutionary. Sheets had tended to be in soft, pastel shades but suddenly the bedroom became a much more stylish bower and space for multi usage. Dorma's early products were quickly joined by roller blinds, paints and wallpapers (the gingham with a border was a particular favourite), and curtains, stretch covers etc extended the influence into living areas. Suddenly the home became the focus. The post-war generation was growing up and putting down roots. Mary had been pivotal in their choice of clothing and now she was influencing and guiding them in their living environment.

In October 1968 the *Financial Times* journalist Sheila Black reported Mary Quant Ltd's healthy estimated surplus in retail values of £8.4 million, tracing the company's extraordinary growth from a profit of £1,200 in 1955, to £254,000 in 1961 and £6.75 million in 1967. McNair's 'down to earth' plans for growth in royalties from licensing hoped for £30 million a year in seven years' time. Black's interview with the company directors reveals the finely tuned three-way relationship built on mutual respect, which harnessed Quant's hunches and

visions, with McNair and Plunket Greene forcing her to fight hard for them, but fundamentally agreeing that they should 'have a go rather than be fearful most of the time'. McNair is described as 'the balance', who 'plans the schedules, slots the deadlines, counts the buttons'. Quant acknowledged in the interview that without McNair, 'I just wouldn't have happened. Not like this.'[4]

By 1969 all three of the Bazaar shops were closed,[5] a decision instigated by Archie McNair who argued that the financial security provided by the more predictable income from licensing made business sense. When interviewed in 2014, McNair reflected that this was difficult for Quant, who argued that the interaction with customers in a physical retail space was necessary to keep her designs in touch with their

159 'It's cherry blossom time for you this spring'
Cosmopolitan, March 1973
Photograph by Norman Eales

requirements.[6] McNair organised the company
finances using the holding company Thomas
Jourdan, which owned various interests including Mary Quant Ltd, and by 1975 Thomas
Jourdan was floated on the stock exchange.[7]
However, fashion remained at the forefront of
the Quant brand, and the Ginger Group wholesale line continued until the middle of the
decade (see below). A semi-couture range was
produced after this point which maintained
Quant's presence in London's fashion week and
continued as a banner for her other designs and
products [159].

As part of the Quant team, Heather Tilbury
Phillips was charged with working particularly
with Plunket Greene on public relations. In
2018 she described some of her responsibilities
and the experience of working for the company
[160]:

I joined Mary Quant Limited in 1970,
based at Ives Street, working in the
slightly chaotic atmosphere of the upper
floor where Mary, Pamela Howard,
Alexander and I had offices. There was
Mary and Pamela's secretary as well –
successively Amanda, Margaret, Linda,
Sara were all a tremendous support during
their tenures. Officially this space was a
flat with a small kitchen, bathroom and
an extremely useful closet which divided
the bigger rooms and was used to store
the current seasonal collection of clothes
and accessories.

We were a very small team. Mary,
Alexander and Archie, the original
triumvirate, each had another board
member working with them. Mary had
Pamela Howard with design, fabrics
and workroom responsibilities. Archie's
right hand man was John Rowlerson
who looked after the business side and
ensured that the licensees complied with
their carefully drawn up contracts and
Alexander and I worked on the marketing

and public relations disciplines. Alexander
was really clever at devising names for
the garments and ranges which were
both witty and apposite and made the
promotional activities such fun to devise
and undertake.

There was often a requirement to put on
shows outside the UK. The importance
of the market in the USA, mainly provided
by the JC Penney stores and mail order
operation, was crucial as a background
for all the other licensees, not only to
boost garment sales but also to ensure
that Mary's total look was portrayed and
evident to the media, the trade and the
consumer. A number of the leading New
York stores stocked Mary's garments and
in the September I went over to the Big
Apple, where the temperatures were well
into the 90s [sic], to mount a press show
at Sardi's. I was met at the airport and
taken straight to the model casting which

160 Heather Tilbury Phillips, wearing a design of Liberty-printed Varuna wool, outside the Ginger Group office, 9 South Molton Street, 1973

Photograph by Tony Boase

about policy, strategy and future plans took place, as in any international company. It was always a condition to listen and try to understand everyone's views so that, however controversial, the most appropriate decisions were reached. Juggling timings, liaison and diplomacy with licensees, constantly dealing with retailers and media so that messages were projected accurately, was an integral part of daily life. We were all united by support of Mary's extraordinary design ability, her engaging personality and magnetism, but also her steely determination that everyone involved with the brand maintained its integrity.

Mary, Alexander and Archie's charm, inspirational and clever motivation resulted in each day, however testing during the long hours that were required, being fascinating and fun. Every day was different. One moment it might be trying to find the right accessories for a photographic session which were so ahead of their time that they just weren't out there! Or responding to demands by international press for interviews, stories, details about new ranges, quotes as varied as, 'What will we be wearing to work in 50 years time?' or 'How does the modern woman juggle being a wife, mother, running the home and being at work all day?' etc as well as generating interest amongst the grandes dames of the world of journalism before a particularly important collection launch.

Orlando, Mary and Alexander's son was born on 4 November 1970, almost the very day that the whole interior design concept was launched! No wonder she was otherwise occupied and Alexander, Pamela and I toured the UK with the 'road show' of mock beds and interior displays to all the major retail stores. Such was the popularity and practicality of Mary's concept that later it was extended to

went on until late that evening. Again only very few girls would be chosen although it seemed hundreds wanted to audition in the hope of being selected! Sizing was also rather different and finding those with the rather boyish proportions which Mary favoured, the understanding of how to show with the right look and hairstyling, provided quite a challenge. It was my first trip across 'the pond' and I was thrilled to be staying at the Algonquin Hotel but a real surprise to see how behind London New York seemed at that time. Alexander arrived a day later (Mary was seven month's pregnant so couldn't fly), accompanied by our model, Lady Sarah Courage. A hefty programme of interviews and media activity followed crammed into our three days!

Of course, life was not always media launches with popping flash bulbs and delicious meals. Extended meetings to thrash out details of collections, debates

161 Moon and Hazel Collins modelling hooded dresses, by Mary Quant, 1973
Photograph by Wieczorek

162 Mary Quant and Orlando Plunket Greene, c.1972
Mary Quant Archive

163 Mary Quant's Ginger Group
Jacket and skirt, 1972
Printed viscose

Given by Linda Kirby in memory of her godmother, Pamela Howard Mace
V&A: T.31:1 to 2–2013

incorporate kitchen accessories, tablewear, carpets and even beds and bedheads.

Even today, Mary's brilliance touches almost everyone's lives in some way. Her far sighted instincts nurtured ambition, hope, a sense of freedom and opportunity, a rejection of rules and her reaction to, 'You can't do that' was, 'Oh yes I can!' And she did.[8]

Heather Tilbury Phillips owned several Mary Quant designs from her time working with the designer, including a kaftan-like long hooded dress called 'Manhattan' printed with a design of skyscrapers by Eddie Squires of fabric firm Warners [161]. When she married in 1973 she wore a going-away outfit designed by Mary Quant of a soft printed crepe jacket and skirt printed with a repeating pattern of a silhouette of a woman

dressed in Edwardian clothing [163]. The example illustrated comes from the collection of Tilbury Phillips's colleague Pamela Howard Mace.

A significant group of clothes designed by Mary Quant was generously donated to the V&A in 2013 by Linda Kirby, the god-daughter of Pamela Howard Mace. Howard Mace worked for Mary Quant Ltd first for a short time from 1964, leaving for a while, and returning in 1968 [166]. A letter from Archie McNair offered her the position of Quant's PA with a salary of £2,600, a company car (in the range of a Ford Cortina 1500cc) and pension benefits.[9] This time, Howard Mace remained with the company until the late 1970s, having been promoted to design director. Her story illustrates some of the opportunities offered in the post-war period by pursuing an interest in fashion and design. Her school friend, Dorothy Kirby, remembered Pamela for her 'tremendous flair for style and fashion right from the word go, despite the fact that at school she was not even able to wear the correct uniform, due to her father's restrictions and the lack of coupons.'

Pamela left school at 16 to work in the beauty department of the weekly magazine *Home Notes*, and now that she had her own money, astounded her friends by wearing 'the most stylish of outfits, a soft grey skirt in the "new look", topped by a cropped royal blue jacket and the required hat.[10]

Howard Mace couldn't afford a winter coat, which worried her friend's mother so much that she gave her the money to buy one. Aged 19, in about 1951, Howard Mace moved on her own to Rhodesia, South Africa (now Zimbabwe), taking advantage of a Rhodesia-subsidised ticket, and working for the government there. While in

164 Mary Quant
Tunic and knickerbockers, 1974
Machine-knitted wool

Given by Linda Kirby in memory of her
godmother, Pamela Howard Mace
V&A: T.28:1 to 2–2013

165 Pamela Howard Mace with Mary Quant
staff and models, 1971

South Africa she changed career to work for a clothing company, and on her return in 1964, began working for Mary Quant. A photograph given along with the clothes shows Pamela promoting one of the Quant collections for 1971 [165]. She is at the centre of an informal group of staff and models showing a selection from that year's collection, which included Pop style knickerbockers and laced boots, army style shorts and exaggerated harem trousers.

High quality fabrics remained a priority and Liberty-printed wools were often part of Mary Quant's Ginger Group collections [168]. The V&A owns one example from 1971, called 'Alice', which has an additional Marshall Field's label, showing that the Ginger Group collections were still exported to American department stores. The dress, which retailed for £20[11] was photographed for promotion to retailers on location in a rural setting, the caption explaining that it would be equally suitable for dinner in town. Many of the Mary Quant flared trousers and skirt styles demanded the high platform soled shoes of the early 1970s and a range was produced under licence, after a launch in 1971 at the London department store Marshall & Snelgrove [167].[12]

166 Mary Quant
Liberty-printed dress, *c.*1973
Printed silk with elastic shirring

Given by Linda Kirby in memory of her
godmother, Pamela Howard Mace
V&A: T.25–2013

167 Mary Quant
Platform shoes, 1972

Worn and lent by Christy Kingdom-Denny

The following year saw the introduction
of new licensed products – ties for men, which
were modelled by celebrities including Vidal
Sassoon and Michael Parkinson and a range
of spectacles and sunglasses, made by the
manufacturer Wiseman. Quant would go
on to design Polaroid sunglasses in 1977.
International licensing deals included a bedlinen
range launched by Berg River in South Africa
and stationery was made by a company called
Forer for the North American market.[13] Quant
also designed uniforms for staff working on the
charter airline Court Line, in 1973. Most significant however, was a visit to Japan to accompany
the launch of the Special Recipe skin care and
cosmetics range; after Mary Quant Cosmetics
Japan was established in Tokyo in November
1970, a flourishing connection with the
Japanese market was established (see p.163).

Mary Quant's Ginger Group became one of
many brands established in the 1960s offering
greater choice on the high street into the 1970s,
but the prices remained relatively high, meaning
that often people purchased Ginger Group
clothes specifically for particular occasions.
Vivien Wearing wore a striped Mary Quant
Ginger Group dress as her 'going-away' outfit

168 'Alice' dress from Mary Quant's Ginger Group collection for autumn 1971
London College of Fashion and Woolmark Archive

169 Mary Quant's Ginger Group 'Alice' dress with waist tie, 1971
Liberty-printed Varuna wool
Retailed at Marshall Field, Chicago
V&A: T.84:1 to 2–2018

following her wedding in 1972 [170, 171].
When she donated the dress to the V&A she
also mentioned that she bought her clothes
from Biba and Jeff Banks, but that Quant had
been a particular influence on her interest in
clothes as a teenager. After a course at Lucie
Clayton's modelling school, Wearing worked as
a house model for Verona Fashions, a wholesale
company on Berners Street. She explained in
2018 that the 'Mary Quant dress was such a joy
to wear and the photo is a memory of the start
of our 46 years of fun together'.[14]

In 1973 Lord Snowdon (Quant's friend,
Antony Armstrong-Jones) photographed ten
of Britain's leading designers for a programme
for a British Overseas Trade Board event rec-
ognising the contribution of fashion designers
for export.[15] The image shows Quant at the
pinnacle of the group, with her enduring contemporaries Jean Muir, Gina Fratini and Thea
Porter amongst some of the younger generation
who had been inspired by Quant and Bazaar,
represented by John Bates, Tim Gardner, Bill
Gibb, Alice Pollock, Zandra Rhodes and Ossie
Clark (National Portrait Gallery: P1937).

Perhaps one of Quant's most memorable
spin offs was the Daisy doll, launched in January
1973 at the Harrogate Toy Fair, as described by
Heather Tilbury Phillips [172, 173, 174]:

Mary often favoured an androgynous
look although she flirted with girlie
dresses and trimmings and, of course,
Daisy her much loved doll, had a mass of
long blond hair – every little girl's dream
to style. Mary used to joke that 'Havoc',
Daisy's 'sister' doll with her leather jacket
and trousers was really her alter ego.
The dolls were launched at the Toy Fairs,
the first in Harrogate being almost
immediately in the New Year (when
everyone was still feeling a bit jaded from
being surrounded by toys at Christmas)
and then on to Brighton. It was always
freezing cold, the wind cutting but it was
really exciting to see the innovations and
clever ideas that would be around for the
following festive season.

Life size versions of Daisy's wardrobe
were modelled by Quant's regular
girls, dancing down the catwalk and
entrancing the sometimes rather staid
buyers who ended up applauding
enthusiastically and singing, 'Daisy,
Daisy, give me your answer do'! Later,
when Daisy was joined by Havoc, the
red-haired, tomboy doll she drove in
on a powerful motorbike, the vibration
from which promptly caused plaster to
cascade onto the audience from the
ceiling!! It was a hugely entertaining,
although unintentional, publicity stunt![16]

These dolls were the brainchild of
Second World War fighter pilot and entrepreneur Sir Torquil Norman, whose company
Bluebird Toys, which he established in
1980, later manufactured some of the most
popular pastimes for children, including
Polly Pocket. He met Quant and Plunket
Greene while shopping at Bazaar; they
became family friends and Norman later
became Orlando Plunket Greene's godfather.
While Sindy, launched in 1963 had already
had fashionable outfits designed by Marion

Lola
CS20/8

More stunning fashions for Daisy by

MARY QUANT

Internationally famous designer, Mary Quant, makes Daisy the best-dressed doll in the world.

Fashions for Daisy by
MARY QUANT

Daisy ® a girl's best friend

Fashions for Daisy by ❀ **MARY QUANT**

For ages 4 years and above   ❀ **MARY QUANT**

Flossie
65221

More stunning fashions for Daisy by

MARY QUANT

Internationally famous designer, Mary Quant, makes Daisy the best-dressed doll in the world.

Fashions for Daisy by
MARY QUANT

For ages 4 years and above.

Huckleberry
CS20/1

More stunning fashions for Daisy by

MARY QUANT

Internationally famous designer, Mary Quant, makes Daisy the best-dressed doll in the world.

Fashions for Daisy by
MARY QUANT

Foale and Sally Tuffin and was a bestseller
by 1968, Daisy was different, offering the
younger generation the chance to own a
smaller, cheaper doll with designer outfits
for £1.30 each. The dolls could be dressed
from collectable daisy-logoed fashion packs,
which ranged from accessories like platform
boots, hats and bags for 30p, to full garments
with hangers for 60p, and bumper fashion
packs for 90p each.[17] Made in Hong Kong
by Model Toys, Daisy was designed and
marketed by Flair Toys, part of British
Company Berwick Timpo.[18] Daisy was
9 inches (23 cm) high, a little smaller than
both Sindy and Barbie, but with a head
modelled by mannequin sculptor Adel
Rootstein, she combined innocent blonde
good looks with full-on grown up glamour.
Outfits were scaled down versions of the
official Quant collections, with Lurex
and satin party dresses with
names like 'Razzle Dazzle'

and 'Frou Frou', fake fur 'Teddy Bear' cropped
jacket and platform boots, and shiny red
mac 'Singing in the Rain', all accessorized
with appropriately chunky but tiny red
plastic mules. The small samples for these
were made by the same workroom staff who
produced the full-size versions, in the Quant
headquarters at Ives Street in Chelsea.

Sticker books and paper doll albums were
also published which revealed Daisy's lifestyle,
showing her at home in her pine kitchen,
complete with vintage willow pattern china
and gingham apron, or trying on a dress in an
'old clothes shop'. Increasing Daisy's aspirational
appeal for girls, a series of books was issued,
between 1973 and 1977, with *My Fashion
Diary*, followed by five more titles including
My Exciting Life as a Reporter and *My
Glamorous Life as a Ballerina*. Illustrator
Joan Corlass created interesting yet easy-to-
cut-out props for each of her backdrops, all
perfectly selling the Mary Quant lifestyle of

175 Display from *Mary Quant's London*, London Museum exhibition, 23 November 1973 to 30 June 1974

176 Mary Quant 'Arundel' ensemble, 1973 Wool jersey

Given by Mary Quant
V&A: T.114 to C–1976

shopping, going out and eating, with fashion firmly at the top of Daisy's priorities in life. Corlass trained in Australia but enjoyed a long career in London, initially in the advertising department at clothing company C&A Modes in Marble Arch, but later working freelance, producing a wide range of styles of artwork for women's and trade magazines before focusing more on book illustration.

Clearly representing a very different style to Quant's own looks, Daisy later acquired a rebellious younger sister named Havoc, launched in 1974, who is said to have had a tomboy personality and style closer to Quant's own. Daisy dolls were equipped with a portable cottage, with stylish furniture to match the clothes; like the dolls and clothes these were made in Hong Kong for the company Model Toys Ltd, which was based in Shotts, Lanarkshire.

At least one Daisy doll was featured in the London Museum's exhibition *Mary Quant's London* which opened in November 1973 [175]. The exhibition, first suggested to Quant by Museum Director John Hayes in March 1971, consisted of 55 outfits, ranging in date from a 1956 pair of spotted pyjamas, to the Arundel group, which was chosen to represent the current 1973 collections [176]. Heather Tilbury Phillips explained how Quant hesitated at first, before agreeing to the exhibition:

One of the most difficult aspects of Mary's life was her modesty and the agony she felt about being interviewed. Media from all over the globe constantly asked for time with her – wanting her to explain the thinking behind a current product launch or collection as
well as her views on current events. Whether it was film, television, radio or even a friendly journalist for a UK newspaper she would have to physically fight her diffidence and shyness. That was when the support of Alexander was so crucial. He had such charm, humour and easy manner that the atmosphere would relax and gradually Mary would regain her articulate, entertaining and natural confidence. Her previous reluctance would be transformed as she explained her passion and commitment to what she was doing and why.

One example of this was when we were approached by Dr John Hayes, the then Director of the London Museum. His foresight that the closing exhibition at its Kensington Palace home should celebrate Mary's achievements led to a long period of persuasion! 'But they only give you that sort of recognition when you are dead,' she responded. However, her hesitation was overborn and the exhibition, which ran from November '73 until June '74, proved extremely popular and an outstanding success.[19]

The exhibition catalogue reveals that while many garments were lent by donors, some

of whom were closely connected with the company (such as Pamela Howard Mace and Heather Tilbury Phillips), others were lent from individuals who had responded to a public call out for Quant garments, helping to display a chronological survey of key designs. Perhaps understandably, given the pace of Quant's output created over the years, the company had not considered the need to keep an archive. Most however were lent by Mary Quant herself, and some had been re-made according to original sketches, often by workroom staff who had been employed the first time the clothes were created.[20] The printed catalogue of this exhibition provides useful contextual images showing fashion photography of the time, and some window displays from Bazaar. The exhibition itself also incorporated fashion photography, and showed the clothes on dynamic mannequins. Exhibition designer Michael Haynes had also worked with Quant on her window displays. The display included a room-set with a brass bedstead made up with a set of Quant bedlinen, and an art nouveau-era dressing table complete with Quant Natural Recipes cosmetics, and the quintessentially 1970s spider plants on a stand.

In 1974 an hour-long documentary about Mary Quant was made for the BBC2 Lifestyle series, which followed Quant and Plunket Greene as they visited factories and held meetings to assess progress with various projects. This included with the British chemical company ICI – their collaboration continued with a launch of Crimplene dressmaking fabrics in 1975 (see p.194). These fabrics were previewed in an article for *Fibres Post*[21] and praised for being 'distinctive as well as saleable' and it was noted that as they were in co-ordinating groups and small-scale in design, it meant they were 'easier making up for the busy housewife or career girl'. Further diversification came with the Mary Quant jewellery range and a wine label, as Heather Tilbury Phillips described [177]:

Mary was always spotting gaps and opportunities – like the wine. In 1974 it was very much still the women who shopped for family meals. Carrying heavy bottles from a corner shop or supermarket wasn't easy so the concept of wine by mail order was born. David Stevens, a family friend and Master of Wine, Mary and Alexander (over a glass or two) conceived and then marketed the idea by using whole page ads in the Sunday colour supplements offering basic, but delicious, favourite wines, like Côtes du Rhône, Côte de Beaune Villages, Bourgogne Aligoté, Blanc de Blancs and even champagne. On a Monday morning (there was a postal collection on Sundays in those days) the front door could hardly be opened for the volume of post, or even a separate Royal Mail van would arrive with sacks of envelopes containing the order form and a cheque. It was amazing to witness the confidence which people had in Mary's ability to recommend a winner. And it worked![22]

178 Mary Quant socks, 1976
Mary Quant Archive

179 Mary Quant and models, 1975
Photograph by Central Press
National Portrait Gallery: x182403

The last Ginger Group collection was for spring–summer 1975 and the South Molton Street showroom and office closed that year. Involvement with fashion continued with a small semi-couture collection, and Mary Quant hosiery remained a staple brand for fashion editors. Also in 1975, Quant's friend Shirley Conran published *Superwoman*, an empowering manual for the working wife and mother. She asked Quant, as one of Britain's most conspicuous career women at the time, to write the introduction. This is typically self-deprecating, deploring Quant's own disorganised approach to home life, which was dominated by work and travel. With more trips to Japan to develop the licensing business selling cosmetics, tights and furnishings there, Mary Quant's business had an increasing focus on new markets.[23]

Selling the Total Look: Quant and Interiors

Johanna Agerman Ross

'Well I don't think it will end up a Mary Quant room at all. The permutations are infinite so I think everyone will arrive at their own variation of this. And I think also it is very easy to add to it, to buy a bit more.'[1]

I n 1970 the British chemical company ICI Fibres released its first homewares collection in collaboration with Mary Quant: 'Wonderful News! ICI Fibres and Mary Quant bring high fashion to home furnishings!' stated the advert featuring Mary Quant holding a length of Bri-Nylon fabric. The first collection included curtains, blinds, stretch covers for furniture and bedding and in its second year expanded into paints and wallpapers through ICI Paints.

The now defunct ICI was one of the largest chemical manufacturers in the UK for parts of the twentieth century and was formed through the merger of four companies: Brunner Mond, Nobel Explosives, the United Alkali Company and British Dyestuffs Corporation, in 1926.[2] The company manufactured a broad range of chemical products, from pharmaceuticals to pesticides, and pioneered developments in plastics, paints and synthetic fabrics. With its partners it developed Perspex, alkyd-based paints and polyethylene in the 1930s, the fabric Terylene in the 1940s and Crimplene in the 1950s. Mary Quant promoted Terylene through adverts featuring Quant fashions in the 1960s and Quant also designed and advertised a range of dress fabrics in Crimplene that launched in 1974. In the late 1960s, Mary Quant and her business partners entered into discussions with ICI about a range of interior textiles. 'She had already used coordination very successfully in the fashion business and ICI decided they wanted to bring that fashion experience to bear in domestic textiles' said Jillian Hurst, ICI's marketing manager in 1972, in a BBC interview about the new interior collection by Quant.[3]

The arrival of the lifestyle accessory

The interior range represented a new sector of business for the Mary Quant brand and reflected the broader trend for interior styling and lifestyle accessories – a growing field in post-war Britain: 'As they were increasingly confronted by desirable goods in the shops they frequented, and by seductive images in the newspapers and magazines they read on a daily basis, consumers began to see these artefacts as lifestyle accessories.'[4] Interior magazine *House & Garden* launched in the UK in 1947; the traditional society magazine *Queen* was restyled as a lifestyle magazine aimed at a younger readership in 1957 and in 1962 the *Sunday Times* released the first colour supplement to be published with a UK newspaper, followed by the *Observer* magazine in 1964.

While interior styling had been portrayed initially as an exclusive pursuit by high-end design-led stores such as Heal's and Liberty's in the 1950s, the 1960s saw the field expand to reach a broader and younger audience through new enterprises such as Habitat, founded by designer Terence Conran in 1964, and fashionable food writer Elizabeth David's eponymous store that opened on Bourne Street in Pimlico in 1965 selling imported cookware. 'Iron shelves hold tin moulds and cutters of every description, glazed and unglazed earthenware pots, bowls and dishes in traditional colours, plain pots and pans in thick aluminium, cast-iron, vitreous enamel and fireproof porcelain, unadorned crockery in classic shapes and neat rows of cooks' knives, spoons and forks,' wrote the *Observer*'s style writer Heather Standring of David's store in 1966.[5] More established design stores tried to appeal to a younger customer by staging exhibitions and events with a focus on easy and inexpensive home-making, as an invitation to Heal's in April 1965 makes clear, citing both the caché of Conran's wife Shirley, a design writer, and the *Observer* colour supplement: 'Come to Heal's and see the simple girl's guide to home design, an exhibition devised by Shirley Conran and based on her recent series of articles in The Observer Colour magazine.'[6]

180 Mary Quant in her
apartment at Draycott
Place, Chelsea, 1967

Besides her wide-reaching visibility as
a proponent of a unique London look, Mary
Quant also frequently appeared in magazines
as a commentator on the home as an extension
of personal style throughout the 1960s. In a
special insert in *Honey* from 1967, for example,
Quant writes in a section called 'Quant on
Designed Living': 'A certain amount of perversity
is a good thing. Take the decoration of your
room. People want to be surprised by it, in
the sense that they will be refreshed by your
individuality.'[7] For a feature promoting a homeware exhibition at Liberty's in *Vogue* in October
1960, Quant had been asked to select a table
setting that reflected her entertaining habits.
The writer observes:

> Mrs Plunket-Greene chose a pine table
> and an unconventional mixture of the old
> and new that echoes her highly original
> flair for clothes.... They treat the antique
> without undue reverence and mix colours,
> textures, good new things from Scandinavia
> with old things from Europe in an
> uninhibited way.[8]

When Quant described her Chelsea
apartment for a feature in *Ideal Home*
magazine in 1964 she said:

> I like space and I feel you must relieve the
> monotony of simplicity with pieces of shapely
> nonsense. Colours matter to me, of course,
> though I change my instinct about these.
> When I was designing this flat last year my
> fashion colours were scarlet and ginger,
> so I use them here, but, just as with dress-
> designing, I like to keep colour held up
> against a neutral background, such as beige
> for clothes, putty for furnishing.[9]

The Plunket Greene home is captured showing an eclectic mix of antique and modern – Vico
Magistretti Carimate chairs (then contemporary
in design) surround a round Italian table with
a marble top, traditional Chesterfield sofas in
red leather sit next to fashionable Habitat coffee
tables, the lithe look of Gio Ponti's Superleggera
chairs (designed in the late 1940s) contrast
nicely with what are described as 'Spanish
rugs'. It reflects a taste for the modern without

Within the image (top left):

Shop in Knightsbridge

designers: Conran Design Group

The clients required a simple, unobtrusive design which would not conflict with the clothes on display, and a large number of storage and display units. This has been achieved by a combination of white walls, grey carpet, natural timbers and muted leather colours.
4, the shop front has an unusually low transom of Honduras mahogany.
5, louvred timber doors to the fitting rooms under the mezzanine.
6, the display fitting on the mezzanine and above it the pine slats of the false ceiling.
7, the staircase leading to the mezzanine display area and offices has teak treads, a Columbian pine string and steel brackets.
8, on the facing page ☞, the central counter for jewellery display is of rosewood with brass trim and has a leather top. It is lit by a cluster of 35 lamps with the lamp-holders encased in brass sleeves.

---

being too minimal or sterile and always with a view to how your home reflects and shapes individual identity. The writer Ruth Jordan observes: 'Mary Quant considers that, in this country, decorative ideas are held back because so many people inherit old-fashioned furniture and feel they must build their rooms round them.... This young woman, still in her twenties, is tuned to her times like a violin, and often composes ahead of time!'[10]

Styling Bazaar

The interior styling of the Bazaar stores similarly became an extension of the brand, as Christopher Breward has observed in *Fashioning London*: 'This strong street presence was partly achieved by an attitude towards window display that prioritized visual impact over the necessity to make sales.'[11] But while the first Bazaar shop was the result of in-house design, the second store, opening in Knightsbridge at the end of 1958, was a more calculated attempt at creating a look for the Bazaar and Quant brands, reflecting Quant's ideal 'to keep colour held up against a neutral background'. Terence Conran and his recently founded Conran Contracts was commissioned to design the interior and Quant observed of Conran's design: 'There was a great feeling of excitement, he designed an open staircase leading to the mezzanine above, which also gave tremendous life to the place.'[12]

According to *Architectural Review* from April 1959: 'The clients required a simple, unobtrusive design which would not conflict with the clothes on display,' and the space had: 'white walls, grey carpet and natural timbers and muted leather colours.'[13] The stairs had a teak tread, the slatted ceiling rippling above the double-height space was executed in pine. Conran remembers:

We designed it so that there was a huge plate glass window so that you could see straight into the shop. It had a double height ceiling and we added a mezzanine, which together with the teak staircase was the most expensive thing in the shop. They wanted it to be constantly on the move with customers and models changing clothes and coming up and down the stairs, they didn't want anything to confuse the fashion show so to speak.[14]

181
'Interior Design:
A Shop in Knightsbridge'
Architectural Review,
April 1959

It's as simple as SUMMA

to build all the storage you'll ever need. With the new range of Summa storage units you can plan sideboards, desks, wall units, dividers, dressing tables—literally hundreds of different practical permutations of just a few basic units.
Summa is simple to set up—each cabinet is complete in itself with pins to locate with cabinets above and below and a floor levelling device if it is needed. Summa is available in teak or ash: bookcase, cupboard, drawer and desk units; adjustable shelves: sliding trays in white, aquamarine, deep olive and orange. Summa needs no wall fixings—just stand it in place and when you want to—add to it or re-arrange it in minutes. Component prices of Summa start as low as £1.8.6. and no single unit costs more than £16.15.0. There is a matching wardrobe too, at £33.18.0. and the 6 foot long dining table in the photograph retails at £20.5.0.* Selected retail stores have Summa already or you can see it and get details of your nearest stockist at CONRAN Showroom 5 Hanway Place, London W.1. Langham 4233.
*prices include purchase tax: slightly higher in some areas to include packaging and delivery.

Advertisement by
Conran Design Group
dress by Mary Quant

itized over making sales when Bazaar first opened on the King's Road, it seems that the stores gradually became vehicles for the promotion of the Quant look, where the merchandise, not the real estate, was the focal point for anyone entering the stores. It was the clothes that created the identity, rather than the stores' design. As the *Vogue* editorial emphasizes: 'A smooth, smooth look all round, smooth shades and no angles, neutral colours and black, leaving the merchandise to jump up and down with colour.'[17]

'It is very easy to add to it, to buy a bit more.'

For the budding entrepreneur Conran, the first two Bazaar shops were an inspiration: 'I remember thinking "gosh if they can do this to fashion, maybe I can do the same for furniture." I was very aware of how taste was changing around the country and realized that just like with clothes, people wanted furniture that they could take away with them.'[18] This aspect of the shopping experience as something incorporating 'taking something away' was a key feature of the interior design store Habitat that Conran opened at 77 Fulham Road in 1964. The first Habitat brochure featured mostly interior accessories such as kitchen utensils, towels, fabric and tote bags wittily described as: 'Rush Turkey bags for rushing to the shop'.[19] In the store the female shop staff were encouraged to wear Quant because as Conran observed: 'it was important to give people a feeling that the staff who served in the shop were also involved in the Mary Quant-movement if you like' [87].[20] This stretched to Conran's own advertising campaigns for the Summa modular storage system where the text at the bottom of the advert states: 'Advertisement by Conran Design Group, dress by Mary Quant' [182].

It would seem that Mary Quant had become shorthand for a certain fashionable lifestyle and attitude. She embodied a new type of fashionability, created rather than inherited, which perfectly

It is clear that the objects for sale took centre stage in this design and the colours and patterns of the season influenced the mood of the space [181]. Conran Contracts redesigned the shop window of the King's Road store in 1957, before the Knightsbridge store opened and the window display also utilized this pared-back approach. Although no reference is made to this design by either Quant or Conran, it seems that there might have been an effort to unify the look of the two stores, creating a Bazaar identity. Designed by Conran in-house designer Lydia Sharman the modular system for the window of Bazaar Chelsea used black-enamelled metal rods as uprights with interchangeable shelves and boards covered in dove-grey felt for the display of merchandise.[15]

When Bazaar opened a third store on New Bond Street almost ten years later, in 1967, it utilized the same neutral approach to its design. Created by yacht designer Jon Bannenberg, a short editorial in *Vogue* from the month it opened described it as: 'No frills, but flowers on the floor and marvellous neutral tones will break the ground for Mary Quant's spanking new shop at 113 New Bond Street.'[16] If, as Breward suggests, the visual impact was prior-

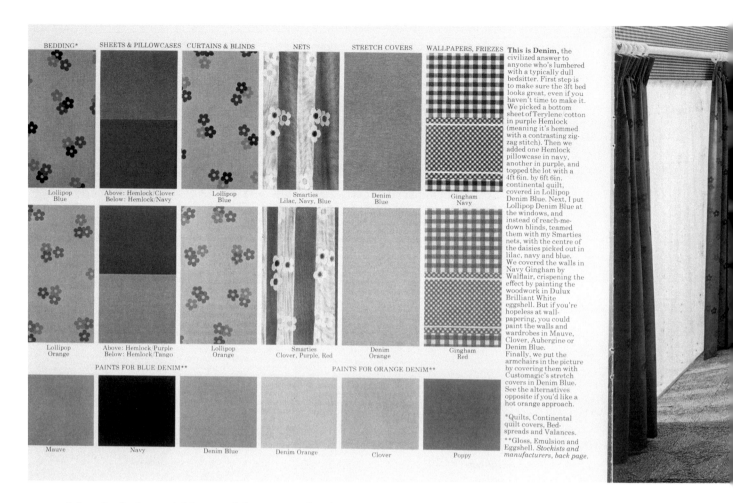

captured the zeitgeist for youthfulness and the need for new attire that personified this. As we have seen in other chapters, this could be applied to a broad array of goods through licensing deals. Conran observes: 'I think it's interesting that Mary and Alexander were very aware that they had a valuable brand, but people hadn't really focused on brands having a value before.' The concept of licensing was a relatively new field in fashion at the time and the Quant formula was naturally applied to fashion-forward make-up, underwear and stockings. In contrast, Quant's homewares seemed less at the cutting edge. There was a range of mugs produced by Staffordshire Potteries Ltd in the early 1970s, the collection contained a number of glazed tea mugs, with transfer print designs of fashionable girls wearing the latest fashion. The stamp at the bottom of the mug featured the Mary Quant daisy, the Mary Quant name and the details 'Staffordshire Potteries Ltd, Ironstone, Made in England.' but it seems this collaboration was short-lived.[21] In comparison, the ICI collaboration, which began in 1970, was a much bigger

undertaking that lasted into the 1980s, including several of the brands either incorporated in the ICI group or involving its synthetic fibres such as Terylene and Bri-Nylon. The range included Dorma sheets, Mellalieu & Bailey quilts, Sunfield fabric curtains, Stiebel net curtains, Customagic stretch covers, Glamorline roller blinds, ICI Paints' wallpapers and friezes and Dulux paints. 'In the late 1960s ICI realized that if they were going to do anything much with their polyester fibre they had to link it with the market place and a brand,' says Peter White, who was the Managing Director of one of the leading British bedlinen manufacturers Dorma at the time of the launch of the collaboration.[22]

The combination of these ranges could completely transform a room without changing the furniture, instead giving it a fashionable 'look' that could be endlessly changed by addressing the less expensive parts of the interior, as Quant herself urged: 'it is very easy to add to, to buy a bit more'. In the booklet that ICI released as a promotional tool handed out to retailers as a free giveaway for customers with the 1972 range, the copy instructs:

'This is Denim, the civilized answer to anyone who's lumbered with a typically dull bedsitter. First step is to make sure the 3ft bed looks great, even if you haven't time to make it' [183].[23] The language is relaxed and informal, clearly aimed at a customer who will undertake the decorating themselves ('But if you're hopeless at wallpapering, you could paint the walls and wardrobes in Mauve, Clover, Aubergine or Denim Blue.'). To assist in the decision-making, each group of bedding had a corresponding fabric curtain, net curtain, paint colour and wallpaper, offering a total Quant look.

The Quant range sold in specialist retailers across the UK[24] and ICI supported them with point of sale materials ('Mary Quant's familiar symbol, synonymous with fashion and good design, cannot fail to draw attention to your displays') and an extensive advertising campaign: 'Full-colour ads featuring room sets will appear in *Good Housekeeping*; *Brides*; *Homes & Gardens*; *Honey*; *House & Garden*; *Ideal Home*; *Nova*; *Reader's Digest*; *She*; *Woman*; *Woman, Bride & Home*,' informs a trade brochure ahead of the 1972 launch.[25]

The bedding in particular pushed the technical capabilities of the manufacturers that Quant worked with as she insisted on using deep dyes for these ranges, breaking with the more commonplace pastel shades widely available on the market at that time. Instead she experimented with strong and dark colours such as navy, purple, cerise, brown, red and greens in co-ordinating designs and patterns. 'The collection created such a stir when it launched in 1970 because it was the first time that deep dyes had been included in bed-related products in easy-care, poly-cotton fabrics,' remembers Heather Tilbury Phillips who was a director of Mary Quant when the range first launched. 'Technically this was extremely difficult as the colours were inclined to bleed and a way had to be found to minimize this to an acceptable level. It is an illustration of where Mary pushed manufacturing in order to achieve the look which she wanted and generating change.'[26] The bedding was considered top of the range in Dorma's collection, as Peter White explains: 'Mary's designs were the top end, a premium brand which appealed to a niche market and would be in a small, select range of colours.' He continues: 'To a certain extent this was reflected in the price and Quant would sell in certain outlets. For instance, Debenhams were middle market and they used to take the Dorma standard middle range. On one or two occasions they took Mary Quant … to make a statement in the store.'[27] The retail prices for the ICI–Quant range supports this. Duvet covers by Dorma in multicoloured Terylene cotton retailed £9.50 for a double (£8.50 for a single). Today this is the equivalent of £121.75. In comparison, Habitat's plain, single-colour double duvet covers were almost half the price and retailed at £4.90, or £67.27 today.

A blanket change

Around this time, duvets were becoming increasingly common in the UK, taking over from blankets as the preferred way to make a bed and many claimed to be the first to

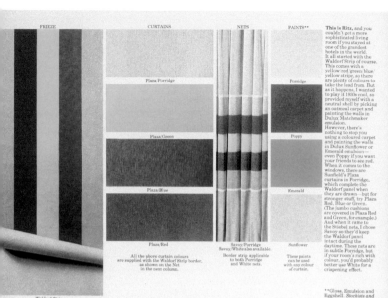

This is Ritz, and you couldn't get a more sophisticated living room if you stayed at one of the grandest hotels in the world. It all started with the Waldorf Strip of course. This comes with a yellow/red/green/blue/yellow stripe, so there are plenty of colours to take the lead from. But as it happens, I wanted to play it 1900s cool, so provided myself with a neutral shell by picking an oatmeal carpet and painting the walls in Dulux Matchmaker emulsion. However, there's nothing to stop you using a coloured carpet and painting the walls in Dulux Sunflower or Emerald emulsion—even Poppy if you want your friends to see red. When it comes to the windows, there are Sunfield's Plaza curtains in Porridge, which complete the Waldorf panel when they are drawn—but for stronger stuff, try Plaza Red, Blue or Green. (The jumbo cushions are covered in Plaza Red and Green, for example.) And when it came to the Stiebel nets, I chose Savoy so they'd keep the Waldorf panel intact during the daytime. These nets are in subtle Porridge, but if your room's rich with colour, you'd probably better use White for a crispening effect.

FRIEZE

CURTAINS

Plaza/Porridge

Plaza/Green

Plaza/Blue

Plaza/Red

Waldorf Strip

All the above curtain colours are supplied with the Waldorf Strip border, as shown on the Net in the next column.

NETS

Savoy/Porridge Savoy/White also available.

Border strip applicable to both Porridge and White nets.

PAINTS**

Porridge

Poppy

Emerald

Sunflower

These paints can be used with any colour of curtain.

**Gloss, Emulsion and Eggshell. Stockists and manufacturers, back page.

introduce the duvet on the British market. White claims Dorma were the first, while Conran says he found them on a trip to Sweden in the mid-1960s and brought them back to sell at Habitat.[28] Quant later recalled that she and Plunket Greene had 'lugged an enormous duvet back from Norway by plane.'[29] A piece in the *Daily Mail* from 19 November 1965 credited Christopher Riddle from Crawley as one of the earliest importers of duvets, having found them on a trip to Sweden while buying timber in 1957. 'But I found that an Englishman does not like his habits tampered with. I took them along to Heal's and Debenhams. But there was no mad rush,' reflects Riddle in the article. But fast forward to 1965 and the picture was different: 'Now Heal's are selling 20 duvets a week. John Lewis are selling 30 a week. And Mr. Riddle, the main supplier to Britain, estimates there are about 50,000 of his duvets on British beds.'[30]

'ICI wanted to make them popular here,' remembers Quant in her autobiography.[31] The reason being that ICI produced synthetic P3 fibre stuffing for the duvets, as an alternative to natural down stuffing. As a result there was a big drive to market fashionable accessories around the duvet. 'In those days you could only buy plain duvet covers, hidden away in a single deep drawer at one store, Heal's, in London.'[32] In contrast Quant filled that plain surface with swirls, seed-packets, pixies, and, of course, daisies. And when looking at the promotional pictures of the Quant and ICI collaboration

it becomes clear that the photographs are elaborate attempts at building acceptance for the duvet as the preferred choice of bedding. Habitat was equally keen to promote the virtue of the duvet or slumberdown to its customers: 'Slumberdowns, which with their covers, take the place of top sheets, blankets and eider-downs, simply have to be shaken out each morning, plumped up, and laid over the bed. Until you've tried this method of making a bed, it's difficult to believe it could be so easy, and so comfortable.'[33] Looking back at the collaboration with ICI, Quant also reflects on the ease and comfort that the duvet brought, connecting it to larger socio-economical changes in society at the time: 'The timing of the ICI deal was perfect, as the washing machine was becoming a new booming household essential, and duvets made bed making easy. The new career girl was our customer, so this was a lovely design job for me.'[34]

Designed by Quant

In a lot of the consumer literature around the ICI ranges, Quant is the voice behind the promotions. For example: 'I've kept the papers simple – and you can't get much simpler than gingham.' Or: 'Friezes are back and I have done three.' And: 'Basically I designed six patterns....' The concept of Quant as a designer is very much based on the idea of an active

184 'This is Ritz...' *The Mary Quant Book of Room Design,* 1972

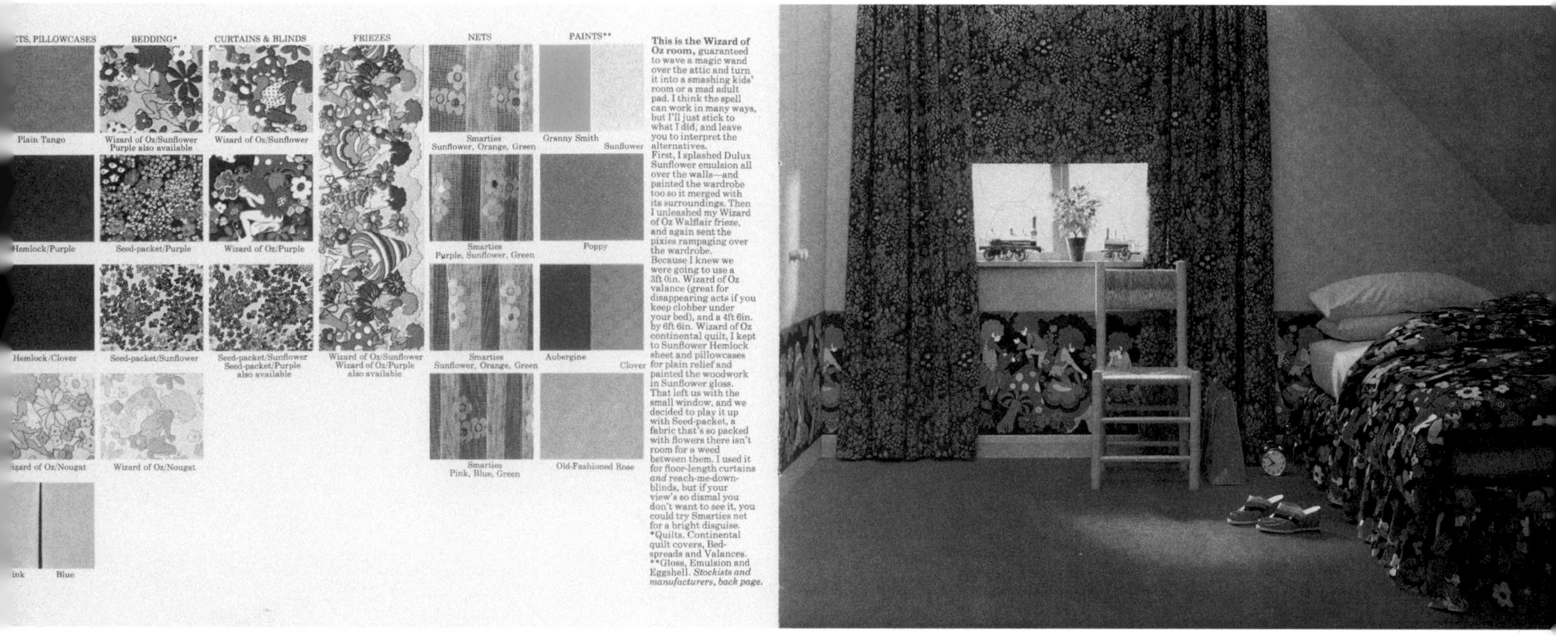
BEDDING*
CURTAINS & BLINDS
FRIEZES
NETS
PAINTS**
Plain Tango
Wizard of Oz/Sunflower Purple also available
Wizard of Oz/Sunflower
Smarties Sunflower, Orange, Green
Granny Smith
Sunflower
Seed-packet/Purple
Wizard of Oz/Purple
Smarties Purple, Sunflower, Green
Poppy
Hemlock/Clover
Seed-packet/Sunflower
Seed-packet/Sunflower Seed-packet/Purple also available
Wizard of Oz/Sunflower Wizard of Oz/Purple also available
Smarties Sunflower, Orange, Green
Aubergine
Clover
Wizard of Oz/Nougat
Smarties Pink, Blue, Green
Old-Fashioned Rose
Blue
This is the Wizard of Oz room, guaranteed to wave a magic wand over the attic and turn it into a smashing kids' room or a mad adult pad. I think the spell can work in many ways, but I'll just stick to what I did, and leave you to interpret the alternatives.
First, I splashed Dulux Sunflower emulsion all over the walls—and painted the wardrobe too so it merged with its surroundings. Then I unleashed my Wizard of Oz Walflair frieze, and again sent the pixies rampaging over the wardrobe.
Because I knew we were going to use a 3ft 0in. Wizard of Oz valance (great for disappearing acts if you keep clobber under your bed), and a 4ft 6in. by 6ft 6in. Wizard of Oz continental quilt, I kept to Sunflower Hemlock sheet and pillowcases for plain relief and painted the woodwork in Sunflower gloss.
That left us with the small window, and we decided to play it up with Seed-packet, a fabric that's so packed with flowers there isn't room for a weed between them. I used it for floor-length curtains *and* reach-me-down-blinds, but if your view's so dismal you don't want to see it, you could try Smarties net for a bright disguise.
*Quilts, Continental quilt covers, Bedspreads and Valances.
**Gloss, Emulsion and Eggshell. *Stockists and manufacturers, back page.*

185 'This is the Wizard of Oz room...' *The Mary Quant Book of Room Design*, 1972

hand, that she had a part in everything that the brand got involved with. 'Mary didn't want any product released that she hadn't designed and this worked out to be a huge restriction on what we could do as a business,' said Mary Quant's business partner Archie McNair in a 2004 interview.[35] But it seems that Quant did not in fact design all the patterns for the ICI collaboration. As the homewares branch of her business expanded, Quant strengthened her workforce accordingly. By the late 1970s the Mary Quant headquarters on Ives Street had a growing design studio that carried out work based on her ideas. Jane Edgeworth, who worked in the Quant design studio from 1977 to 1985, recalled that 'the studio girls didn't really have that much to do with the fashion projects ... we concentrated on all the other products – bedlinen, wallpaper, carpets, stationery etc.'[36] There seem to have been around four to six designers in the design studio at this time, all dedicated to the Quant homeware licenses, that expanded in the late 1970s to incorporate American licenses via Nigel French Enterprises.[37]

> With an in-house studio, Mary could have more control over the final designs, and could be more adventurous ... It was my job to make sure Mary's wishes were carried out – a go-between – and that all designs for a client were presented in the right format in a finished state, allowing no room for subsequent interpretation after leaving Ives Street.[38]

Despite Quant's insistence that her extensive homeware range for ICI wouldn't create 'a Mary Quant room', it nevertheless seems that this was the specific intention of the collaboration. The infinite possibilities of different pattern and colour combinations were made to feel safe with the help of booklets explaining which went together. Quant herself was omnipresent, through the daisy logo, daisy designs, her image and her words. Quant introduced the 1972 collection: 'There are lots of variations on each theme, so you'll have the freedom to express yourself without having to take the usual risks.'[39] With its broad possibilities and the emphasis on ease of use and application, the ICI range was aimed to appeal to the nascent homemaker and the budding market of female DIY-ers. And maybe this is the collaboration's real achievement – again Quant's ability 'to compose ahead of time', to use Jordan's words. While many adverts contemporary with the Quant–ICI collaboration portray men as the doers and the women as the passive and beautiful appreciators of DIY, the words in the *The Mary Quant Book of Room Design* are in fact a call to action for women to do it themselves.

PART SIX

1975–2000 Lifestyle Brand

The later 1970s offered Mary Quant more opportunities to bring fashion to the home, as Britain's most well-known designer at the time. Quant brought out ranges of carpets for Templeton's of Glasgow in 1978 and beds designed with her daisy logo for Myers in 1979. Coordinating table and kitchen linen for Dorma ranges were also produced that year. The carpets were promoted with distinctive advertising and a quote from the designer; 'Too many people's carpets have become dull and boring necessities simply because they have lagged behind other home furnishings in terms of design and colour. My aim has been to produce, in collaboration with Templeton's, a range of Axminsters which puts fun back into flooring, but at the same time, fulfils a genuine consumer demand' [187].[1]

Quant's reputation for designing functional, well-made separates resulted in a collaboration with Viyella's London Pride label which produced a line of classic separates from 1976. These were promoted in women's weekly magazines such as *Woman*, and were available in department stores across the country. The caption for this fashion photograph shows that the diagonal print Viyella brushed cotton shirt was called 'Gitanes' and cost £9.95, (approximately £75 today) while the wrapover skirt, 'Hugs and Kisses', in a wool/angora mix, retailed for £16.50 (approximately £125) [189].[2] The Viyella range also included a range of girls dresses and smart outfits for boys.[3] The hosiery business manufactured by the Curry brothers continued to flourish (see p.136), with 50 styles in production in 1981, while the international cosmetics business brought in £60 million a year.[4] Other licenses agreed into the 1980s included a Mary Quant range of stationery, a range for Schoenfeld Industries in America in 1981, K shoes in the UK, and in 1982, a range called MQ At Home Cameo including a dinner service made by Johnson Brothers, and a toaster and an iron produced by Morphy Richards. The same year, a range of

stylish, Victoriana-inspired party dresses and co-ordinating separates for boys and girls retailed through Pollyanna, the high-end Fulham Road shop and mail-order catalogue company, reintroducing the Mary Quant name into the world of children's retail [188].

Archie McNair continued to develop interests in his investment company Thomas Jourdan, which incorporated a diverse range of 'nuts and bolts' companies across the UK.

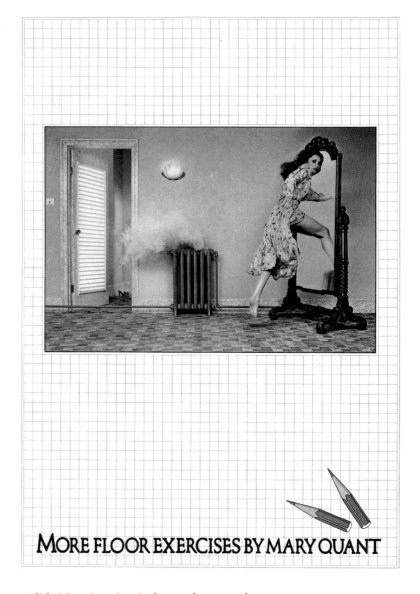

MORE FLOOR EXERCISES BY MARY QUANT

PREVIOUS PAGE
186 Mary Quant-designed limited edition Mini, 15 June 1988

187 *More floor exercises by Mary Quant* Advertisement for Axminster carpets by Templeton's, 1978

27. **Crumpets**
A beautiful velvet full floral dress with frilled hem and collar, lined and edged in contrasting plain cotton. Colours: (a) Floral on dark ground and (b) Floral on light ground. Fabric: 100% cotton velvet. Ages: 4, 5, 6 £34.00 / 7, 8, 9, 10 £37.00

28. **Sugar and Spice**
Delightful, full frill hemmed dress, leg o' mutton sleeves with button fastening. Made in top quality Viyella floral print. Colours: Floral on Cream and Floral on Navy. Fabric: Viyella's 55% wool / 45% cotton mixture. Ages: 4, 5, 6 £33.00 / 7, 8, 9, 10 £36.00

VIYELLA

27.

28.

28

29

188 'Exclusive Mary Quant Designs for Pollyanna' Pollyanna catalogue, autumn–winter 1982

These included manufacturers of street lamp bases and tyre manufacturing machinery, but most notably, the Corby trouser press, which sold and leased equipment for hotels on a massive scale.[5] For Mary Quant Ltd, the 1980s were marked by an increasing emphasis on Japan. At a time when Japanese women were living according to traditional gender roles, Quant was one of the first women to travel and conduct business there, in a society which was rapidly transforming with increasing Westernization. Her style connected with Japanese consumers, and with considerable foresight, Quant developed clothing and hosiery lines, and home textiles, as well as her cosmetics, which enjoyed huge success there, with the opening of Mary Quant Colour Shops in 1983. Quant's reputation as a key authority on cosmetics was furthered with the publication of *Colour by Quant* (1984) and *Quant on Make Up* (1986). Photographer Jill Kennington, previously a Quant model known particularly for the dynamic images

she created with John Cowan, captured Mary Quant in an intimate portrait of 1987 [190].

In 1988, 30 years after the introduction of the Morris Mini, an official collaboration between Mary Quant with the Mini car came to fruition, merging two icons of British popular culture, following discussions that had lasted a decade.[6] In 2006 Quant recalled that her first car was a Mini Classic, 'black with black leather seats…. I felt totally free and emancipated because with a tank full of petrol one could go anywhere and one had a mobile roof over one's head. With those bucket door pockets there was room for a pair of boots, a bottle of wine, a toothbrush, a ham sandwich and a bathing suit' [186].[7] Her white 'Limited Edition Mini Classic' of 1988, manufactured by Rover, had op-art style black and white striped seats with red piping, and a daisy logo at the centre of the steering wheel, and is now a highly collectible car. Also in the late 1980s, Quant's close identification with the mini skirt was reconfirmed when many younger women (possibly mostly students) were wearing classic Doc Martens lace up shoes with short jersey skirts. Quant was photographed with two models demonstrating the look for *People Weekly* magazine in 1988 [192].

Towards the end of 1988, three decades after the opening of the Knightsbridge Bazaar, Archie McNair retired from Mary Quant Ltd. At around the same time, he was hit by a taxi in London, suffering serious injuries that resulted in the removal of his spleen. He moved to his house in southern Spain, and spent many active years in retirement before his death in London aged 96, in June 2015, almost exactly a year after the death of his wife Cathy. The beginning of the 1990s was marked by the tragically early death of Alexander Plunket Greene, at the age of 58.

Mary Quant Ltd, the creation of the three perfectly matched entrepreneurs, continued to operate under the name Mary Quant, but now in her sixties, the designer herself began to work more independently. In October 1990, Quant won the British Fashion Council's 'Hall of Fame' award for her contribution to the fashion industry. In the early 1990s, a range of duty free products sold at airports was introduced, including sunglasses, brightly coloured printed T shirts, beach sarongs, and rain ponchos. In the following years, many further acknowledgements of Quant's unique contribution to British design were made. She was made a Senior Fellow of the Royal College of Art, and given honorary fellowships of Goldsmiths University and the Royal Society, and made a Fellow of the Society of Industrial Artists and Designers. From 1997, Quant was a non-executive Director of House of Fraser, and a Mary Quant Colour Shop opened at Montpelier Street, close to the site of the second Bazaar on Knightsbridge. These replaced short-lived ventures led by Mary Quant Japan Ltd in Carnaby Street and Ives Street. Shops were also opened in Paris, Rue Bonaparte, St. Germain (1996) and Madison Avenue, New York (1998). In 2000 Quant retired from her directorship of Mary Quant Ltd (which is now based in Japan), but remained a consultant to the business.

Conclusion
Fashion for Everyone

I n the twenty-first century, Quant has continued to receive recognition for her extraordinary career, with further honorary doctoral degrees awarded from Winchester School of Art (2000) and the University of Wales (2001). In 2006, Quant participated in the Women of Achievement reception at Buckingham Palace, and gave a lively presentation to a packed lecture theatre at the V&A in January 2007, as part the Costume Society's 'Reconstructing Sixties Fashion' study day. That same year, the V&A celebrated the 150th anniversary of the opening of the Museum at the South Kensington site; Quant was one of 150 artists and designers invited to contribute to an album that collected ideas about how the Museum had provided inspiration [191]. Quant's response – a finely drawn design for a white swimsuit, with a mauve, zipped bra-effect top – was annotated in the distinctive style recognizable from many of her design sketches already donated to the Museum collections. Her 'Banana Split' mini dress of 1967 was chosen to feature on a series of Royal Mail Special Stamps in 2009, recognizing British design icons of the twentieth century (also included was the London underground map by Harry Beck, Sir Giles Gilbert Scott's telephone box and George Cawardine's Anglepoise lamp). Quant continued to give interviews to journalists, and appeared on Radio 4's *Woman's Hour* in February 2012. This was the year that her second autobiography was published – a series of recollections and ideas on design and lifestyles from the current perspective.[1] In 2015, Quant was made a Dame in the New Year's Honour's List, just under 50 years after she was awarded an OBE in 1966.

The story of Mary Quant and her journey from art school to international label undoubtedly helped to shape the global brand of British fashion we know today. During London Fashion Week, in September 2018, the British Fashion Council (BFC) reported that the fashion industry had contributed £32.3 billion to the UK GDP in 2017, a 5.4 per cent increase on the previous year. British fashion is positioned as young, new and multicultural by the BFC, reflecting the world-leading fashion education offered by British universities, and London Fashion Week is promoted as 'a city-wide celebration of individualism, openness and diversity ... a melting pot for creativity and innovation'.[2]

Quant's role in developing the concept of young, exciting, mass-produced British fashion – and its export potential – is one of the key legacies of her brand. Another, perhaps overarching achievement, was to understand and skilfully employ the art of marketing, providing an exemplary model for others to emulate. As branding specialist Mark Tungate has written: 'When clothes leave the factories where they are made, they are merely "garments" or "apparel". Only when the marketers get hold of them do they magically become "fashion".'[3] With her two business partners, several decades before internet shopping, albeit during an earlier media revolution, Quant successfully built a creative and commercial international brand which was free from the constraints of running factories, and which did not rely on pushy salesmen or a long chain of retail outlets. Even in 1966, her brand was published as a success case story in the trade magazine *Marketing*.[4]

At the core of this success were Quant's designs, and her products, which were perfectly suited to the realities of young working women around the world. To sell these, she created an exciting retail environment, with imaginative window displays, and promoted what would now be called 'visual merchandising'. She employed interesting staff wearing her look and designs, and perceived the value of consistent labelling and packaging – the little extras that helped to make the brand stand out amongst all the competition. Newsworthy ideas and innovative presentation of the clothes at dynamic fashion shows and personal appearances by the designer, helped to secure extensive PR and media coverage for her products and ideas. The Mary Quant brand was so consistent and strong that advertising for her licensed products nearly always relied on a common understanding of who Mary Quant was, what she looked like and the innovative ideas she represented. All these elements

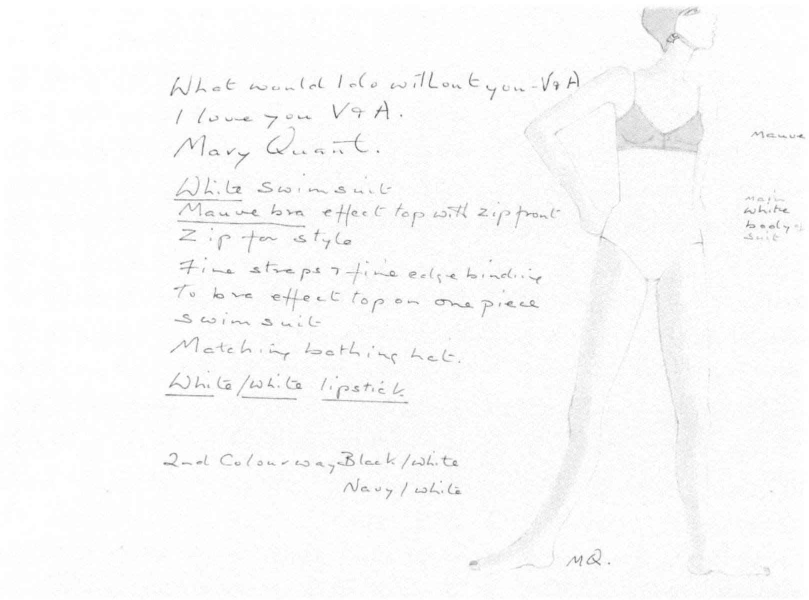

191 Mary Quant
Design for swimwear,
created for the V&A's
150th anniversary
V&A: E.479:20–2008

[handwritten notes in image:]

What would I do without you – V&A
I love you V&A.
Mary Quant.
White swimsuit
Mauve bra effect top with zip front
Zip for style
Fine straps + fine edge binding
To bra effect top on one piece
swimsuit
Matching bathing hat.
White/white lipstick

2nd Colourway Black/white
Navy/white

MQ.

Manue

Main
white
body's
suit

formed part of her brand identity, and all are vitally relevant to fashion brands today – especially with the additional dimension of twenty-first century social media.

Quant and her team also understood the power of a logo. The simple daisy motif applied to packaging allowed for the creation of licensed products that would carry the same emotional appeal of a Mary Quant dress. This encouraged huge numbers of customers to engage with Quant herself, the brand essence and personality, even by buying nail varnish or a pair of tights. The publication of *Quant by Quant* also made sure that her journey from schoolteachers' daughter to jet-set fashion designer was well understood by her customers, increasing the authenticity of her brand. Above all, Quant and the daisy logo represented a spirit of fun, a reaction against the establishment and the older generation. The logo and the brand ensured that customers built up loyalty to the concept and products, a loyalty that is clearly still felt today judging by the thousands of people who responded to the V&A campaign #WeWantQuant.[5]

Trend prediction, a discipline that developed in the nineteenth and twentieth centuries to become a vital force in today's fast fashion culture, underpins fashion marketing.[6] Quant felt that her tendency to get bored quickly was behind her ability to move on and keep ahead of current trends. Yet then, as now, this depended on spending time at the places where street culture could be observed: '... going to night clubs, seeing colours in the streets. It's a sort of flair within me'.[7]

Quant's ability to 'anticipate changes of mood' was crucial to harnessing the new spending power of the younger generation and women who were now earning their own income.[8]

Quant foresaw the ubiquity of unisex fashion and especially jeans, remarking that this was the one garment she wished she had designed.[9] 'A fashionable woman wears clothes, the clothes don't wear her', she wrote, pre-empting the individualism that characterizes the creativity and no rules of fashion today worn by the 'Z generation' – the current youth market. Recent research shows that, like Quant's generation, this group expresses disillusionment with mainstream institutions and big brands, instead valuing uniqueness and celebrating diversity.[10]

While not a political feminist, Quant supported female emancipation, offering options for dress reform and developing a working wardrobe. She reacted against the Paris designers who she said took 'an abstract architectural shape and put a woman into it.... I want free-flowing, feminine lines that compliment a woman's shape, with no attempt at distortion. I want relaxed clothes, suited to the actions of normal life.'[11] In 1966, Quant acknowledged research that showed that clothes were psychologically motivating – a 'tool to compete in life outside the home' – arguing that wearing the right clothes was not trivial, but rather functional and enabling. Beyond the brand, as a visible and vociferous working woman, consistently presenting herself with a direct assertive gaze, Quant remains an iconic image of fashion as a force for female empowerment.

Appendix
Mary Quant Labels

For today's fashion historians, garment labels are a vital way of recognizing, and often dating, a designer's work. They were first used in European fashion in the mid-to-late nineteenth century. Charles Frederick Worth is often credited as one of the first couturiers to attach distinctive woven 'signature' labels inside his dresses as a hidden but powerful element of his brand appeal.[1]

Mary Quant's garment labels provide a unique insight into the development of her business and her brand. There are more than 40 different styles of Quant labels in existence, reflecting Quant's engagement with innovative graphic designers to strengthen her brand identity. By studying a group of over 200 items, in the V&A's collection, Quant's archive, and examples in other collections, it has been possible to piece together the following chronology.

Perhaps unsurprisingly the earliest known example of Quant's work from this sample, a pink cotton blouse, c.1956, does not have a label. Created as part of a small-scale production cycle, Quant's early pieces were probably all unlabelled. Consequently, the earliest Quant designs are almost impossible to trace, unless they survive with strong provenance or in the collection of the original wearer. The earliest labelled garment from our survey dates to 1959. The label is simply designed; the shop's name Bazaar is printed in black on a silver ground. By 1960, however, Quant's name had gained recognition and was a key part of her brand. By 1961 a new Bazaar label, with the tag line 'Designed by Mary Quant', had been introduced to capitalize on this. With one exception, all subsequent labels featured Quant's name.

Early Bazaar labels illustrate a new business creating its brand identity. They also reflect a modest production cycle. Between 1959 and 1961 Quant produced at least four different label designs, some of which were used concurrently. In contrast, the wholesale company, Mary Quant's Ginger Group, which opened in 1963, with the backing of the long-established manufacturer Steinberg & Sons, only had one label design. Ginger Group designs were produced in multiples of thousands. The label was reissued with small additions only twice in its lifecycle, demonstrating a brand with a confident and considered visual identity, as well as the factories and infrastructure to support it.

Alongside Bazaar labels, alternative 'Mary Quant' labels were introduced in the 1960s. Influenced by the broader flourishing of graphic design, these labels used strong colours and a bold font. A particularly striking version emerged in about 1962 with the 'M' and the 'U' from Mary Quant cleverly joined together. These labels existed in different colours but with a consistent visual identity. It is possible that these 'Mary Quant' labels, separate from the Bazaar labels, were related to Quant's wholesale range, started in 1961. A portion of these garments have a second label from a retailer, such as the British department store Debenham & Freebody and the New York department store, Lord & Taylor. Other designs may have been exclusive to the Bazaar shops, and these may have been differentiated by a coloured label.

From its inception, developments in Quant's business were reflected in the garment labels. The 1970s and 1980s were no different and many new 'Mary Quant' label designs were produced. There are also more than a dozen label designs for Quant's collaborations. These all reiterate the currency or 'brand authenticity' represented by the name Mary Quant.

In the following chronology, date ranges are given based on garments with a documented date. Where no dated garments exist a probable decade has been suggested. It is likely that some of the labels existed for longer periods of time than indicated here and that there are more label designs in existence. This simply serves to highlight the rapid development of Quant's business and the scale and diversity of the operation.

BAZAAR
The first Bazaar shop opened on the King's Road in 1955 although Quant did not sell her own designs until a year or so later. She opened a second shop in Knightsbridge in 1958 and a third on New Bond Street in 1967. By 1970 all three shops had closed, in order for Quant to increase her focus on the licensing business. The design of Bazaar labels changed in the 1950s and early 1960s as the business established itself. This evolution in visual identity was mirrored in other branded items, including letterheads and receipts.

1959–61. Printed
V&A: T.55:1–2018

1961–2. Printed. Fashion Museum, Bath: BATMC I.09.869

Probably 1961–2. Woven
Private collection

1961–2. Printed
V&A: T.41–2013

1961–3. Woven
V&A: T.22–2013

1963–6. Woven
Private collection

MARY QUANT

By the 1960s Quant's name was a key part of her brand identity. 'Mary Quant' labels were made from about 1962. Garments with these labels were sold both from Bazaar shops and from retailers including independent boutiques and department stores. The label was redesigned in the early 1970s, changing from a large coloured label to a slim, discrete black and white design. The 1980s were marked by an increasing emphasis on the Japanese market and this was accompanied by multiple new label designs in a variety of colours and sizes.

1962–4. Woven
V&A: T.52–1985

1962–5. Woven
Private collection

1962. Woven
V&A: T.42–2013

1962–3. Woven
V&A: T.34:1–2013

1964–6. Woven
V&A: T.30:1–2007

1970–5. Woven
V&A: T.23–2013

1970–5. Woven
V&A: T.100–1976

Probably 1980s. Woven. Fashion
Museum, Bath: BATMC.2003.41

Probably 1980s. Woven
Private collection

Probably 1980s. Woven
Private collection

Probably 1980s. Woven
Private collection
Also pink and white colourway

Probably 1980s. Printed
Private collection

Probably 1980s. Printed
Private collection

Probably 1980s. Printed
Private collection

MARY QUANT'S GINGER GROUP

Mary Quant's Ginger Group opened in 1963, marketing her designs to a wider audience. It utilized a fresh, fun, label design in a ginger colour to complement the name and had a playfully inverted 'I'. The only changes made to this label were the addition of the phrase 'Made in England' (although many designs were in fact made in a factory in Wales) and later the addition of the trademark sign ®.

1963–5. Woven
V&A: T.40–2013

1964–5. Woven
V&A: T.383–1988

1965–72. Woven
V&A: T.86–1982

MARY QUANT – OTHER LINES

A prolific designer, Quant also produced unique labels for her supplementary ranges, including ties, hats and underwear.

*Ties: c.*1970–5. Woven
V&A: T.76–2018

Hats: From 1960s. Woven
V&A: T.77–2018

Underwear: 1970s–80s. Printed
V&A: T.93:2–2018

COLLABORATIONS

All of Quant's collaborations were identified with a unique label, often designed in keeping with Quant's visual identity. An early JC Penney label, for example, shows clear parallels in its design with a 'Mary Quant' label from the same time. The same style of type can also be found on the 'Alligator by Mary Quant' labels.

Knitwear collaboration, *c.*1961–6.
Woven. V&A: T.1707–2017

JC Penney collaboration.
Examples from, *c.*1965–7
Woven. Private collection

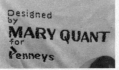

JC Penney collaboration.
Examples from, *c.*1968–9
Woven. Private collection

JC Penney collaboration, 1970s
Woven. Private collection

Underwear collaboration, from
1965. Printed. V&A: T.442–1988

Puritan Fashions collaboration,
from 1965. Woven
Private collection

Taffs, Australia collaboration,
1965. Woven. Private collection

Alligator Rainwear Limited
collaboration, from 1965.
Woven. V&A: T.89–2018

Towelling outfits, made in
Germany, *c.*1966. Printed
V&A: T.96–2018

London Air collaboration,
example from 1967. Printed
Manchester Art Gallery, 1985.187

London Pride collaboration, from
1976. Woven. Private collection

Viyella House collaboration, from
1976. Woven. Private collection

Viyella House collaboration, from
1976. Woven. V&A: Misc.91–1979

Viyella House collaboration, from
1976. Woven. V&A: Misc.86–1979

Pollyanna collaboration, from 1982
Woven. Private collection

Notes

INTRODUCTION Making Fashion History

1 For discussion of the historical development of lifestyles, see Ashmore 2008, pp.73–90.
2 'Miss Kooky OBE', *Daily Mail*, 11 June 1966.
3 Quant 1966, p.66.
4 Ibid.
5 Ibid., p.30.
6 Pringle 1988.
7 *Women's Wear Daily*, 19 August 1959.
8 Fashion Museum, Bath: BATMC I.24.73 A–C.
9 The development of the mini skirt is explored in detail on p.126.
10 Ernestine Carter, 1962; this features the second wholesale collection.
11 Breward and Wilcox 2012.
12 Liz Tregenza, *London Before it Swung: British Ready-to-Wear Under the Model House Group and Fashion House Group 1946–66*, V&A/RCA History of Design Postgraduate Programme. Thesis/dissertation 2014. Thanks to Liz Tregenza for sharing several useful images and information relevant to sizing from her forthcoming PhD thesis, University of Brighton, 2018.
13 An advertisement for Ginger Group appears in *Vogue*, 15 September 1963, p.112.
14 In the early 1960s the company manufactured garments in an underwear factory on the Fulham Road, this closed after the agreement with Steinberg & Sons to manufacture the Ginger Group line. See Harry Miller, 'Secrets of Success: Quantrary Mary OBE', *Marketing*, July 1966
15 McNair and O'Neill, 2008, track 1.
16 Available on www.youtube.com.
17 'Already, a Mary Quant Retrospective', *New York Times*, 12 December 1973.
18 *Annabel: The New Magazine for the Young Wife*, April 1966, p.29.
19 Email from Barbara Fowkes to the author, 18 June 2018, responding to #WeWantQuant. Barbara Fowkes is a writer, designer, and consultant to the fashion and creative industries.
20 Suzy Menkes, 'If Clothes Could Talk', www.harpersbazaar.com, 28 May 2013 and 'In My Fashion: The Suzy Menkes Collection', Christie's New York, 11–22 July 2013.
21 All three shops are listed in the 1969 Post Office directory, however this probably published data collected in 1968.
22 Cecil Beaton, *Fashion: An Anthology*, exh. cat., V&A, 1971, p.39 featured four Mary Quant dresses of 1966 and 1967, all incorrectly dated to 1964.
23 Brian Morris, *Mary Quant's London*, exh. cat., London Museum, 1973.
24 Exhibition files at the Museum of London. Tickets cost 20 pence, about the same as a paperback book. Concessionary tickets for children and 'OAPs' were 10 pence.
25 Ernestine Carter, 'Introduction', *Mary Quant's London*, exh. cat., London Museum, 1973, p.11.
26 Email from Kevin Roberts to the author, 7 July 2018. See also Kevin Roberts, *Lovemarks: The Future Beyond Brands* (New York, 2006).
27 Quant 1966, p.82.

PART ONE Before Bazaar 1919–1955

1 Veronical Horwell, Archie McNair obituary, *The Guardian*, 17 July 2015 and McNair and O'Neill, 2008, track 1. Thanks to Hamish McNair and Camilla Mair for generous access to eulogies by family and friends.
2 McNair and O'Neill, 2008, track 1. Thanks to Charlie Morgan, Oral History Archivist, National Life Stories, British Library.
3 General Register Office; United Kingdom; Marriage Register Indexes at www.ancestry.co.uk.
4 Quant 1966, p.3. No relevant records survive at Goldsmiths College to confirm the dates of Quant's or Plunket Greene's attendance. Thanks to Lucy Nagar, Senior Development Manager, Goldsmiths, University of London. In Quant 1966, p.3, the author states that she met Plunket Greene at Goldsmiths when they were both 16, while she was probably 20 and he 18, as Quant was in fact two years older than Plunket Greene. In Quant 2012, she states 1953 as the year she met Plunket Greene. From the evidence of articles in magazines Quant's age is quoted variously as younger than she actually is from at least 1957, and by 1962, they are stated as both being 28 in the *Sunday Times* colour supplement (rather than 32 and 30). This may have been agreed to disguise the age gap between the two, to comply with conventions of the time, and also to heighten Quant's youthfulness, or to increase her appeal to her market. At the time, it was not considered socially acceptable to enquire about or discuss a woman's age.
5 Quant 1966, p.3.
6 General Register Office; United Kingdom; Marriage Register Indexes at www.ancestry.co.uk.
7 Quant 2012, pp.21–3 and Quant 1966, p.23.
8 Quant 1966, p.23.
9 Quant 1966, p.23. See also Georgiana Blakiston, *Woburn and the Russells* (London, 1980) and *Letters of Conrad Russell 1897–1947* (London, 1987).
10 Conversation with Esther Fitzgerald, who worked as Orlando Plunket Greene's nanny, 7 June 2018.
11 Quant 2012, p.23.
12 Ibid., p.10.
13 General Register Office; United Kingdom; Marriage Register Indexes at www.ancestry.co.uk.
14 Email from Tony Quant to Heather Tilbury Phillips, 9 August 2018.
15 Quant 1966, p.5.
16 Ibid., p.14.

17 John Steeran, *Introducing Sam Rabin* (Dulwich Picture Gallery, 1985), p.30.
18 'Mary Quant "student" sketchbook auctioned', www.bbc.co.uk/news.
19 AIM25, Archives in London and the M25 Area, Goldsmiths College identity statement, www.aim25.com.
20 Patricia Stacey, 'Recollections from my time working for the milliner, Erik Muller', as told to Alison Collyer-Bristow, 11 April 2018 (unpublished).
21 Ibid.
22 Ibid.
23 Ibid.
24 London, England, Electoral Registers, 1832–1965 at www.ancestry.co.uk.
25 Quant 1966, p.31.
26 Ibid., p.30.
27 Ibid., p.32.

PART TWO Boutique to Wholesale 1955–1962

1 Quant 1966, pp.32–7.
2 Adburgham 1964, p.18.
3 Quant 1966, p.53.
4 'London's Young Designers: Two Shops Offer "Chelsea Look" for British Beatniks', *Women's Wear Daily*, 19 August 1959, p.4.
5 McNair and O'Neill, 2008, track 3.
6 The 1950 Shop Act, consolidating previous legislation, attempted to regulate and restrict opening hours especially on Sundays. For detailed discussion about the campaigns for relaxation of trading laws and anti-secularisation movement see Lynda Nead, 'An English Sunday Afternoon' in *The Tiger in the Smoke: Art and Culture in Post-War Britain* (New Haven and London, 2017), pp.277–305.
7 Quant 1966, p.42.
8 Thanks to Tereska and Mark Peppe who donated a hat (V&A: T.77–2018) and shared a scrapbook and slides from the time. Mark Peppe, an artist and illustrator, worked at 85a King's Road in the studio of Enzo Plazzotta.
9 Email from Shirley Conran to Heather Tilbury Phillips, 18 June 2018.
10 Leonard S. Marcus, *The American Store Window* (New York, 1978); Yasuko Suga, 'Modernism, Commercialism and Display Design in Britain: The Reimann School and Studios of Industrial and Commercial Art', *Journal of Design History*, vol. 19, no. 2, 2006, pp.137–54; Bernard Lodge, 'Natasha Kroll: Brilliant designer who brought about a style revolution at BBC Television', *The Guardian*, 7 April 2004. Thanks to Edwina Ehrman and Dr Mirsini Trigoni, London College of Fashion at the University of the Arts, London.
11 Quant 1966, p.41. See also www.universaldisplay.co.uk/news. John Bates (1937–2018) began his career in what became the field of visual merchandising in 1954, at the age of 17, at John

Lewis on Oxford Street, in a temporary building as the shop had been bombed and the new building was not completed until 1960. After four years at Liberty on Regent Street, Bates worked for Barway Display, becoming friends with Quant and Plunket Greene. He went on to become display manager for the innovative chain Wallis shops, and then for Bata Shoes in the Netherlands. In 1973 John Bates purchased Gem's Wax Models and renamed it Gemini Mannequins, and the company became known for high end mannequins for retail and museum displays. This company was later bought by Proportion London. With many thanks to Thomas Swinburne Sheldrake for sharing the eulogy read at John Bates's funeral by his business partner Joe Jacquest. Michael Haynes also assisted with window displays in the 1960s; he went on to design the London Museum's 1973 exhibition 'Mary Quant's London'.

12 Quant 1966, p.36.
13 Thanks to Juliet Nicolson and *Harper's Bazaar* for finding this reference.
14 Quant 1966, p.39.
15 Ibid., p.67.
16 MacCarthy 2006, p.57.
17 Anne Fogarty, 'Wife Dressing No.5: Look out Ladies, Men do notice', *Woman and Beauty*, July 1960, pp.70–1. Thanks to Liz Tregenza for sharing this article. Price converted at www.nationalarchives.gov.uk/currencyconverter.
18 See Beatrice Behlen, 'London & UK' in de la Haye and Ehrman (eds) 2015, p.213.
19 'The Young Face of Old Chelsea', *Tatler and Bystander*, April 1959.
20 Ibid.
21 Paul Gorman, *The Look: Adventures in Rock and Pop Fashion* (London, 2006). Joan Bakewell describes her arrival at Cambridge University in 1951 with her meagre wardrobe of mostly homemade clothes, chosen and paid for by her mother, and her later acquisition of the black polo neck sweater, tight black trousers and flat pumps of the Beatnik look glamorized by Juliette Greco. Joan Bakewell, *The Centre of the Bed* (London, 2003), pp.87 and 91. See also Brigid Keenan, *Full Marks for Trying: An Unlikely Journey from the Raj to the Rag Trade* (London, 2016), chapter 6.
22 Dylan Jones, quoted by Paul Gorman, 'À la mod: how the Jam and mod style transcended fashion', *The Guardian*, 12 August 2015.
23 Conversation with the author, 20 September 2018.
24 Janey Ironside, 'The Young Outlook in Fashion Design', *Harper's Bazaar*, July 1957, pp.48–51.
25 *Vogue*, December 1958; Quant 1966, p.84.
26 Quant 1966, p.79.
27 Ken and Kate Baynes, 'Behind the Scene', *Design*, 1966, pp.18–29.
28 Bazaar and Mary Quant were rarely promoted by paid-for advertisements, but some appeared in *Queen*, 1960 and *Tatler*, September 1962, *Harper's Bazaar*, October 1962. Wolsey's full influence as an art director has yet to be the subject of extended study. See Mike Dempsey's blog 'Tom Wolsey: no compromise',14 August 2015, www.mikedempsey.typepad.com and Tom Wolsey, *New York Times*, death notice,

12 May 2013. Quant discusses the development of the daisy logo in Quant 2012, pp.82–3.
29 Gwen Robyns, 'Oh! The Chic of the Girl: Miss Quant finds it pays to be quaint', *Daily Mirror*, 24 October 1960.
30 'Young Idea: Double Take', *Vogue*, December 1960.
31 Gwen Robyns, 'Oh! The Chic of the Girl: Miss Quant finds it pays to be quaint', *Daily Mirror*, 24 October 1960.
32 'Beat the Beatniks', *Queen*, February 1960.
33 Telephone conversation with Nicky Hessenberg, 2 August 2018.
34 Michael Pick, *Shoes for Stars* (Woodbridge, 2015), p.126.
35 Rough sketches and cotton toiles labelled 'Mary Quant designs for S. London', V&A Furniture, Textiles and Fashion department archive. Thanks to Susan North for bringing these to our attention.
36 Email from Shirley Conran to Heather Tilbury Phillips, 18 June 2018.
37 Bernadette Snell, who worked for Mary Quant from 1962 until 2003.
38 Shirley Shurville, 'How it all began for me' unpublished memoir, 17 November 2017.
39 Email to the V&A, 25 June 2018.
40 'Tutti Frutti', remade for the 1973 exhibition, V&A: T–104 to D–1976. Another example is at the National Museums of Scotland, K.2004.222.1&2. 'Greenery Yallery' design, V&A: E.253–2013. Other designs in this group include 'Tantrum' and 'Feckless', V&A: E.250 to 256–2013.
41 Miller 1966, p.1067; McNair and O'Neill, 2008, track 6.

Modelling Quant

1 Caroline Evans, *The Mechanical Smile: Modernism and the First Fashion Shows in France and America, 1900–1929* (New Haven and London, 2013).
2 For more see Valerie Mendes, *John French Fashion Photographer* (London, 1984), pp.19–26.
3 Brigid Keenan, *The Women We Wanted to Look Like* (London, 1977), p.146.
4 Shrimpton 1964, p.37.
5 Mary Quant, quoted in Keenan 1977, p.127.
6 Shrimpton 1964, p.58.
7 Quant 1966, p.46.
8 Quant 2012, p.96.
9 Shrimpton 1964, p.157.
10 *Sunday Times*, 4 February 1962.
11 Coddington 2002, p.44.
12 Ibid., p.74.
13 Ibid.
14 Quant 2012, p.163.
15 Coddington 2002, p.67.
16 www.vogue.co.uk/article/grace-coddington-on-her-iconic-vidal-sassoon-haircut.
17 Mary Quant interview with John Pepper, ITV Cymru, 1966.
18 Twiggy 1975, p.7.
19 *Daily Express*, 23 February 1966.
20 *Paris Match*, 8 April 1967.
21 Jill Kennington interview with author, 2018.
22 *Newsweek*, 10 April 1967.
23 Quant 1966, p.78.
24 Ibid., p.81.

25 Ibid., p.83.
26 Coddington 2002, p.67.
27 Quant 1966, p.94.
28 Mary Quant speaking on BBC2 documentary, *The Real Blow Up: Fame, Fashion and Photography*, 2002.
29 Mary Quant interview with John Pepper, ITV Cymru, 1966.
30 Pamela Howard Mace, Mary Quant Design Director, 1968–79.
31 Heather Tilbury Phillips interview, 2018.
32 Quant 1966, p.165.
33 Ibid., p.175.
34 Ibid., p.187.
35 Lucie Clayton, *The World of Modelling and How to Get the London Model-Girl Look*, (London, 1968).
36 Beverly Johnson was the first black woman to appear on the cover of US *Vogue*, in August 1974.
37 *Time*, 1 April 1966.
38 Suzy Menkes, *How to be a Model* (London, 1969), p.106.
39 Amanda Lear, *My Life With Dali* (London, 1985).
40 April Ashley, *The First Lady* (London, 2006), p.106.
41 Quant 2012, p.70.
42 *Sunday Telegraph* magazine, 25 May 1973.

Photographic Interpretations

1 MacInnes 1959.
2 Ibid.
3 Archie McNair obituary, see www.telegraph.co.uk/news/obituaries.
4 Mary Quant interviewed by Hilary Alexander, 12 January 2009, see www.youtube.com.
5 Mary Quant in conversation with Philippe Garner, September 1998, published in Garner 1999, p.12.
6 Garner 1999, p.9.
7 Ibid.
8 Martin Munkácsi, 'Think While You Shoot', *Harper's Bazaar*, November 1935.
9 Models are discussed in greater detail in Stephanie Wood's essay, see pp.61–79.
10 Shinkle 2017, p.118.
11 Garner 1999, p.8.
12 Ibid., p.47.
13 Quant 1966, p.127.
14 Ibid., p.129.
15 Robin Muir, *Norman Parkinson: Portraits in Fashion* (London, 2004), p.109.
16 Quant 1966, p.75.
17 MacInnes 1959.
18 The image was first used to illustrate a *Daily Mirror* article by Felicity Green celebrating the launch of the cosmetics line and Quant's world-wide success. Felicity Green, 'From rags to rouges', *Daily Mirror*, 6 April 1966, p.15.
19 Hugo Vickers (ed.), *Beaton in the Sixties: More Unexpurgated Diaries* (London, 2004), p.303.
20 Shinkle 2017, p.89.
21 BBC2 documentary, *The Real Blow Up: Fame, Fashion and Photography*, 2002, 9:40.
22 Ibid., 18:07.
23 Nicky Haslam, 'How Bailey changed my life in a flash', *Daily Mail*, 20 January 2012, see www.dailymail.co.uk.

24 BBC2 documentary, *Fame, Fashion and Photography: The Real Blow Up*, 2002, 43:45.

25 Grace Coddington and Robin Muir, 'The Fashion Photographs of Terence Donovan, *Daily Telegraph*, 2 November 2012.

26 Twiggy photographed on 3 June 1966, image published in *Woman's Mirror*, 27 August 1966.

27 *Daily Mail*, June 1965, quoted in Garner 1999, p.17.

28 Bosley Crowther, 'Blow-Up', *New York Times*, 19 December 1966.

29 Marion Hume and Tamsin Blanchard, 'Fashion Through a Lens Backwards', *The Independent*, 28 April 1993.

30 Stephen Gundle, *Glamour: A History* (Oxford, 2009), p.295.

31 *Vogue*, 1 October 1966 and 15 September 1967.

32 *Vogue* cover, 1 March 1966, Donyale Luna photographed by David Bailey.

PART THREE Into the Big Time 1963–1964

1 *Vogue*, 1 October 1963.

2 Quant 1966, p.113.

3 Ibid., p.121.

4 Ken and Kate Baynes, 'Behind the Scene', *Design*, 1966, pp.18–29.

5 Further details about Ames Mill have not been possible to establish so far.

6 Quant 1966, pp.124–6.

7 See Betty Keep, 'Styled by the With-It Girl', *Australian Women's Weekly*, 15 March 1964; with thanks to Paola di Trocchio, Senior Curator, Fashion and Textiles, National Gallery of Victoria.

8 Jill Butterfield, 'A girl like this makes you want to gamble', *Daily Express*, 6 November 1963, p.8.

9 Felicity Green, *Sex, Sense and Nonsense: Felicity Green on the 60s Fashion Scene*, p.12.

10 Annabel Taylor (Mackay), *Some memories of a career in the Rag Trade*, unpublished, 1 February 2018.

11 Quant 1966, p.159.

12 www.butterick.mccall.com/our-company/ butterick-history and Joy Spanabel Emery, *A History of the Paper Pattern Industry The Home Dressmaking Pattern Revolution* (New York, 2014), p.181.

13 Anna Buruma, *Liberty & Co in the Fifties and Sixties: A Taste for Design* (Woodbridge, 2008), pp.124–5.

14 For example, see *Tatler*, November 1964, p.152, Grace Coddington modelling an ankle-length dress reproduced with Victorian style graphics.

15 Quote from a 1992 interview with Alistair Gauld who was a designer in the Trowbridge weaving mill McCalls between 1959 and 1974. The interview is part of the oral history interviews made with previous mill workers in the beginning of the 1990s, held at Trowbridge Museum. From Hanne Dahl, 'Research into Mary Quant garments Made of West of England cloth Woven in Trowbridge' unpublished report, February 2018.

16 These 'West of England' labels have been found on a dress at Leeds Museums and Art Gallery and others in private collections.

17 The design comes from the horse blankets used originally at Tattersall's horse market in London, which became used for riding waistcoats, and waistcoats in general. See Wiltshire and Swindon History Centre ref 1387/880.

18 Elizabeth Gibbons correspondence with V&A, 2013. Coddington 2002, p.67.

19 Quant 2012, pp.168–9.

Doing Business in Transatlantic Fashion: the Experience of Mary Quant

1 'U.K. Designer Mary Quant in Penney Tie-in', *Women's Wear Daily* [hereafter cited as *WWD*], 19 September 1962; Mort Sheinman, 'Giant Fashion Step Taken by Penney's', *WWD*, 3 October 1962.

2 'New York Dress Market Dominant, Survey Shows', *WWD*, 8 December 1954.

3 Bobbie Brooks, Inc., *Annual Report for the Year Ended April 30, 1961*, pp.17, 19, folder 3, box 1, Ms. 5157, Research Library, Cleveland History Center, Cleveland, Ohio.

4 Apparel and Fashion Industry's Association, *London Presents* (London 1957), MSS222/ AP/4/2/2, Modern Records Centre, University of Warwick.

5 Blaszczyk 2006.

6 Mark Abrams, 'Spending on Clothes', *Financial Times* [hereafter cited as *FT*], 6 October 1956.

7 'London Group Bases Fashion Show on Teen Preferences', *WWD*, 9 November 1955.

8 'Fashion Comes to the Market', *FT*, 20 May 1960; 'Women's Clothing – How the Money Is Spent', *FT*, 31 March 1960.

9 The sizing story can be traced in *WWD*. Some of the history is also summarized in Florence H. Forziati, 'Changes in Body Sizes of Young Women', address presented at the Second Annual Conference of the Apparel Research Foundation, Washington, D.C., 8 October 1968, in folder: Sizing Studies, accession 2215: DuPont External Affairs, Hagley Museum and Library, Wilmington, Del.

10 Forziati, 'Changes in Body Sizes of Young Women'; Board of Trade, *Women's Measurements and Sizes: A Study Sponsored by the Joint Clothing Council Limited* (London 1957); Geoffrey Henry, 'Trade Lines', *The Maker-Up*, vol. 48, 1943, p.856; Julia Felsenthal, 'A Size 2 Is a Size 2 Is a Size 8', *Slate*, 25 January 2012. See www.slate.com.

11 JC Penney Company, *Sizing Up Women's Fashions* (1965; revised 1966), JC Penney Collection, DeGolyer Library, Southern Methodist University, Dallas, Tex. (hereafter cited as Penney-SMU). The role of home economics can be traced Penney's magazine for teachers, *Fashions and Fabrics*; Penney-SMU.

12 Rachel Worth, *Fashion for the People: A History of Clothing at Marks and Spencer* (London, 2006).

13 See, for example, 'Steinberg & Sons (London & South Wales)', *FT*, 11 September 1952.

14 'Office Will Assist U.S. Buyers at London Openings', *WWD*, 19 October 1955; 'Britain Pushes Ready-to-Wear Exports to U.S.', *WWD*, 16 January 1956.

15 'Group in London Credits Showing for Export Rise', *WWD*, 18 January 1962.

16 'Frederick Starke Heads London Group', *WWD*, 14 December 1959; 'Fashion House Group of London Ceases Activities', *WWD*, 28 January 1966.

17 Starke quoted in 'The American "Mind" Is Ripe for British Fashion', *WWD*, 21 July 1965.

18 'British RTW Firms Cast Eager Eye on U.S. Market', *WWD*, 2 June 1965.

19 'Frederick Starke Operates on Two Distinct Price Levels', *WWD*, 3 October 1960.

20 Blaszczyk 2018b.

21 JC Penney Company, *Annual Report 1960*.

22 John McDonald, 'How They Minted the New Penney', *Fortune*, July 1967, reprint, Penney-SMU.

23 Blaszczyk 2018a.

24 *Penneys Fall and Winter 63*, Penney-SMU.

25 Quant 1966 (2012 edn), pp.101–2; Quant 2012, p.68; 'Mary Quant Visits N.Y.O and West Coast Stores', *Penney News*, vol. 28 (September 1963), p.5, Penney-SMU.

26 'Looking Back – into the Future', *Penney News*, 30 August 1965, pp.10–11, Penney-SMU.

27 The 'Chelsea Girl' line of apparel that Quant designed for JC Penneys predated and was unrelated to the Chelsea Girl apparel chain that operated on the British high street from 1965 to 1991, when it was rebranded as River Island. James Hall, 'From Chelsea Girl to Concept Man: History of River Island', *Telegraph*, 20 March 2011.

28 *Penneys Fall and Winter 63*; JC Penney Company, *Sizing Up Women's Fashions*.

29 'Mary Quant Designs New Collection for Spring and Summer', *Penney News*, vol. 28 (April 1963), pp.1, 10, Penney-SMU.

30 Blaszczyk 2018b, p.107; Quant 1966 (2012 edn), pp.104–5; *Penneys Spring and Summer 64*, pp.8–9, Penney-SMU.

31 *Penneys Fall & Winter 1964*, pp.88–9; *Penneys Fall and Winter 1965*, pp.6–8; *Penneys Spring and Summer 1966*, pp.2–9; *Penneys Fall and Winter 1966*, pp.2–31, all in Penney-SMU.

32 Quant 2012, p.69.

33 Blaszczyk 2018b, p.109; *Penneys Fall and Winter 1965*, pp.2–31; *Go Young in Spring and Summer 1967 Penneys*, pp.2–13; *1969 Penneys Spring & Summer American on the Go*, pp.58–65, all in Penney-SMU.

34 'New Fashion Company Formed', *FT*, 21 February 1963; 'Steinberg & Sons (London and South Wales)', *FT*, 9 October 1963.

35 'The Far-Out Stockings', *Daily Mail*, 2 May 1963.

36 Felicity Green, 'Girls Will Be Boys', *Daily Mirror*, 21 August 1963.

37 'Burgeoning Quant', *WWD*, 27 August 1963.

38 'Sure-Footed for Spring', *Tatler*, 29 January 1964.

39 'Better Prospect for Steinberg & Sons', *FT*, 17 September 1964.

40 Tom McDermott, 'The Swingingest Giant of Them All', *WWD*, 17 August 1966; 'Puritan Confirms Young Appointment', *WWD*, 14 April 1965; Robert S. Taplinger Associates, 'YOUTHQUAKE', press release (June 1965), Mary Quant Archive.

41 McDermott, 'The Swingingest Giant'; 'Puritan Confirms Young Appointment'; Paul Hanenberg, 'First of 25 Paraphernalia Shops to Bow in May Co., Cleveland', *WWD*, 7 March 1966.

42 Mort Sheinman, 'Puritan Swings', *WWD*, 17 March 1965; Mort Sheinman, 'Puritan Keeping Its Eye on Durable Press, Youth', *WWD*, 20 May 1965.

43 'Minneapolis Units Go "Feminine" in Dress Sections', *WWD*, 22 July 1965.

44 'What They Really Buy', *The Economist*, 20 November 1965, p.862.

45 'Spring Check-Up', *WWD*, 1 December 1965.

46 Sheila Black, 'G.B. Britton to Make Women's Shoes', *FT*, 14 March 1967.

47 'Current Problems at Steinberg', *FT*, 20 March 1968.

48 Sheila Black, 'Fashion: No Place for the Amateur', *FT*, 28 January 1966; Carol Bjorkman, 'Carol', *WWD*, 17 September 1965; 'WWDeadline', *WWD*, 2 August 1967; 'New Names – In London RTW', *WWD*, 3 October 1967; 'In Philadelphia: Gimbels and Clairol Reveal How London Sees Blondes', *WWD*, 3 November 1967.

49 'Mary Quant Deal', *FT*, 13 March 1970; 'Quant Is Back', *WWD*, 15 April 1970.

50 'More Stores Are Buying But Orders Are Small', *WWD*, 28 April 1971; Sheila Black, 'British Fashion Needs Quality to Go with Its Style', *FT*, 6 October 1972; 'Steinberg & Sons (London & South Wales) Ltd', *FT*, 11 October 1973.

51 Tom McDermott, 'Puritan Fashion's Rosen: Revolution Toward Youth', *WWD*, 28 October 1971.

52 *JC Penney Fall and Winter 1971*, pp.4–5, Penney-SMU.

53 *JC Penney Fall and Winter 1972*, author's collection.

54 'Archie McNair Obituary: London Entrepreneur Whose Vision Transformed King's Road, Chelsea', *The Guardian*, 10 July 2015.

55 Grumbach 2014, p.212.

56 'In Fashion the Name Is the Game', *The Economist*, 17 March 1984.

57 For *WWD* quotation, see 'In Fashion the Name Is the Game'.

PART FOUR The Shock of the Knee 1965–1967

1 Quoted in Dominic Sandbrook, *Never Had It So Good: A History of Britain from Suez to the Beatles* (London, 2005), p.465, who is in turn quoting from Asa Briggs, *The History of Broadcasting in the United Kingdom*, vol. 5, 1995, p.204.

2 *Life*, 5 December 1960.

3 Telephone conversation, Nicky Hessenberg and the author, August 2018.

4 John Ayto, *Twentieth Century Words*, (Oxford, 1999), p.422. Ayto quotes from *The Economist*, 1965, but doesn't give a precise reference.

5 Quant 1966, p.175.

6 Quant 2012, pp.275–8.

7 Email from Toyah Willcox to V&A, following announcement of #WeWantQuant campaign, 8 June 2018.

8 Patricia Peterson, 'Courrèges Is Star of Best Show Seen So Far', *New York Times*, 3 August 1964. See also Roma Fairley, *Bomb in the Collection: Fashion with the Lid Off* (London, 1969), p.47.

9 *Vogue*, January 1965.

10 Alexander Fury, 'Does it matter who invented the mini? Fashion's a free-for-all', *The Independent*, 11 January 2016.

11 Quant 1966, pp.66–7.

12 Shrimpton 1996, p.109. The Furniture, Textiles and Fashion department at the V&A sometimes receives enquiries about the dress Shrimpton wore in Melbourne, however it is not at the V&A. In 1974 Jean Shrimpton donated a short white skirt, c.1966, with a label from the New York store Henri Bendel, V&A: T.68–1974.

13 See 'Mod Fashions made in Australia', *Australian Woman's Weekly*, 29 April 1965, (with thanks to Paola di Troccio, National Gallery of Victoria), and *Crossroads: The Memoirs of Sidney Sernack, 'The Man For Your Wardrobe'* as narrated to Linda Bermeister (Canberra, 2014), pp.170–1. With thanks to Tracey Sernack-Chee Quee.

14 Green 2014, pp.114–5.

15 Fashion Museum, Bath: BATMC 94.23; V&A: T.110–1976.

16 Ernestine Carter, 'Quantuples of Four', *Sunday Times*, 11 April 1965; thanks to Hanne Dahl for bringing this to my attention.

17 Beatrice Behlen 'London & UK' and Ben Whyman, 'Hardy Amies' in de la Haye and Ehrman (eds) 2015, p.204; p.162.

18 Interview with Gerald Farraday, 26 May 2015.

19 Email from Jack Isenberg to Heather Tilbury Phillips, February 2018.

20 Ernestine Carter, 'Introduction', *Mary Quant's London*, p.11; see also Alexandra Palmer, *Dior*, (London, 2009), p.92; *M&S News* (in house magazine) February 1963. Thanks to Katie Cameron, Archive and Outreach Officer, M&S Company Archive, Leeds.

21 An early mention of Mary Quant stockings is found in US *Vogue*, 15 September 1964, p.164.

22 Email to author from Roger Curry, 29 June 2018.

23 Interview with Derry Curry, June 2015.

24 See 'Corset making' A Tale of One City, www.ataleofonecity.portsmouth.gov.uk (accessed 22 August 2018); thanks to Edwina Ehrman for helping to identify the Weingarten Brothers factory as manufacturers of the Qform underwear line, and Alison Carter for further references.

25 'Yiperoonee it's party time', *Petticoat*, 3 December 1966.

26 Black rabbit fur with leather trimmings, private collection.

27 *Tatler*, 19 January 1965.

28 www.nationalarchives.gov.uk/currency-converter.

29 *Honey*, October 1966, p.101.

30 Examples have been found in two private collections.

31 Reverse of design headed 'Coat length & very short', private collection.

32 *Vogue*, 1 October 1966 p.135. Price converted at www.nationalarchives.gov.uk/currency converter.

33 V&A: T.72:1&2–2018 and V&A: T.73:1&2–2018. Donated by Diane Harris.

34 V&A: T.56–2018. Donated by Sue Robertson.

35 'Odd gear at the Palace', *Daily Mail*, 16 November 1966.

36 For example see V&A: T.353–1974.

37 Discussion with Suzanne Isaacs (now Russell) with the author and Stephanie Wood, 22 May 2018.

38 Various websites suggest that Stevcoknit was located in North Carolina. More research is needed to establish any further links with Mary Quant's designs.

39 Quant 2012, p.74, also email from Shirley Shurville to the author, 25 September 2018.

40 Christopher Laverty, *Fashion in Film* (London, 2016), pp.144–7.

41 *On the Quant Wavelength – a Honey special*, (London, 1967), p.1.

42 Suzy Menkes, 'The Daisy Trail', *The Times*, 16 August 1967, p.9, where prices are quoted at between £2 9s 11d and £3 19s 11d (£44 and £70 today, www.nationalarchives.gov.uk/currencyconverter.)

43 Alison Adburgham, 'Mary Quant talks to Alison Adburgham', *The Guardian*, 10 October 1967.

44 Quant 2012, pp.117–8. Quant mentions that historic clothing at the house was given to the V&A. All files relating to the Plunket Greene and Russell family have been checked and no mention of these garments being offered to the Museum has been found. See V&A archive, file MA/1/R/2092 (Lady Dorothea Russell), MA/1/R/2097 (Miss Flora Russell), and MA/1/B.1632 (Mrs Noel Blakiston).

45 www.gracesguide.co.uk/File:Kangol3-1955.jpg.

46 *Vogue*, 1 October 1967, p.53.

47 Heather Tilbury Phillips, 'I first met Mary Quant', unpublished, 28 May 2018.

Quant and Cosmetics

1 CBC (Canadian Broadcasting Corporation), *British Fashion Icon Mary Quant*, 1968, CBC Archive.

2 Oral History Interview, Mary Quant and Marketa Uhlirova, 15 September 2004, Museum of London 2008.64.

3 McNair and O'Neill, 2008, session 5, track 8.

4 Oral History Interview, Mary Quant and Marketa Uhlirova, 15 September 2004, Museum of London 2008.64; and Quant 2012, p.109.

5 Oral History Interview, Mary Quant and Marketa Uhlirova, 15 September 2004, Museum of London 2008.64; and Quant 2012, pp.108–9.

6 *On the Quant Wavelength – a Honey special* (London, 1967), p.3, italics in original; see also Quant 1986, p.ii.

7 Ibid.

8 Oral History Interview, Mary Quant and Marketa Uhlirova, 15 September 2004, Museum of London 2008.64.

9 Prudence Glynn, 'The package deal', *The Times*, 28 November 1967, p.9.

10 CBC, *British Fashion Icon Mary Quant*, 1968, CBC Archive.

11 Ibid.

12 Intellectual Property Office, Trade Mark Number UK00000888980.

13 www.trademarks.ipo.gov.uk. Helen Quin, 'The image is the message', *The Guardian*, 3 April 1969, p.9. According to another source the packaging was designed by Tom Wolsey: Ken and Kate Baynes, 'Behind the Scene', *Design*, 1966, p.23.

14 Prudence Glynn, 'The package deal', *The Times*, 28 November 1967, p.9.

15 'Mary Quant Starkers', *Cosmopolitan* NY, October 1966, vol. 161, issue 4, p.44.

16 *On the Quant Wavelength – a Honey special*, (London, 1967), p.3.

17 Allen 1981, p.79.

18 *On the Quant Wavelength – a Honey special*, (London, 1967), pp.3–4.

19 Joy Debenham-Burton (née Ingram) during conversation with Patricia Gahan (née Mash) and Heather Tilbury Phillips, all formerly working for Mary Quant/Gala, on 21 January 2018.

20 Ibid.

21 Ibid.

22 Patricia Gahan (née Mash) during conversation with Joy Debenham-Burton (née Ingram) and Heather Tilbury Phillips formerly working for Mary Quant/Gala, on 21 January 2018. The cartoons might have been inspired by the successful 'cookstrips', recipes drawn in black and white that Len Deighton produced for *The Observer*, 1962–6.

23 'The Beauty Part – It's a Barefaced Happening', *WWD*, vol. 112, issue 124, 24 June 1966, p.9; see also Angela Taylor, 'Mary Quant Makes Make-up for Mods', *New York Times*, 8 September 1966, p.78.

24 Notes provided by Patricia Gahan via email on 11 May 2018.

25 Anne Braybon, 'About Town: A Case Study from Research in Progress on Photographic Networks in Britain, 1952–1969', *Photography and Culture*, vol. 1, issue 1, 2008, pp.95–106, DOI: 10.2752/175145108784861446. The advertisement appeared in *Vogue*, June 1966.

26 Paul Jobling, *Advertising Menswear: Masculinity and Fashion in the British Media Since 1945* (London, 2015), n.23, p.51; Felicity Green, 'The Magical Miss-Tree-Tour', *Daily Mirror*, 21 March 1968, p.15; email to the author from Heather Tilbury Phillips on 6 August 2018.

27 Quant 2012, p.132.

28 Patricia Gahan (née Mash) and Joy Debenham-Burton (née Ingram) during conversation with the author attended also by Heather Tilbury Phillips formerly working for Mary Quant/Gala, on 21 January 2018.

29 A.M. P.M. perfume advertisement, *Vogue*, December 1967, p.15.

30 'Hers: Mug's game a success', *The Observer*, 12 March 1967, p.28.

31 'Help!', *The Times*, 13 June 1967, p.9; see also examples at Museum of London: 74.330/32x and 74.330/32y, see www.collections. museumoflondon.org.uk.

32 'The lure of the lash', *Women's Wear Daily*, vol. 153, issue 4, 15 February 1969, p.44.

33 Patricia Gahan (née Mash) and Joy Debenham-Burton (née Ingram) during a conversation with the author attended also by Heather Tilbury Phillips formerly working for Mary Quant/Gala, on 21 January 2018.

34 Simon 1971, p.17.

35 Sheila Black, 'Trio who put the Quant theory into practice', *Financial Times*, 24 October 1968, p.13; Jo-An Jenkins, 'Inside Out – Mary Quant', *Women's Wear Daily*, vol. 117, issue 125, 27 December 1968, pp.14–15; for an extant box of the vitamin pills see Museum of London: 74.330/32as.

36 Sheila Black, 'Trio who put the Quant theory into practice', *Financial Times*, 24 October 1968, p.13.

37 Advertisement: Mary Quant's Beach Paints, *Harper's Bazaar*, New York, vol. 102, issue 3088, March 1969, p.80; see also 'Variations on a Tan', *Harpers and Queen*, London, May 1972, p.89.
See copy on examples in Museum of London's collection: 74.330/32an and 74.330/32ao; *The Chemist and Druggist*, 19 May 1973, p.648.

38 'Beauty Bulletin', *Vogue*, 1 October 1966, p.128; also: From a London Correspondent, 'Changing face an art form', *Canberra Times*, 4 October 1967, p.18.

39 Examples of each product are in the Museum of London's collection: 74.330/32lla and 74.330/32llc.

40 'The Cosmetics: The Beauty Part' sections in *Women's Wear Daily*, vol. 117, issue 73, 11 October 1968, p.28 and vol. 121, issue 47, 4 September 1970, p.18.

41 Katie Stewart, 'Counterpoint', *The Times*, 11 February 1972, p.9; *The Chemist and Druggist*, 19 May 1973, p.648.

42 Email from Toyah Willcox to V&A on 8 June 2018.

43 Twiggy 1975, p.94.

44 Notes provided to the author by Jill Saxton (née Lauderdale), Creative Manager at Gala 1968–9, 25 July 2018.

45 Simon 1971, p.65.

46 Ibid., p.66.

47 Jody Jacobs, 'Fall Cosmetics: Make-up To Make Love', *Women's Wear Daily*, vol. 120, issue 109, June 1970, p.20; *Gala Gossip*, company's inhouse magazine, sent by Patricia Gahan, 1970, p.30.

48 Notes provided to the author by Jill Saxton (née Lauderdale), Creative Manager at Gala 1968–9, 25 July 2018.

49 *Make-up To Make Love In*, sales brochure, c.1970 (in the possession of the author).

50 Allen 1981, p.80.

51 Mary Quant Special Recipe advertisement, 1976, Alamy Stock Photo.

52 Prudence Glynn, 'The natural thing', *The Times*, 14 May 1972, p.9.

53 Quant 2012, p.140.

54 Special Recipe advertisements: *Harpers and Queen*, June 1973, p.42; *Women's Wear Daily*, vol. 129, issue 56, 18 September 1974, p.3; *Seventeen*, November 1975, p.131.

55 Advertisements in *Seventeen*, September 1973, p.53 and November 1973, p.33. Already in 1967 Quant had launched 'Shadow Shapers, fine thin sticks of solid colour for the lids', 'British Beauty Firsts', *Harper's Bazaar*, vol. 76, issue 5, pp.56–7.

56 Quant 2012, p.137.

57 Stanley Reynolds, 'Bronze age', *The Guardian*, 29 January 1974, p.13.

58 Anthony Parkinson, 'Mainly for Men: Charlie is a darling with his mascara', *Newcastle Evening Chronicle*, 26 May 1975, p.4; Angela Taylor, 'Best Face Forward', *New York Times*, 30 April 1976, p.35.

59 Alastair Thain, 'Warrior of the wasteland', *The Times*, 10 April 1993, p.9.

60 Quoted in Allen 1981, pp.82–3.

61 Margaret Pagano, 'Max Factor busy three UK brands', *The Times*, 13 November 1980, p.19; Margaret Dibben, 'Max Factor buys Mary Quant', *The Guardian*, 13 November 1980, p.17.

62 Kasai Usui, *Marketing and Consumption in Modern Japan*, (London, 2014), p.49; 'Brand Story', see Club Cosmetics company website, www.clubcosmetics.co.jp.

63 Roger Berthoud, 'Encounters: The Two Sides of Woman', *Illustrated London News*, 1 April 1986, p.63; Libby Purvis, 'From mini skirts to maxi millions', *The Times*, 13 October 1990, p.4; Noreen Taylor, 'The woman who refuses to stay stuck in the Sixties', *The Times*, 4 January 1996, p.15.

64 McNair and O'Neill, 2008, session 6, track 11.

65 Ibid.

66 Libby Purvis, 'From mini skirts to maxi millions', *The Times*, 13 October 1990, p.4.

67 Mary Quant and Felicity Green, *Colour by Quant*, (London, 1984).

68 Mary Quant, *Classic Make-up & Beauty* (London, 1998) originally published as *Ultimate Make-up & Beauty* in 1996.

69 Mary Quant Cosmetics Ltd website, www.store.maryquant.co.uk.

Quant and Advertising: Collett Dickenson Pearce

1 Mary Quant is in *Harper's Bazaar*, October 1962 and *Tatler*, September 1962

2 Quant 2012, p.112

3 The 'creative revolution' in advertising refers to the time when creative talent became known to be the most valued asset of agencies, as modelled by DDB – where art and copywriting teams worked in intuitive, rather than formulaic ways. This new creative approach is outlined most thoroughly in Cracknell 2011 – a publication that informs this essay, along with writings by Sir John Hegarty.

4 Bill Bernbach, Ned Doyle (1902–1989) and Mac Dane (1906–2004) co-founded Doyle Dane Bernbach (DDB) in 1949.

5 Bernbach had previously worked on the 1939 New York World Fair and for various agencies. See Cracknell 2011, p.55.

6 Maurice Saatchi, email to Jenny Lister, 10 July 2018.

7 Hegarty 2011, p.33; 'John Hegarty on the Power of Advertising' in 'Celebrating Five Decades Of The Observer Magazine' *The Observer Magazine*, 31 July 2018.

8 *Honey*, February 1967.

9 Daniel Farey-Jones, 2012. 'D&AD honours 50 years of industry talent' see www.campaignlive. co.uk/article.

10 Co-Founder of Wight Collins Rutherford and Scott (WCRS), 1979–99.

11 Ministry of Education, 'Art Education' Pamphlet No. 6. His Majesty's Stationery Office London, 1946.

12 According to *Quant by Quant*, Mary Quant left Goldsmiths before graduating, p.25.

13 Sassoon 1968, pp.120–5; Jones 1990, p.53.

14 Simon Forbes established Antenna hair salon in London in 1981.

PART FIVE Liberated Fashion 1968–1975

1 *Vogue*, September 1968, p.73.

2 Interview with Janie Ranger, June 2015 and responses to the V&A #WeWantQuant campaign.

3 Discussion with author, 26 June 2018.

4 Sheila Black, 'Trio who put the Quant theory into

practice', *Financial Times*, 24 October 1968. Thanks to Regina Lee Blaszscyck.

5 According to London telephone directories, thanks to Camilla de Winton for meticulous research.
6 McNair and O'Neill, 2008, track 5.
7 'Thomas Jourdan recovery', *Investors Chronicle*, date illegible, p.690, from a scrapbook kept by Archie McNair, thanks to Camilla Mair for sharing this.
8 Heather Tilbury Phillips, 28 May 2018.
9 A copy of this letter, dated 16 July 1968, is held in the V&A acquisition file, 2012/841.
10 Correspondence with the V&A, acquisition file, 2013.
11 Decimal day had taken place on 15 February 1971, converting the British currency from pounds, shillings and pence to the current system.
12 Timeline of Mary Quant Ltd, Heather Tilbury Phillips (unpublished).
13 Ibid.
14 Email from Vivien Wearing to V&A.
15 Programme for 'Designs on Fashion' event, foreword written by Lord Thorneycroft, Chairman of the BOTB. Thanks to Gerald Farraday for sharing this.
16 Timeline of Mary Quant Ltd, Heather Tilbury Phillips (unpublished).
17 Daisy promotional poster, Museum of Childhood, V&A: B.144–2017.
18 Frances Baird, *British Teenage Dolls 1956–1984* (London, 2004), pp.85–95.
19 Timeline of Mary Quant Ltd, Heather Tilbury Phillips (unpublished).
20 Museum of London files. Many thanks also to Naomi Tarrant and Valerie Osborne.
21 *Fibres Post*, 12 July 1974.
22 Timeline of Mary Quant Ltd, Heather Tilbury Phillips (unpublished).
23 Shirley Conran, *Superwoman: Everywoman's Book of Household Management* (London, 1975), pp.9–10.

Selling the Total Look: Quant and Interiors

1 Undated BBC interviews, marking the launch of the second Quant–ICI interior design range, c.1972.
2 Julia Kollewe and Graeme Wearden 'ICI: from Perspex to paints', *The Guardian*, 18 June 2007.
3 Undated BBC interviews, marking the launch of the second Quant–ICI interior design range, c.1972.
4 Penny Sparke, 'At Home with Modernity: The New Domestic Scene' in Christopher Breward and Ghislaine Wood (eds), *British Design from 1948: Innovation in the Modern Age* (London, 2012), p.131.
5 Heather Standring, 'Cook's Tour', *The Observer*, 19 June 1966, p.28.
6 Found in Heal's archive at the V&A Archive of Art and Design: AAD/1994/16/2869.
7 'Quant on Designed Living' a special insert in *Honey*, 1967, p.6.
8 'Talk Round the Table', *Vogue*, October 1960, p.118.
9 Quote in Ruth Jordan, 'The Ginger Touch', *Ideal Home*, September 1964, p.69.
10 Ibid.

11 Christopher Breward, *Fashioning London* (London, 2004), p.155.
12 Nicholas Ind, *Terence Conran, the Authorized Biography* (London, 1995), p.106.
13 'Shop in Knightsbridge', *Architectural Review*, April 1959.
14 Interview with Terence Conran by the author, 10 April 2018.
15 Interview with Lydia Sharman by the author, 3 July 2018, in which Sharman showed her Conran Contract drawings for the window display system, dated 12 November 1957. She will give more detail in a forthcoming book.
16 'Quant by Bannenberg', *Vogue*, February 1967, p.15.
17 Ibid.
18 Interview with Terence Conran by the author, 10 April 2018.
19 Folded broadsheet with illustrations by Juliet Glynn-Smith and text by Caroline Conran, found in V&A Archive of Art & Design: AAD/1995/12/5/1.
20 Interview with Terence Conran by the author, 10 April 2018.
21 Email interview with Janie Ranger, 16 August 2018.
22 Interview with Peter White by Heather Tilbury Phillips, 18 June 2015.
23 *The Mary Quant Book of Room Design – From ICI*, 1972, in the Daphne Sanderson Archive at the V&A Archive of Art and Design: AAD/2009/5.
24 While this essay focuses on the impact on the UK market, Peter White told the author in an interview on 20 September 2018 that this range was also distributed in France, Germany, Holland, Switzerland, the USA and Japan where Quant altered some of her ranges to fit the Japanese market.
25 ICI marketing booklet for retailers, 1971, in the Daphne Sanderson Archive at the V&A Archive of Art and Design: AAD/2009/5.
26 Interview with Heather Tilbury Phillips by the author, 3 September 2018.
27 Interview with Peter White by Heather Tilbury Phillips, May 2015.
28 Interview with Terence Conran by the author, 10 April 2018.
29 Quant 2012.
30 Desmond Zwar, 'I'm as snug as a duck in my duvet', *Daily Mail*, 19 November 1965.
31 Quant 2012.
32 Ibid.
33 Habitat catalogue, 1971, p.96, in the Habitat archive at the V&A Archive of Art and Design: AAD/1995/12/5/5.
34 Quant 2012.
35 McNair and O'Neill, 2008, track 5.
36 Interview with Jane Edgeworth by Heather Tilbury Phillips, May 2015.
37 Regina Lee Blaszscyk and Ben Wubs (eds), 'Beyond the Crystal Ball', *The Fashion Forecasters: A Hidden History of Color and Trend Prediction* (London, 2018), p.22.
38 Interview with Jane Edgeworth by Heather Tilbury Phillips, May 2015. Edgeworth also added that she worked closely with Pamela Howard and Pay Hyduk on interpreting Quant's wishes for the homeware designs.
39 *The Mary Quant Book of Room Design – From*

ICI, 1972, in the Daphne Sanderson Archive at the V&A Archive of Art and Design: AAD/2009/5.

PART SIX Lifestyle Brand 1975–2000

1 'Friday Gem from the Stoddard-Templeton Design Archive: Mary Quant' see: www.universityofglasgowlibrary.wordpress.com.
2 National Archives Currency Converter
3 Museum of Childhood: Misc.86,87 and 91–1979.
4 *Sunday Telegraph* magazine, 29 March 1981, pp.28–34.
5 Veronica Horwell, Archie McNair obituary, *The Guardian*, 17 July 2015.
6 Heather Tilbury Phillips, in discussion with the author.
7 BMW, *MINI The Book* (Hamburg, 2006), p.69.

CONCLUSION Fashion for Everyone

1 Quant 2012.
2 'Fashion boss hails £32bn earner for UK as London labels take centre stage', *The Metro*, 13 September 2018, p.8. See also LFW February 2018 Facts and Figures: www.britishfashion council.co.uk/pressreleases
3 Mark Tungate, *Fashion Brands* (London, 2012), p.1.
4 Miller 1966, pp.1066–70.
5 www.vam.ac.uk/blog/news/we-want-quant.
6 Regina Lee Blaszscyck, *The Color Revolution* (Boston, Mass., 2012).
7 Quant 1966, p.66; J. Aitken, *The Young Meteors* (London, 1967), p.15.
8 Christopher Breward, 'Clothing Desire: The Problem of the British Fashion Consumer c.1955–1975', *Cultures of Consumption Working Paper Series*, Royal Society, public lecture, 17 March 2004.
9 Mary Quant perfume sample packaging, c.1970, Mary Quant Archive.
10 Sarah Owen, WGSN, Senior Editor, Digital Media & Marketing, 'The Gen Z equation', WGSN www.lp.wgsn.com/en-download-gen-z-equation.
11 'Young Marrieds Today: Mary Quant and Alexander Punket Greene', *Annabel: The New Magazine for the Young Wife*, April 1966, p.29.

APPENDIX Mary Quant Labels

1 Elizabeth Ann Coleman, *The Opulent Era: Fashions of Worth, Doucet and Pingat* (London, 1989).

Bibliography

Adburgham 1964
Alison Adburgham, *Shops and Shopping 1800–1914*, London 1964

Allen 1981
Margaret Allen, *Selling Dreams: Inside the Beauty Business*, London, Melbourne, Toronto 1981

Ashmore 2008
Sonia Ashmore, 'Liberty and Lifestyle: Shopping for Art and Luxury in Nineteenth-Century London' in David Hussey and Margaret Ponsonby (eds), *Buying for the Home: Shopping for the Domestic from Seventeenth Century to the Present*, London 2008, pp.73–90

Blaszczyk 2006
Regina Lee Blaszczyk, 'Styling Synthetics: DuPont's Marketing of Fabrics Wand Fashions in Postwar America', *Business History Review*, vol. 80 (2006) pp.485–538

Blaszczyk 2018a
Regina Lee Blaszczyk, 'The Rise and Fall of European Fashion at Filene's, in Boston', in Regina Lee Blaszczyk and Véronique Pouillard, eds., *European Fashion: The Creation of a Global Industry*, Manchester, 2018, pp.170–200

Blaszczyk 2018b
Regina Lee Blaszczyk, 'What Do Baby Boomers Want? How the Swinging Sixties Became the Trending Seventies', in Regina Lee Blaszczyk and Ben Wubs, eds., *The Fashion Forecasters: A Hidden History of Color and Trend Prediction*, London, 2018, pp.102–5

Breward and Wilcox 2012
Christopher Breward and Claire Wilcox, *The Ambassador Magazine: Promoting Post-War British Textiles and Fashion*, London 2012

Coddington 2002
Grace Coddington, *Grace: A Memoir*, London 2002

Cracknell 2011
Andrew Cracknell, *The Real Mad Men*, London 2011

de la Haye et al 2014
Amy de la Haye, Jeffrey Horsley and Judith Clark *Exhibiting Fashion: Before and After 1971*, London 2014

de la Haye and Ehrman 2015
Amy de la Haye and Edwina Ehrman, eds, *London Couture 1923–1975: British Luxury*, London 2015

Drewniany and Jewler 2014
B. Drewniany and J.A. Jewler, *Creative Strategy in Advertising*, London 2014

Frayling 1987
Christopher Frayling, *The Royal College of Art. One Hundred and Fifty Years of Art and Design*, London 1987

Garner 1999
Philippe Garner, *John Cowan: Through the Light Barrier*, Munich 1999

Grumbach 2014
Didier Grumbach, *History of International Fashion*, Northampton, Mass., 2014

Hegarty 2011
John Hegarty, 'Celebrating Five Decades of the Observer Magazine', *The Guardian*, 31 July 2011

Jones 1990
Dylan Jones, *Haircults: Fifty Years of Styles and Cuts*, London 1990

Lewis 2000
David Lewis, *The Incomplete Circle: Eric Atkinson, Art and Education*, Aldershot 2000

London Museum 1973
Mary Quant's London, exh. London Museum, 29 November 1973–30 June 1974

MacCarthy 2006
Fiona MacCarthy, *Last Curtsey: The End of the Debutantes*, London 2006

McInnes 1959
Colin MacInnes, *Absolute Beginners*, London 1959

McNair and O'Neill 2008
Archie McNair interviewed by Alistair O'Neill, *An Oral History of British Fashion*, British Library, 2008

Ministry of Education, *Art Education Pamphlet No. 6.*, London 1946

Outside Collett Dickenson Pearce, exh. Leeds Arts University, Leeds 2015

Pringle 1988
Alexandra Pringle, *Very Heaven: Looking Back at the 1960s*, London 1988

Quant 1966
Mary Quant, *Quant by Quant*, London 1966

Quant 1986
Mary Quant, *Quant on Make-Up*, London 1986

Quant 2012
Mary Quant, *Autobiography*, London 2012

Quant and Green 1984
Mary Quant and Felicity Green, *Colour by Quant*, London 1984

Salmon and Ritchie 2000
J. Salmon and J. Ritchie, *Inside Collett Dickenson Pearce*, London 2000

Sassoon 1968
Vidal Sassoon, *Sorry I Kept You Waiting, Madam*, London 1968

Shrimpton 1964
Jean Shrimpton, *The Truth About Modelling*, London 1964

Shinkle 2017
Eugenie Shinkle, *Fashion Photography: The Story in 180 Pictures*, London 2017

Simon 1971
Rosemary Simon, *The Price of Beauty*, London 1971

Twiggy 1975
Twiggy, *Twiggy: An Autobiography*, London 1975

Wilcox 2004
Claire Wilcox, *Vivienne Westwood*, London 2004

Further Reading

Mary Alexander, 'Women, Clothes and Feminism', *Feminist Arts News*, no.9, August 1982, pp.4–7

Beatrice Behlen, 'A Fashionable History of the King's Road' in Anjali Bulley (ed.), *Cadogan & Chelsea: The Making of a Modern Estate*, London 2017

Barbara Bernard, *Fashion in the 60's*, London 1978

Christine Boydell, *Horrockses Fashions: Off-the-Peg Style in the '40s and '50s*, London 2012

Christopher Breward and Ghislaine Wood (eds), *British Design from 1948: Innovation in the Modern Age*, London 2012

Christopher Breward, David Gilbert and Jenny Lister (eds), *Swinging Sixties: Fashion in London and Beyond 1955–70*, London 2006

Caroline Charles, *Caroline Charles: 50 Years in Fashion*, Woodbridge 2012

Becky E. Conekin, 'Eugene Vernier and "Vogue" Models in Early "Swinging London": Creating the Fashionable Look of the 1960s', *Women's Studies Quarterly*, vol. 41, no.1–2 (2012) pp.89–107

Max Décharné, *King's Road: The Rise and Fall of the Hippest Street in the World*, London 2005

Marnie Fogg, *Boutique. A '60s Cultural Phenomenon*, London 2003

David Gilbert (ed.), 'Shopping Routes: Networks of Fashion Consumption in London's West End 1945–1979', *The London Journal*, vol. 31, no. 1 (2006)

David Gilbert and Sonia Ashmore, 'Mini-skirts, Afghan Coats and Blue Jeans: Three Global Fashion Happenings of the Sixties' in Mirjam Shatanawi and Wayne Modest (eds), *The Sixties: A Worldwide Happening*, Amsterdam 2015, pp.162–77

Paul Gorman, *The Look Adventures in Rock and Pop Fashion*, London 2001

Felicity Green, *Sex, Sense and Nonsense: Felicity Green on the 60's Fashion Scene*, Woodbridge 2014

Martin Harrison, *Shots of Style: Great Fashion Photographs Chosen by David Bailey*, London 1986
–, *Appearances: Fashion Photography Since 1945*, London 1991
–, *Young Meteors: British Photojournalism 1957–1965*, London 1998

Barbara Hulanicki and Martin Pel, *The Biba Years 1963–1975*, London 2014

Brigid Keenan, *Full Marks for Trying: An Unlikely Journey from the Raj to the Rag Trade*, London 2017

Richard Lester, *John Bates: Fashion Designer*, Woodbridge 2008
–, *Photographing Fashion: British Style in the Sixties*, Woodbridge 2009
–, *Boutique London: A History King's Road to Carnaby Street*, Woodbridge 2010

Joel Lobenthal, *Radical Rags: Fashions of the 1960s*, New York 1990

Phyllis Magidson, *Mod New York: Fashion takes a Trip*, New York 2017

Geoffrey Rayner, Richard Chamberlain and Annamarie Stapleton, *Pop! Design, Culture, Fashion 1956–1976*, Woodbridge 2012

Geoffrey Rayner and Richard Chamberlain, *Conran/Quant: Swinging London – A Lifestyle Revolution*, Woodbridge, 2019

Dominic Sandbrook, *Never Had It So Good: A History of Britain from Suez to the Beatles, 1956–63*, London 2005
–, *White Heat: A History of Britain in the Swinging Sixties, 1964–70*, London 2006
–, *State of Emergency: The Way We Were: Britain, 1970–4*, London 2010
–, *Seasons in the Sun: The Battle for Britain, 1974–9*, London 2012

Penny Sparke (ed.), *Did Britain Made it? British Design in Context 1946–86*, London 1986

Iain R. Webb, *Foale and Tuffin: The Sixties. A Decade in Fashion*, Woodbridge 2009

Richard Weight, *MOD: From Bebop to Britpop, Britain's Biggest Youth Movement*, London 2015

Notes on contributors

Johanna Agerman Ross, Curator: Twentieth Century and Contemporary Furniture and Product Design, V&A

Beatrice Behlen, Senior Curator: Fashion and Decorative Arts, Museum of London

Regina Lee Blaszczyk, Professor of Business History, University of Leeds

Susanna Brown, Curator: Photographs, Word and Image Department, V&A

Jenny Lister, Curator: Furniture, Textiles and Fashion Department, V&A

Elisabeth Murray, Curator: Furniture, Textiles and Fashion Department, V&A

Janine Sykes, Senior Lecturer, Creative Advertising and Course Leader, Curation Practices, Leeds Arts University.

Stephanie Wood, Exhibition Project Curator: Furniture, Textiles and Fashion Department, V&A

Index

192 Mary Quant
People Weekly, 1988
Photograph by Terry Smith

Sponsored by

KING'S ROAD

With support from

GROW
ANNENBERG

The ⚘ daisy device is a registered trade mark of the
Mary Quant group of companies throughout the world
and is used with the kind permission of those companies.

First published by V&A Publishing to accompany the
exhibition *Mary Quant* on view from 6 April 2019 to
16 February 2020 at the Victoria and Albert Museum,
South Kensington, London SW7 2RL

© Victoria and Albert Museum, 2019

Distributed in North America by Abrams,
an imprint of ABRAMS

The moral right of the authors has been asserted.

ISBN 9781 85177 995 6

10 9 8 7 6 5 4 3 2 1
2023 2022 2021 2020 2019

A catalogue record for this book is available from the
British Library.

Designer: Raymonde Watkins
Copyeditor: Rebeka Cohen
Origination: DL Imaging Ltd, London
Indexer: Nic Nicholas

Printed by Printer Trento, Italy

Front cover Mary Quant, 18 July 1963
Photograph by Terence Donovan

Back cover Advertisement for Triumph Herald
convertible, February 1967

pp.2–3 Mary Quant and Ginger Group models,
Market Street, Manchester, 1966

p.4 Kellie Wilson and an unknown model, wearing satin
shirts and shorts and for Mary Quant's intimate apparel
range, 1966
Photograph by Brian Duffy

p.8 Op art-style skirt and coat by Mary Quant, 1964
Photographs by Murray Irving for John French
Mary Quant Archive

p.10 Kellie Wilson modelling dress with tie by Mary Quant's
Ginger Group, c.1966
Photograph by Gunnar Larsen
Mary Quant Archive

V&A Publishing

Supporting the world's leading
museum of art and design,
the Victoria and Albert
Museum, London

Photography Credits

By figure number, unless otherwise stated.

Courtesy of The Advertising Archives: 137, 139, 143, 145
Image courtesy of The Advertising Archives/Image
 © David Bailey: 151, 152, 153
© Associated Newspapers/REX/Shutterstock: 42
© Bettmann/Getty Images: 140
Image courtesy of BNPS: 11
© Bokelberg: 131
Courtesy of Christy Kingdom-Denny/Victoria and Albert
 Museum, London: 167
The Collett Dickenson Pearce (CDP) Archive at the
 History of Advertising Trust: 147, 148, 149, 150
© Condé Nast Publications Ltd/Illustrated London News
 Ltd/Mary Evans: 72
© The Cowan Archive, courtesy of the Mary Quant
 Archive: 21
© David Bailey: 5, 46
© David Bailey. Image courtesy of the Mary Quant
 Archive/Victoria and Albert Museum, London: 63, 84
© David Hurn/Magnum Photos: 89
© David Montgomery. Image courtesy of Victoria and
 Albert Museum, London: 44
Courtesy of DeGolyer Library, Texas: 99
© Duffy Archive: p.4, 64
Courtesy of Emma Gaunt/Image © Victoria and Albert
 Museum, London: 10
© Getty Images: 179, 180
Image courtesy of Gladys Perint Palmer: 36
© Gunnar Larsen. Image courtesy of the Mary Quant
 Archive/Victoria and Albert Museum, London: p.11,
 59, 60, 61, 62
Courtesy of Hamish McNair and Camilla Mair: 9, 14
Courtesy of Heather Tilbury Phillips/Image © Victoria and
 Albert Museum, London: 160
Helmut Newton/Vogue © The Condé Nast Publications
 Ltd: 136
© Hulton Deutsch/Corbis Historical/Getty Images: 3
© Illustrated London News Ltd/Mary Evans: 7
Image courtesy of Iconic Images © Norman Parkinson:
 27, 68, 69, 85
Image courtesy of Iconic Images. Norman Parkinson/
 Vogue © The Condé Nast Publications Ltd: 26
Image courtesy of Iconic Images © Terence Donovan:
 40, 51, 65, 78, 87, 95, 107, 110
Image courtesy of Iconic Images © Terence Donovan/
 French Elle: 74, 75, 76, 77
Image courtesy of Iconic Images © Terry O'Neill: 56
© 2016 The Image Works, Inc: 186
© INTERFOTO/Alamy Stock Photo: 142
Courtesy of Jean Scott: 2
Jeff Morgan 13/Alamy Stock Photo: 119
© Jill Kennington: 190
© Joan Corlass. Image courtesy of Victoria and Albert
 Museum, London: 173
© John Adriaan/Image courtesy of NPG: 71
Image © John Adriaan. Image courtesy of the Mary Quant
 Archive/Victoria and Albert Museum, London: 154

© John Cowan Archive: 49, 50, 67
© John Cowan. Image courtesy of the Mary Quant
 Archive: 66
Courtesy of Joy Debenham-Burton. © Terence Donovan.
 Image courtesy of Victoria and Albert Museum,
 London: 138
Courtesy of Joy Debenham-Burton. Image courtesy of
 Victoria and Albert Museum, London: 140
© Ken Heyman: 4
Courtesy of Linda Kirby/Image © Victoria and Albert
 Museum, London: 165
Image courtesy of Mardie Gorman/Museum of London
 © Mardie Gorman: 19
Image courtesy of the Mary Quant Archive/Victoria and
 Albert Museum, London: p.8, 17, 22, 29, 47, 48, 52,
 53, 54, 55, 58, 81, 83, 88, 96, 98, 101, 102, 108, 116,
 121, 123, 124, 126, 127, 156, 162, 177, 178, 188, 189
© Michael Wallis. Image courtesy of the Mary Quant
 Archive/Victoria and Albert Museum, London: 33, 38
© MirrorPix: 93
© MirrorPix/Getty Images: pp.2–3
Image courtesy of Museum of the City of New York: 100
Image courtesy of Museum of London: 6
© Museum of London: 80, 146, 175
Courtesy of Nanna Bjornsdottir/Image © Victoria and
 Albert Museum, London: 157
Image © Norman Eales: 159
Courtesy of Patricia Lowe/Image © Victoria and Albert
 Museum, London: 134
Courtesy of Patricia Stacey/Image © Victoria and Albert
 Museum, London: 12
© Roger Jackson/Stringer/Getty Images: 57
© Rolls Press/Popperfoto/Getty Images: 79, 111, 112,
 113, 132
© Sharhrokh Hatami/REX/Shutterstock: 13
Image courtesy of The Sunday Times © David Bailey: 31
Image courtesy of Sweet Jane blog: 144
© Terence Donovan. Image courtesy of the Mary Quant
 Archive/Victoria and Albert Museum, London: 106
Courtesy of Tereska and Mark Peppe: 16
© Terry Smith: 192
ullstein bild/Getty Images: 117, 161
Image courtesy of University of Glasgow library: 187
Image © Victoria and Albert Museum, London: 1, 15,
 18, 23, 24, 25, 28, 30, 32, 34, 35, 37, 39, 41, 43,
 45, 70, 73, 82, 86, 90, 91, 92, 94, 103, 104, 105,
 109, 114, 115, 118, 120, 122, 129, 130, 133, 134,
 135, 141, 155, 158, 163, 164, 166, 169, 170, 172,
 174, 176, 181, 182, 183, 184, 185, 191
Courtesy of Vivien Wearing: 171
Image courtesy of The Western Reserve Historical
 Society, Cleveland Ohio: 97
This image is an orphan work. Attempts have been
 made to contact the owner. The image is held by the
 London College of Fashion and Woolmark Archive
 (The Woolmark Company Pty Ltd): 168